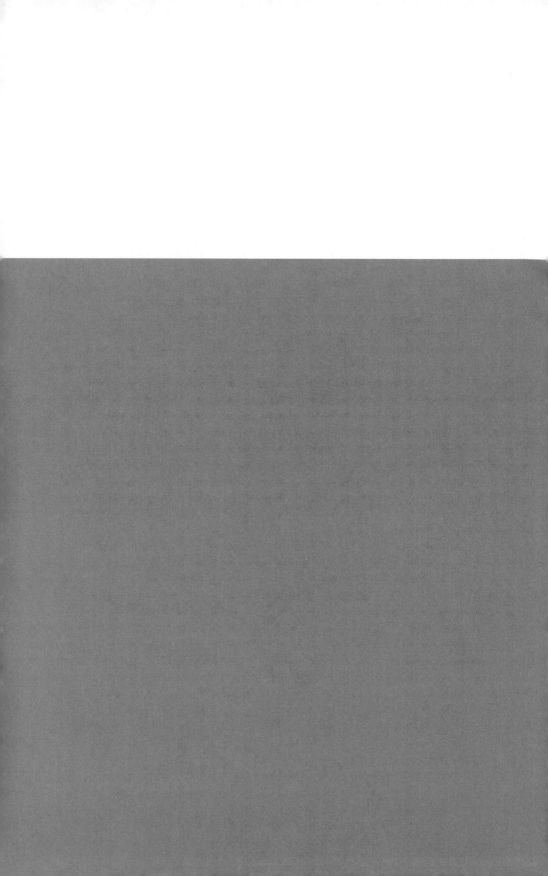

BORN TO BE WILD

A HISTORY OF THE AMERICAN BIKER AND BIKES 1947–2002

Paul Garson
and the Editors of Easyriders

Simon & Schuster
New York • London • Toronto • Sydney • Singapore

SIMON & SCHUSTER
Rockefeller Center
1230 Avenue of the Americas
New York, NY 10020

For information regarding special discounts for bulk purchases, please contact Simon & Schuster Special Sales at 1-800-456-6798 or business@simonandschuster.com

Interior Designed by: Andrea Sepic & Nathan Savage/Red Herring Design

Illustrations provided by: Antique Cycle Supply, Inc.

Manufactured in the United States of America
10 9 8 7 6 5 4 3 2 1

Library of Congress Cataloging-in-Publication Data
Garson, Paul.
Born to be wild : a history of the American biker and bikes / by Paul Garson and the editors of *Easyriders*.
p. cm.
Includes biographical references.
1. Motorcycles—United States—History.
2. Motorcycling—United States—History.
3. Motorcyclists—United States—History.
I. *Easyriders*. II. Title.

TL439.5.U6G37 2003
629.227'5'0973—dc21

2002044610

ISBN 0-7432-2523-6

Acknowledgments

In general I want to thank each and every person appearing in this book, the riders, the builders, the painters, the photographers, the restorers, the manufacturers, the racers, the historians—everyone that made this book possible in the first place. In particular, I would like to thank Tex Campbell, who while an editor at *Easyriders* more than twenty years ago bought my first story and gave me the advice and encouragement to keep at it. Thanks go to all the current staff at Paisano Publications, a.k.a. *Easyriders*, who for more than twenty-five years have created legendary magazines. Thanks to *Easyriders'* publisher, Joe Teresi, for keeping the wheels turning. Thanks to Editor-in-Chief Dave "Phantom" Nichols and Editors "Clean Dean" Shawler and Kim Peterson for leading the way. Thanks to VP/Associate Publisher Gil Luna, Sr., giving of his time when it counted. Thanks to John Nielsen for helping me wade through 10,000 photographs. Thanks to Billy Thornbury, who dug up more images. Thanks to Jim Fitzgerald of the Carol Mann Agency and Chuck Adams at Simon & Schuster for signing their signatures and making the book a reality. Thanks to Susan Brown for her meticulous copyediting. And thanks to Cheryl Weinstein at Simon & Schuster, whose e-mails and kind words facilitated the whole process. And, of course, thanks to the guy who aeons ago blasted by my mother's Oldsmobile on an open pipe bike and got me hooked on motorcycling in the first place.

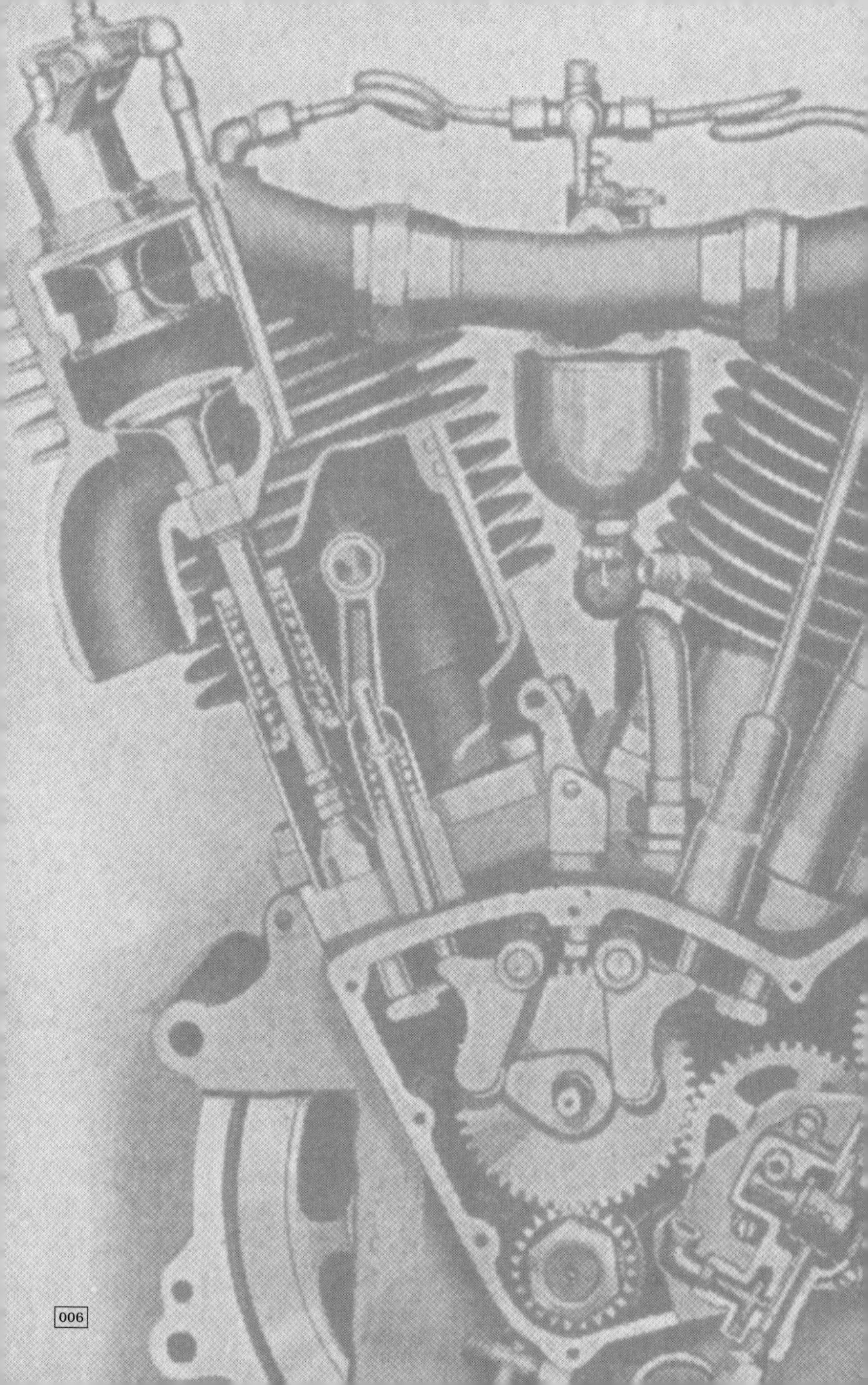

This book is dedicated to my son, Grant Nathaniel Garson, who I trust will read many books and write some of his own.

Contents

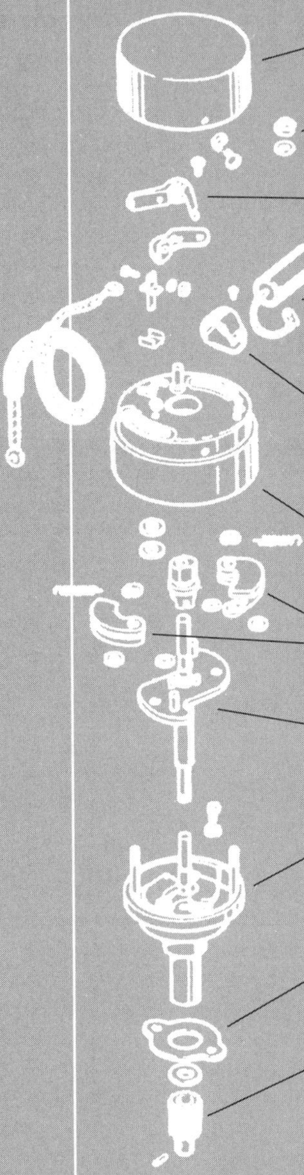

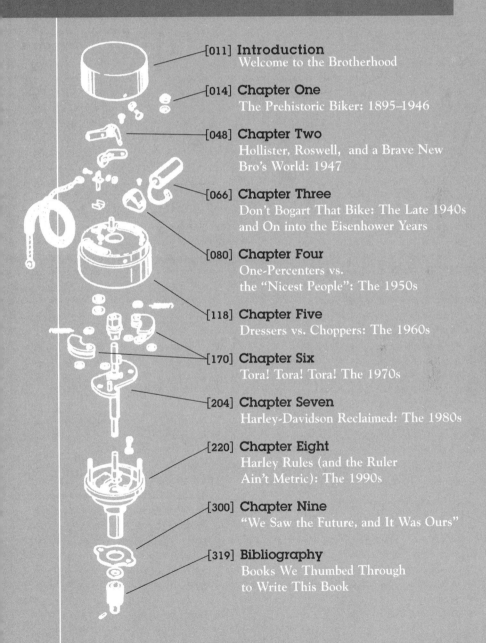

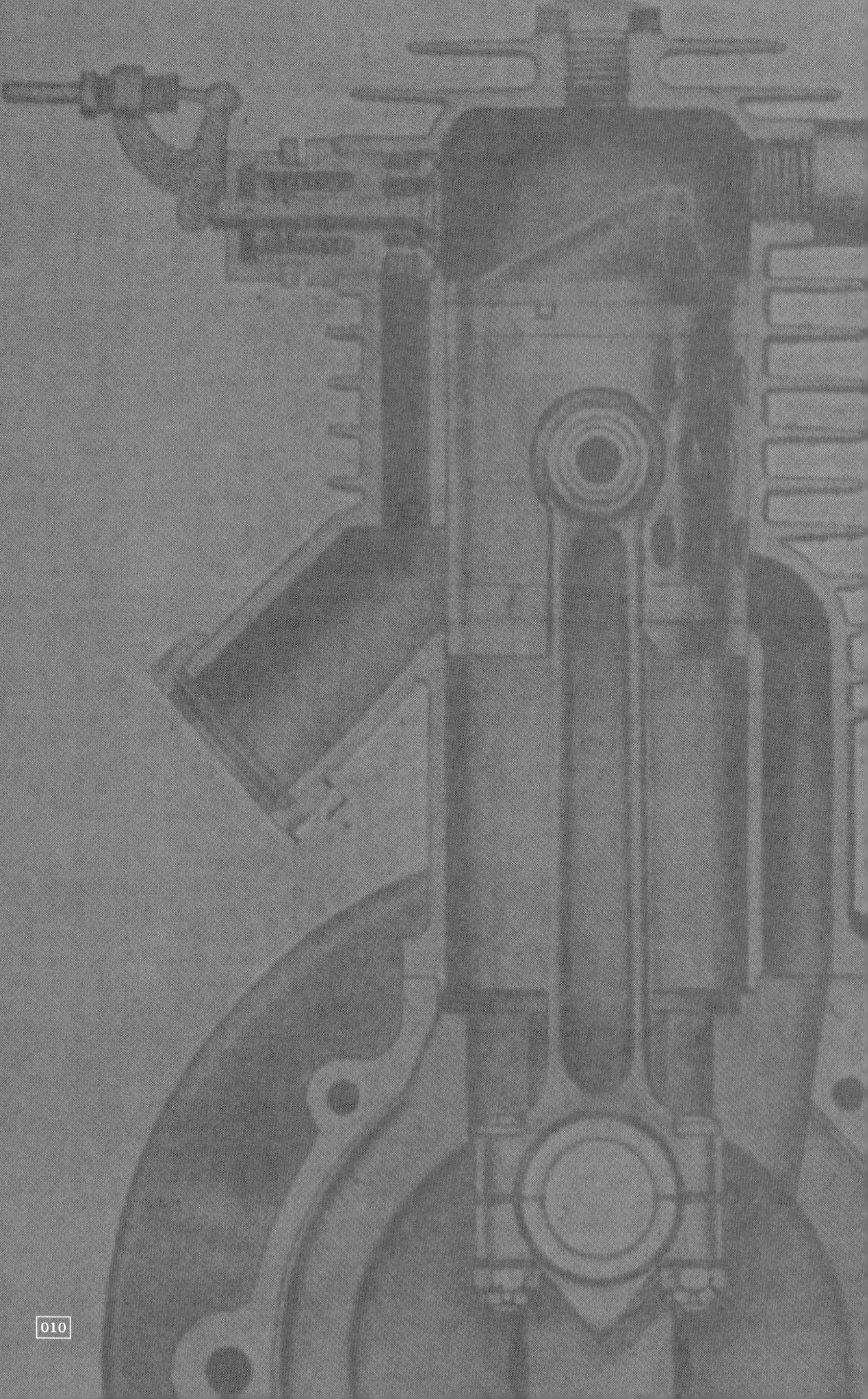

INTRODUCTION

WELCOME TO THE BROTHERHOOD

The concept of the motorcycle outlaw was as uniquely American as jazz. Nothing like them had ever existed. In some ways, they appeared to be a kind of half-breed anachronism, a human hangover from the era of the Wild West.

—Hunter S. Thompson, gonzo journalist

We were depicted as Vikings on acid, raping our way across sunny California on motorcycles forged in the furnaces of Hell.

—Sonny Barger, former leader of the Hells Angels

Which came first, the bike or the biker? Or, for that matter, the biker lifestyle or *Easyriders* magazine, founded in 1971? Or was it the 1969 film *Easy Rider* that gave it all a focus and the biker culture its raison d'etre. Or did it stretch back even further to dapper dudes thumping around in bow ties and spats when motorcycle sidecars and not SUVs carried whole families around America?

The answers are both simple and complex, colorful and controversial, but above all else they constitute one hell of a story.

The story of the American biker is as multifaceted and unique as each individual and his or her motorcycle. In the year 2002, Bro is a transgender concept. Some things change, some things don't. With a million U.S.-registered Harley-Davidsons on the official books, there're at least a million different stories traceable to that one motorcycle icon alone. So the best way to get to know what we're calling the Bro is to mingle.

Motorcyclists, a.k.a. bikers, like to mingle; we're social animals. That's a given, despite the lone wolf stereotype fostered by the media, as in *Then Came Bronson* and similar TV and film variations. We're talking Bro as a term applying to anyone who spends significant time riding a motorcycle, any motorcycle, without any mandatory Milwaukee brand identification, although arguably the two are synonymous.

The Story of the Bro is woven from myth and legend and from the metal marvels created by hundreds of manufacturers, most who've been long consigned to the history books but all who have contributed their well-wrought measure of blood, sweat, and tears, chrome and leather to the threading of that biker cloth indelibly scented over the many decades with burning rubber, nitromethane, Jack Daniel's and, more recently, Chanel No. 5.

The common denominator that eliminates all restrictions of age, sex, politics, ethnicity, nationality, blood type, gene pool membership, polyester vs. 100-percent-cotton preferences, Neil Diamond vs. Smashing Pumpkins fans, and any other of the infinite them-us dichotomies that plague humankind is, at the end of a long, convoluted sentence, the motorcycle/motorcyclist. At one with each other, an androidal fusion of man and machine.

There's a popular biker mantra, "Live to ride, ride to live." Six words easy to print on a T-shirt or ink on an arm. But for all the complex formulas the experts try to use to explain the magic and mystery of the biker experience, those six words sum up the essence. Now we're writing a book, and essence is something best found in concentrated doses within poetry and perfume, but we're giving it our best shot. No doubt you, the reader, have a story that would fit right into these pages. Hell, maybe you're already in here somewhere. In any case, the idea of this book is to give you an inside look at the Bro's world as seen by the people who live it, letting each tell his or her story.

News Flash! Bike Sales Wheelie-ing to New Heights

The year 2000 was a great one for the motorcycle industry, with a sales increase of 27.3 percent. Honda Motor Co. has reported a 34.5 percent sales increase for the last year, selling about 45,000 more motorcycles than the previous year. Honda total unit sales were inching toward 175,000 bikes. Meanwhile Milwaukee, which makes fewer bikes per annum (but all great ones!), announced record sales and earnings (again, of course). The final figure was $2.91 billion, calculating out to a nice 18.5 percent increase for the year. Because of the good news, the Factory is increasing production to 229,000 units. By the way, we call "units" bikes. And how many shares in H-D do you own?

From Russia with Gloves et cetera

There is now a motorcycle club in Moscow that has about fifty members . . . and only one bike to share amongst them all, a Harley, of course. Things are tough in the ex-USSR. Maybe they can melt down all those old Lenin statues into motorcycle parts. In addition, a Los Angeles area bike builder has established an unusual relationship with the Russian military. He got in touch with a tank manufacturer in Kiev who had expertise in the fabrication of titanium, a supertough, superlightweight material good for all kinds of advanced applications. In this case, he had the tank designers create an all-titanium V-twin motorcycle engine, and they did just that, building what is perhaps the most beautiful motor you'll ever see. The new motors are already being bolted in good old Amerikanski frames.

Warning! The Globalization of the Motorcycle May Be at Hand!

That means homogenization, the ultimate threat to all things Bro. Bland, gray, all-the-sameness, anathema to the whole meaning behind motorcycling. In 1999 the United States, Japan, and fifteen member countries of the European Union signed an agreement in Geneva that would standardize safety regulations for motor vehicles. For motorcycles, this might mean leg protectors, air bags, noise limits (well, we got those already), horsepower restrictions, antitampering measures (no customizing!), banning of air-cooled engines (allowing only water-cooled, like with radiators), banning of open chain drives, and even banning of performance tuning. For more news on these gloomy tidings, check out www.aimncom.com, a website run by the Law Offices of Richard M. Lester.

1

H-D factory

1895–1946

THE PREHISTORIC BIKER

History is what the winners say happened. In this case, the winner was Harley-Davidson. The Milwaukee Marvel alone survived the Hundred Years' War, a century of innovation and most often extinction. Scattered across the scrapyard battlefields of the first few decades of the twentieth century, you could count the rusting steel bones of around three hundred different American motorcycle manufacturers. Well, let's call them motorcycle builders, since some built only a handful, literally. So where have they all gone? We gave these machines names—colorful, even memorable names like Apache, Argyle, Black Diamond, Buckeye, Comet, Crouch, Duck (put the latter two together and it described what pedestrians found themselves doing when the spindly things came blatting around the corner on a muddy dirt road)—and so personified them, glamorized them. Then there were the Dusenberg, Elk, Hemingway, Herring, Kokomo, Mack, Marvel, Flying Merkel, Nelk (an Elk relative?), Pansy (don't go there), Pirate, P-T (don't pity its passing), Ruggles, Schickel (not the gruber model), Thiem (remember them?), Thor, Torpedo (yep, it sank from sight), and you certainly can't forget (or pronounce) the Twombly. Built from the

Builder: Ron Simms
Photo: Michael Lichter

late 1890s to roughly 1915, these bikes were all brilliant glints in the eyes of their creators and if found today are regarded still as brilliant, and valuable, jewels. And they do occupy a special niche in a Bro's left ventricle, because they're part of the family, the lineage, the bloodline that holds it all together. Only a silver spoke driven through the carburetor of an old bike can kill it, but its memory can never be done away with.

BICYCLES MET THE INTERNAL COMBUSTION MACHINE AND EVOLVED SEEMINGLY OVERNIGHT INTO MOTORCYCLES.

It was the best of times and the worst of times, technologically speaking, these early spawning years when bicycles met the internal combustion machine and evolved seemingly overnight into motorcycles. The early motorcycle gene pool was afroth with great experimentation and mutation, during a time when blacksmiths and shade tree mechanics and teenage tinkerers conjured up chimeras of two-wheeled locomotion, as often as not H. G. Wells chitty chitty bang bangs that ran on a wild assortment of fuels: kerosene, steam, gasoline, moonshine, you name it. No multimillion-dollar R & D facilities required, no patents, no DMV rule books, no smog certificates, and no limits. It was a wild, open time, when inventors and dreamers harkened to the Gold Rush Fever of motorcycling.

A Brief but Somewhat Tweaked History of Davidson-Harley Time

Most people call them Harleys. But if you read the chrome strip on the tank it says, "Harley-Davidson." What if you had a twin brother named George and your name was Spivey, and people always called both of you George? Well, maybe that would be a good thing. But there's no mistaking a Harley-Davidson for anything else, unless you're one of those uninformed types that say, Hey, all those V-twins look alike to me. So maybe it's time to get the names straight relative to the guys that started the whole ball of wax rolling about a hundred years ago.

Their first prototype bike appeared in 1903, then further developed and eventually sold in 1904 as the "Silent Gray Fellow," a 475-cc, single-cylinder model that would set precedents echoing down to this day. But it was a couple years earlier, in 1901, when William "Bill" Harley and Arthur "Art" Davidson, aged only twenty and twenty-two respectively, started banging away, mixing together little motors and bicycles. While they kept their day jobs, they spent weekends and nights in the little old laboratory, or should we say shed. One of their early accomplishments was a rude form of a carburetor fashioned from a tomato can, something that almost turned Mrs. Davidson's kitchen into Chernobyl. Bill's dad built the ten-by-fifteen-foot shed in the backyard. So with the Davidsons building the "factory" and supplying the real estate, not to mention the tomato can, how come they didn't put their name first?

Owner: Dale Walksler; Photo: Roy Kidney

In any case, Bill Harley was handy with the pencil, a draftsman and the actual designer of the earliest bikes, so maybe he deserves first billing. His 1907 design for the springer front end was part of the package for many years, all the way to the first-year Panheads.

A few bikes got sold, and with sales came expansion, so the new H-D company nailed some more buildings together. Not exactly monolithic structures, one was literally picked up and moved by eight Bros when it was learned that the structure infringed on some railroad right-of-way.

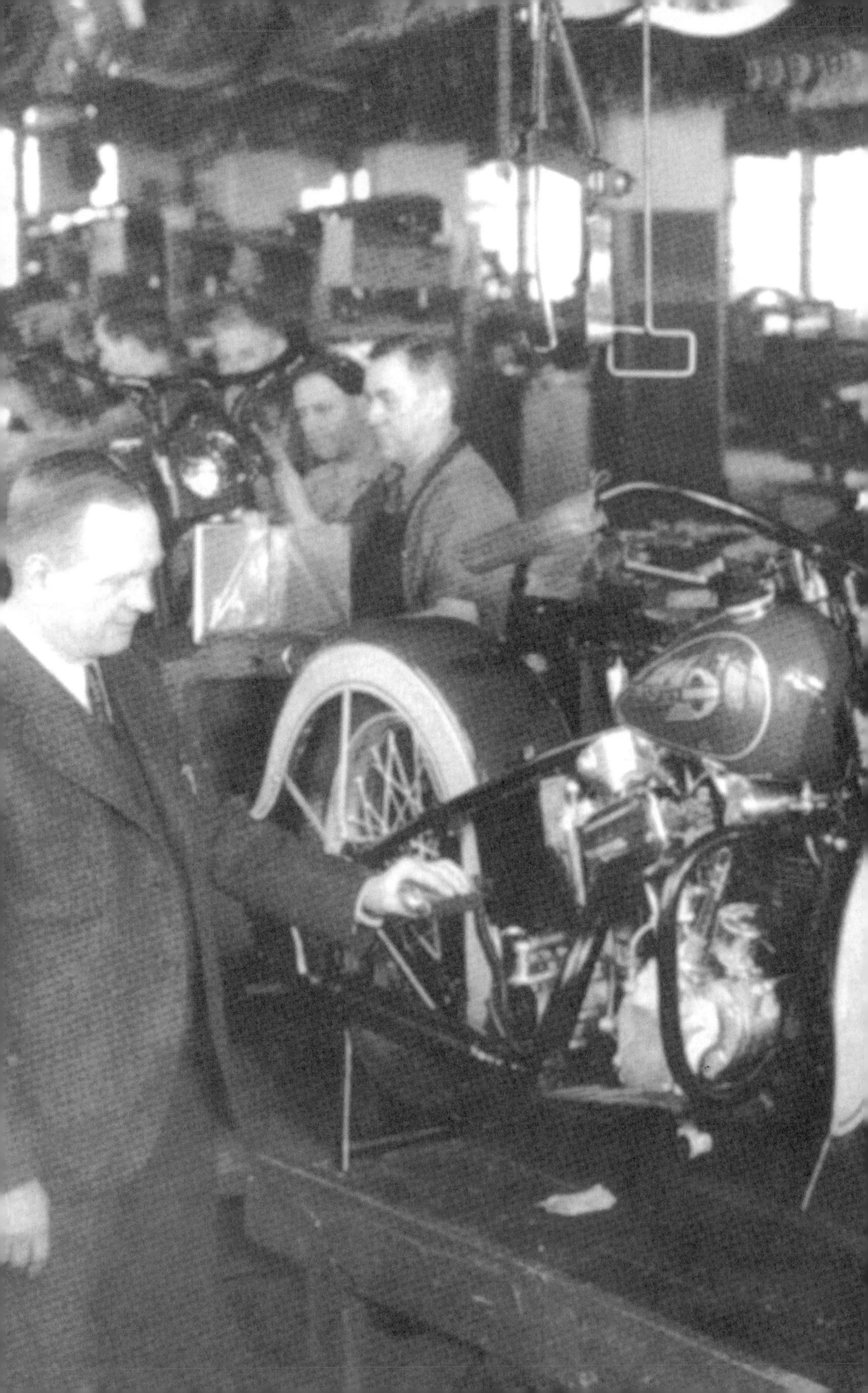

The Harley and Davidsons

Owner: Kevin McDonald
Photo: Kim Peterson

Five years into their efforts, Bill Harley and the Davidsons were pumping out around 450 bikes. Yet another brother, Walt Davidson, was coaxed into joining up. In 1909 he garnered some good press when he squeezed 188 miles to the gallon from a single-cylinder Harley-Davidson during a Long Island Reliability Run.

Reliability became associated with the new company's machines, and H-D began sharing the limelight with Indian, which had been founded in 1901. As a result police motor patrolmen became customers and

A Sidecar Named Desirable

Taking a side trip into the future, let's look at what Arlen Ness, the World's Most Famous Custom Bike Builder (he wouldn't say that, but we would), can do with a sidecar. From his San Leandro, California, facility have rolled trendsetters, mold breakers, unique exotics, a slew of motorcycles that go off the graph when it comes to innovation, artistry, and expertise. We'll see some of Arlen's work later, but right now we want to focus on his treatment of a sidecar.

When asked about his Ness Taxi bike, which takes a motorcycle sidecar and turns it into, well, a sidecar, Arlen says, "We just wanted to do a fun project. Something to cruise the shows and events and not take ourselves too seriously. After being in the transportation industry for years, it seems a taxi is a natural progression, the custom bike as a commercial vehicle, so to speak."

Photo: Mike Chase

Now Arlen has built sidecar setups in the past, but this time, instead of a rider on a bike, the Ness Taxi carries the motor in an outrigger arrangement attached to the sidecar, with the driver and passenger sitting tandem inside the sidehack along with the steering and controls. The fiberglass fabrication is based on a vintage sidecar design, with the body stretched to accommodate the tandem passengers while the power plant is a classic '70s vintage ironhead Sportster fed by dual pumper carbs. Vintage touches include the 21-inch wheels and yellow-and-black "taxi" paint job by John Nelson and Jesse Diaz, with the graphics created by Eric Reyes.

Yep, there's a lot of creativity and imagination out there in Bro-land. Anyone who hasn't figured out it's a legitimate and highly advanced art form needs to hail the Ness Taxi. And don't forget to tip.

But Please Don't Lick it!

Want a nice, safe hobby to go along with your nitromethane drag racer? How about combining motorcyclist with philatelist? No, not the whips thing. Collecting motorcycle-oriented postage stamps could stick with you once you get started, and it's easy and inexpensive enough to do, thanks to M. Fineman Motorcycles, P.O. Box 4323, San Leandro, CA 94579-0323; 510-614-8408. They've got 'em literally from A to Z. There are all kinds of bikes, from a 1939 Ardie to a 1973 Zündapp, in the catalog, which also features such cool ones as a 1918 Cleveland issued by Vietnam in 1985 and a 1955 H-D Bulgarian Police Model. Average price is three to five dollars.

fostered more sales. By 1912 the Harley-Davidson Motor Co. of Milwaukee, Wisconsin, employed almost five hundred workers, production having been spurred in 1909 by the introduction of their trademark forty-five-degree V-twin-powered bikes producing 7 horsepower and capable of 60 mph. Further glory, press, and sales were garnered when a factory rider clocked the then blazing 68 mph at a Bakersfield, California, road race.

Wins at the racetracks, then and today, translate to winning sales from the public. As a result H-D created its own R & D skunk works, designing and building purpose-built racers and prototypes to go against the likes of Indian, Excelsior, Cyclone, and the Flying Merkel. Spearheading the attack was the Model 17, usually referred to as the Eight Valve because it featured four valves per cylinder. That number of valves, a common enough configuration today, provided for better engine breathing (yes, they are alive!), enabling the fearsome Model 17 to grunt out close to fifty fire-breathing horses in 1916, the same year Henry Ford built 500,000 cars and dropped his price to $250. Keep in mind that a 1913 Pope (Hartford, Connecticut) V-twin had a price tag of $250.

Some twenty years later H-D would build one of its most beloved motorcycles, the 1936 Knucklehead. (We'll get to the nicknames in a minute.) The factory built a monster Knuck to race at Daytona Beach, Florida, a name now synonymous with March's Bike Week (and maybe with Biketoberfest in October). They fitted the works racer with full aluminum streamlining, stuffed in Lightning cams and gear wheels, bolted dual over-and-under carbs, and let 'er rip, to the tune of 65 hp, and it cleaned house. The racing glory mantle would later be passed on to the legendary KR 750 flathead (1952–1968), which battled the Brit and European bikes on the road race circuits.

Occasionally an oddity migrated out into the dealer's showroom; for example, the 1919 Sport Model W, with its BMW horizontally opposed engine layout at complete odds with the traditional H-D vertical and V-twin designs. The Model W had one cylinder facing the front wheel, the other pointing rearward. The sewing-machine-smooth-running 584-cc (37-cubic-inch) power plant combined with a weight of 257 pounds allowed this scooter to set some impressive long-distance records. In June 1919, a Model E blitzed from the Canadian border to the Mexican border in a tick shy of sixty-five hours, and that was on roads more aptly called dirt ruts in the summer, mud bogs in the winter.

But the competition in the form of the better-selling Indian Scout spelled the demise of the Harley Sport Model. Weird didn't sell, and

First Names

Next time you meet a wanna-be with more attitude than riding experience, strutting around in a two-thousand-dollar hand-tooled Corinthian leather jacket with baby seal lining, you can deflate his ego by asking, Why did the fledgling H-D company call their first bike the Silent Gray Fellow? Pause a moment while he squirms, then rattle off the following. Consider it part of his education into Bro-hood.

Owner: Dale Walksler
Photo: Roy Kidney

Paint choices were limited in 1904. House of Kolors and PPG and Von Dutch and Ed "Big Daddy Rat" Roth were not around yet. But there was a lot of gray paint with plenty of lead. In any case, the bike got painted a conservative gray. So there's the "Gray" part. And the first Harley had a muffler to squelch the thunderous outpourings of its 35-cubic-inch motor, so it ran on the quiet side of the decibel chart and didn't offend the pedestrians. Call it civil. That sure changed, right? In any case, the third part, "Fellow," was chosen because it seemed a friendly enough word that would inspire a sense of confidence in the machine, reliability being a big selling point. And there you have it, the arcane meaning behind the "Silent Gray Fellow."

FROM THAT WAR, HOWEVER, THE NEW GENERATION OF BIKERS WOULD EMERGE.

the Suits at the Factory clamped the lid on nontraditional designs, although another boxer motor did appear during World War II, when the War Department wanted a motorcycle for courier work that resembled the vaunted BMW of the German Wehrmacht. But it barely saw the light of day even then. From that war, however, the new generation of bikers would emerge. Hardened by the global conflict, disenchanted, perhaps disenfranchised from mainstream America, they would be the pathfinders for the Bros to follow.

The Name Game

Let's get the Founding Fathers' names right for starters. They were William A. Davidson, Walter Davidson, Sr., Arthur Davidson, and William S. Harley. Like we said, heavy on the Davidsons, light on the Harleys, but who knew?

Can we all say Schebler? After 1909 that tomato-can-inspired carburetor was replaced with a more refined design, the Schebler. Of course, now we have carbs with more easily pronounceable names, like Weber, S & S, and Mikuni.

And Now for Motor Mnemonics

We like to give ships and planes names. Remember the *Lusitania* and the *Enola Gay* for example. So it's no wonder Bros conjured up monikers for the various engine configurations generated by the Factory. The intrinsic uniqueness of each evolutionary step lent itself to such personification. In the beginning there was the **Flathead.** Simple enough, the top of the cylinders were flat, like the world, right? The 45-inch motors were used in both the solo and the three-wheeled

Harleys during the 1940s. (There was also a K model 45-inch Flathead that eventually begat the famous Sportster model.) The early 80-cubic-inches also were "flatheads."

Photo: Roy Kidney

The next evolution appeared in 1936 in the form of 61- and 74-cubic-inch power plants. Because the new overhead valve motor had the look of a clenched fist, with the rocker covers forming the knuckles, it took on the appellation of Knucklehead. Retaining the OHV form, the next generation of motor designs was the Panhead, so called because of their distinctive skillet-shaped valve mechanism covers. The Pan came in 61-cubic-inch displacement during the early 1950s as well as in 74-cubic-inch flavor from the time it was introduced in 1948 until it was discontinued at the end of the 1965 model year. That's when the new **Shovelhead** design took over, the name derived from the shovellike shape of its cylinder covers.

Next on the scene was the really revolutionary Evolution motor, at first igniting a controversy because it seemed such a quantum change from the traditional look. But it too earned a nickname, **Evo,** when it made its first appearance in 1983. Continued R & D produced in the mid-1990s the new **Twin Cam 88** A and B motors, which retained their Twin Cam nomenclature, while the biggest news as of the summer of 2001 was the introduction of the all new, totally blow-us-all-out-of-the-water **V-Rod,** a radical departure in all areas for H-D. Sporting a sixty-degree splay of cylinders and double overhead camshaft design, the newest from Harley boasts a 115 hp, is billed as a "performance cruiser," and features a wraparound frame and a water-cooled motor that makes you want to say "quantum leap" over and over again. Yes, H-D has gone metric. Reaction has been intense on both ends of the spectrum.

Photo: Roy Kidney

Owner: Otis Chandler
Photo: Roy Kidney

The 1936 61E is considered by most of the Old School to be the ultimate Harley-Davidson, the pivotal benchmark in a hundred-year saga of change and improvement. Better known as the Knucklehead, it earned its highest achievement award thanks to innovations like being the first of the big V-twins to incorporate overhead valves and a recirculating lubrication system. Plus it looked marvelous, a combination of style and performance (100 mph) that left the competition, like Indian, in the Daytona dust.

Many of the Early Rides forever carved their images into the Bro's memory banks, including the following classics, bravura bikes ridden by brave men, by Bros. Here's a taste of some of them, the few, the proud, the loud.

The Original X-Men: 1913 Excelsior Single Board-Track Racer

While many of the early bikes bore the names of their builders, such as Harley-Davidson, Curtis, Merkel, and Henderson, others have a less egocentric origin. The Excelsior got its name from the Latin *excellus*, roughly translating to "higher and superior." It also came to mean the curled wood shavings used in packing fragile items. The 1913 racer fits both meanings, exceptional quality in a delicate assemblage. During its heyday it battled its major competitors, Harley-Davidson and Indian, for board-track glory, as often as not garnering splinters for the rider, because the racecourses were fashioned from wooden planks.

Photo: Roy Kidney

Born in 1907 in Chicago, the American Excelsior (the Germans and English had their own Excelsiors) was a subsidiary of no less a legend than the Schwinn bicycles dynasty (and eventually the equally legendary Henderson four-cylinder machines). Ultimately, Ignatz Schwinn would shoehorn 30-cubic-inch singles and 45- and 61-cubic-inch V-twins into his beefed-up bicycle frames. The first models, 499-cc,

Photo: Roy Kidney

two-stroke powered, when sent to Europe were labeled American-X, then Super-X, so as not to confuse them with the Continental manufacturers using the same name.

Weighing only 265 pounds, the bikes blasted around the twenty-five to thirty-eight-degree-bank third- and quarter-mile tracks, reaching almost a hundred miles an hour, all without benefit of brakes or a transmission. The resulting injuries and fatalities eventually ended board-track racing, but you could rightly call the Excelsior racers the first X-Men, superheroes of a bygone era.

Photo: Roy Kidney

In the Eye of the Storm: 1914 Cyclone Racer

The following words were in the October 5, 1914, edition of the *Omaha World Herald:* "The mile ridden by J. A. McNeal in 32.5 seconds shatters the previous world's record, made a year ago at Los Angeles by Lee Humiston, who covered the distance on an Excelsior at the remarkable time of 36 seconds flat. McNeal was riding a Cyclone yesterday."

The overhead cam Cyclone was conjured up by Joerns Manufacturing, the same Minnesota firm that had built the long-forgotten Thiem motorcycles. While the Cyclone's glory lasted only four years, it burned bright, a darling of the public's eye not only because of its screaming yellow paint job but because for its time it was high-tech. Introduced in 1913, the 1000-cc V-twin engine featured a roller-bearing crankshaft and connecting rods, a bevel-driven single overhead cam and valve arrangement, plus forged steel flywheels, good for producing 7 solid horses. Because it incorporated "ported" cylinders, basically direct exhaust vents, riders following in the wake of a Cyclone literally were buffeted by intense amounts of noise and a pall of oil smoke since the engine consumed a quart every five miles. At night an extra added attraction were the blue flames licking around the engine and the rider's legs.

An odd feature, and vexing to riders, was the lack of a throttle. You were always on "fast"; the fuel-air mixture was beyond control thanks to the "open port" design that required a rich fuel load, whose correct proportion was reached only at the top of the powerband. The pilot had to manipulate a push-button kill switch to interrupt ignition to control the bike. As a result, the 250-pound bike lurched and leapt back and forth as its supply of spark interrupted, supplied, and interrupted over and over again. And all this with a spindly machine that hit 111 miles an hour.

The bike seen here was restored by the L.A. area master restorer Mike Parti and belongs to the vintage bike fan Jeff Gilbert, who when asked why he wanted a Cyclone responded, "I made a list of the most important racing bikes. Topping the list for American racers was the Cyclone because it had the most drama, the most stories behind it, an overhead cam engine, and the fact that it's a very early built machine. Also, quite a legend had grown up around these screaming yellow bikes."

The bike sits in Jeff's dining room, where else if you're a Bro looking for just the right furniture?

Reliving the Glory: 1936 Harley UX3 and the Great Race

The Bro's world is, above all else, a rich tapestry of history, and there was something about the 1930s that mixed magic and madness and motorcycles to new extremes. In February 1930, New York City decided to install the first red traffic lights; previously they'd used amber.

Drivers were complaining that pedestrians were stepping in front of their vehicles. It also seems the guy who invented traffic lights, Garrett Morgan, invented the gas mask. A guy named Hitler was making waves in Germany, Gandhi was making passive resistance in India, the Empire State Building reached for the clouds (and King Kong climbed it), the Zippo lighter was created, and the guy who invented Vaseline, and ate a spoonful every day, died at age ninety-six. Vaseline was used on many a bike in those days for rustproofing and lubrication, maybe some was even globbed on the Factory's prototype racer the UX3.

Owner: Dale Walksler
Photo: Roy Kidney

Joe Petrali: Record Breaker

Joe Petrali was perhaps the winningest competitor to race Harley-Davidsons, cutting his teeth on dangerous board-track courses at the age of sixteen, back in 1920. While he began racing on Indians, followed by a stint with Excelsior, he brought glory to himself and Milwaukee aboard Harleys, for example, winning all thirteen national calendar events including five nationals in a single day during 1935. In 1937 he blasted across the hard-packed sand at Daytona aboard an OHV 61-cubic-inch Knucklehead built by himself and Hank Syversten, clocking 136.183 mph to crack the solo record. Joe retired from racing in 1938 with a total of forty-eight national wins.

Old bikes sometimes get a chance to relive their youth, often in the hands of men who, though born decades later, find some inner calling to return to yesteryear and the glory of yester-bikes. Such is the story of the UX3. No, not a submarine, but a very rare Harley racer, part of the Wheels Through Time museum collection in Maggie Valley, NC, and under the direction of Dale Walksler, one of the leading "conservators" of classic motorcycles, who enthusiastically believes in putting old bikes through new paces.

You can call Dale one of the leading ambassadors of vintage bikes in particular, and of the Bro's world in general. A highly successful Harley-Davidson dealer for many years, he now concentrates his talents on his museum, which is open free to the public.

In the spirit of an Indiana Jones–type character, Dale and Wayne Stanfield of Tustin, California, decided to go motorcycle racing with a decidedly historical flavor. They entered Dale's fully restored, extremely rare and valuable 1936 prototype factory racer into the famous Great American Races, the competition limited to vehicles built before 1942. The brainchild of Tom McRae and Norman Miller, chairman of Interstate Batteries Systems of America, the timed event in 1995 had grown into the Great North American Race because its route meandered through Canada, the United States, and Mexico.

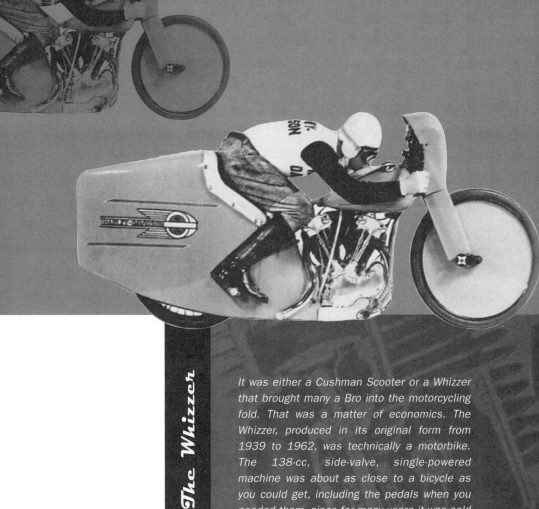

The Whizzer

It was either a Cushman Scooter or a Whizzer that brought many a Bro into the motorcycling fold. That was a matter of economics. The Whizzer, produced in its original form from 1939 to 1962, was technically a motorbike. The 138-cc, side-valve, single-powered machine was about as close to a bicycle as you could get, including the pedals when you needed them, since for many years it was sold in kit form only (for about eighty dollars), the parts usually attached to Schwinn bicycles. Chugging out about 2 horsepower, it wasn't much threat to speed limits, though the postwar models jumped to 3 hp, and then you bought a complete Whizzer called the Pacemaker. Again, it caused no heart attacks in the performance category, but for many a kid it was the very essence of freedom and empowerment, and entry into Bro-dom.

Photo: Pete Chido

For that year Wayne and UX3 were the only motorcycle entry, competing against 111 specially prepared vintage cars. The sixty-year-old bike and forty-seven-year-old rider faced the challenge of 4,400 miles with stops in more than fifty cities along the way. The prize . . . $250,000.

Wayne had won the event in 1994 and thus earned the right to carry the #1 plate on the UX3, which was equipped with a variety of rally-related equipment, including an 8-inch analog quartz clock necessary for precise calculation . . . and a pair of custom-made titanium trifocal glasses that fit under Wayne's goggles. "I must be able to see the instruments, charts, and road very clearly. I also plan to get a close look at the finish line," said Wayne.

He did see the finish line, and was at the head of the pack for a while, but eventually he lost ground to the four-wheelers. However, he did succeed in placing second in their class on the list of finishers, bringing a victory for the UX3 that was savored by both Wayne and Dale.

Harleys as Hero Bikes

Photo: DeJay Monson

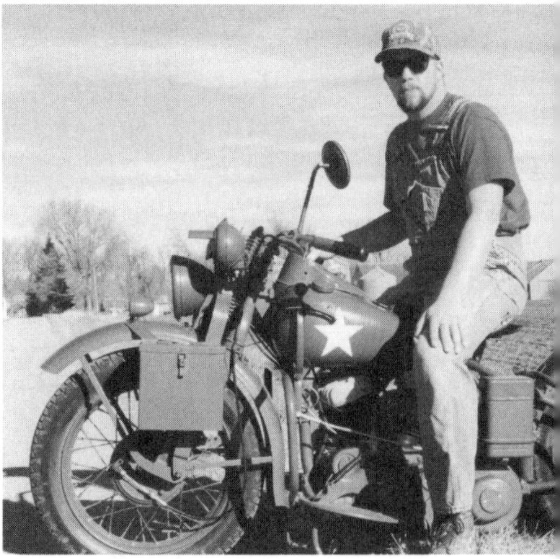

Harley-Davidson enlisted for World War II along with hundreds of thousands of Americans, some of them riding the bikes into battle. While Harleys had been popular for several decades at home, the crucible of war forged new bonds between man and machine, that kind you brought home with you along with the searing memories and maybe a Purple Heart.

Supporting America's fight for freedom and democracy, the factory ad campaigns of World War II, made in cooperation with the War Department, captured grandiloquently the fervor of the times, as in the following 1942 print advertisement:

Off the assembly line they roll—by the hundreds and thousands—sleek, streamlined Harley-Davidson motorcycles for Uncle Sam's forces and the armies of our allies. Day and night, whirring wheels, clicking automatics,

Leave the Driving to Us . . . Harley-Style

From 1915 to 1925 Milwaukee offered sidecars to go along with their bikes, literally to augment their passenger- and load-carrying potential. Manufactured for H-D by the Rogers Company, the little tubs carried family members to church, groceries home, feed to farmers, girlfriends to parties . . . you name it. Sidecars contributed significantly to the budding transportation system and as such had endearing, often bizarre and mystifying names, such as Jenny, Joy, Meadow, Mimic, Mister, Pen, Pie, Plot, Purity, Puritan, Repand, Rescue, Slant, and Slash. After 1925, H-D began building its own "sidehacks" and, although redesigned through the years, they are still available and in use.

Pre-SUV family transportation—The Sidecar

pounding presses roar ceaselessly as raw materials are fashioned into still more Harley-Davidsons.

Today's Harley-Davidson motorcycles are duplicating the splendid record made by their predecessors back in World War I. The hard-riding scouts who lead the advance of the armored divisions to reconnoiter, spot mines, traps and ambushes, report on road conditions, and enemy movements know that the staunch and sturdy construction of their mounts will not let them down. They know that in Harley-Davidsons, reliability and dependability are in-built qualities that make them equal to any task that may be assigned to them. All the exacting care and skill of determined loyal workers—all the resources and experience of the Harley-Davidson organization are enlisted to give freedom's fighters the best in motorcycles. That we pledge until complete victory has been won.

—Harley-Davidson Motor Co., Milwaukee, Wis., U.S.A.

US

Photo: Jim Williams

Photo: Dave Johnson

In the dark, shrapnel-filled days of March 1940, World War II was already six months old. German panzers had blitzkrieged their way through Poland and beyond, oftimes their tanks attended by small herds of snarling BMW and Zündapp motorcycles, as tough as the Wehrmacht armored divisions themselves. The Nazi motorcycles could negotiate the harsh terrain and serve as speedy courier vehicles. And with their sidecar-mounted M-42 machine guns they were literally hell on wheels. While the United States was holding on to its neutrality, the Army saw the storm clouds gathering as far back as 1937, when they visited the Harley Factory to check out its readiness status and soon went looking for the right motorcycle themselves. Anticipating America going to war on Harleys, the dean of the Factory's service school, John Norvak, traveled to every Army camp east of the Mississippi to monitor the school mechanics, logging 200,000 miles on his sidehack EL.

By 1939 the Army had tested various Harleys and Indians as well as a BMW clone made by the Delco Corporation. The Harley model was based on the popular 750 Flathead of the time, but the Army ordered up some tough requirements; the bike had to be able to reach 65 mph, had to ford streams 16 inches deep, and could not overheat when slogging around muddy fields at slow, stump-pulling speeds.

Competition for the government contract was almost as fierce as the fighting overseas, but Harley edged out the others, and it was in March 1940 that Milwaukee received its first order for 745 WLAs, the 45-cubic-inch flathead taking on the new tubular front, which provided an increased travel length of about 2.5 inches, needed to clamber over shell holes and such. Outfitted in the U.S. Army's traditional drab olive green, the bikes wouldn't win any custom paint awards today, but the camouflage helped keep them and their riders out of harm's way. The WLA eventually pumped out 23.5 hp and benefited from several upgrades, including an oil-bath air filter mounted high out of water's

Photo: John Lewis

Photo: D. L. Wilson

way, and improved engine lubrication, clutch, and tranny. Milwaukee met the Army's ruggedness and dependability requirements thanks to their new aluminum heads and their list of modifications, including D-shaped floorboards, blackout lights, crash bars, crankcase-mounted skidplates, and cargo racks. For carrying all those secret communiqués, they were slung with the now famous leather saddlebags and often a scabbard for toting a Thompson .45-cal submachine gun.

The WLA was a success, and orders blossomed, every U.S. armored division listing 540 WLAs in its motor pool. Meanwhile 2,000 were ordered by South Africa, 5,000 by Great Britain, 20,000 by Canada (called WLCs), and later large numbers were shipped to both the Russian and Chinese armies. Such was the importance of these wartime battle bikes that in 1942 H-D's Civilian Training Facility became the Quartermaster School for teaching military mechanics. Beginning in 1941, 88,000 WLAs (plus spare parts for 30,000 more!) were built by the time the last bullets were being fired. When new each

Historic Racing Association

For motorcycle enthusiasts interested in vintage and classic road racers, motocrossers, dirt trackers, and observed trial machines, the American Historic Racing Motorcycle Association (AHRMA) offers riding schools, concours, races, and other events dedicated to reviving motorcycling's racing history. Racers and spectators craving the sights, sounds, and smells (castor bean oil) of yesterday's race bikes can contact AHRMA, P.O. Box 882, Wausau, WI 54402-0882; 715-842-9699.

The American Motorcycle Association (AMA)

Not the American Medical Association by a long shot but rather the long-time (since 1920) governing body for all things motorcycle sport and manufacturing. Sounds pretty all-inclusive and, well, it was. At the outset it was supposed to be this democratically run deal, but trade interests gained the controlling hand. What a surprise. Depending on what side of the fence you were on, they made some interesting rulings. For example, in the 1920s the AMA instituted the 21-cubic-inch engine displacement as a racing class. So what if H-D had just introduced their new single . . . in a 21-cubic-inch format. The ruling generally peeved a lot of other bike manufacturers. Then in 1970 the AMA announced that 750-cc bikes could compete in flat-track racing. And the hot Harley XR750 kicked everybody's butt.

All said, though, the AMA has done great service to the organization of motorcycle sport in the United States, often championing Bros' rights. It was the AMA who decided to create the famous Gypsy Tour, a series of race events including flat-track and hill-climb competitions through the country, eventually contributing to the so-called infamous Hollister event you'll hear more about in the next chapter.

This 1941 WLA was restored by Mike Egan, and could serve well if called up to re-enlist.
Photo: Roy Kidney

cost about $380, but for a few years after the war you could buy surplus WLAs still crated and wrapped in Cosmoline for about a dollar a cubic inch. Not anymore.

Meanwhile, back in the States, the film star and heartthrob Clark Gable was cruising around Tinsel Town on his 1942 EL. Clark, nattily dressed in sportcoat, tie, and two-tone loafers, was often spotted at L.A. bike events.

Another American-built bike, one that seriously challenged every other bike at the time with its performance and quality, was the Crocker. Many a Bro salivated over this machine, though few were able to throw a leg over one. Unfortunately, only a handful were built, and because of wartime restrictions on materials, it went out of production in 1942. But for a few short years it made its mark, and today the Crocker is one of the most venerated footnotes in American motorcycling history.

Even in WWI, all eyes turned to Harley-Davidson.

Metal Money

Old motorcycles don't fade away, thanks to dedicated restorers and a market where old bags are often worth their weight in gold or close to it. While it used to be Bros horse-trading vintage bikes, now it's big business, with "investors" scarfing up "collectible" historic machines and paying a pretty penny. Case in point, the famous Sotheby's auction house.

A while back the Chicago branch produced a weeklong motorcycle event, culminating in an auction that saw some outstanding two-wheelers fetch considerable prices—and praise—from the Windy City's citizens, who flocked to the open-house display of vintage, custom, classic, and exotic machines.

The cornerstones of the sale were fifteen bikes that had belonged to a prominent Chicago family, but all makes and models were added, including the vintage bicycle that Ignatz Schwinn himself had ridden as a child; it went for $106,000! Yeah, a pedal bike. Another hit with the crowd was a spectacular 1939 Indian four-cylinder restored by John Dohnal of Brookfield, Illinois, which took $60,000.

Because of the event's success, more such auctions are scheduled. For the latest dates, call Sotheby's at 312-396-9510.

The First V-Twin Crocker

Some fifty years ago a Crocker, supposedly the victim of a kamikaze attack, was sent to Davy Jones's locker while aboard a U.S. aircraft carrier sunk during the ferocious Battle of the Coral Sea. Now that same Crocker may have surfaced. A Crocker was reportedly spotted years later in New Guinea, its serial numbers said to be those of the missing bike. Only the continuing squabbling between the indigenous people and their government has prevented an expedition to retrieve it. Such is the attraction of the legendary Crocker, perhaps the ultimate American classic.

The Crocker, built in a shop on Pico Boulevard, in Los Angeles from 1936 to 1942, was, and is, considered by many the Dusenberg of American Motorcycles. Featuring an advanced engine design, agile handling, and enduring styling, the Crocker V-twin provided unsurpassed performance; each limited production machine was handmade to customer specifications.

Photo: Roy Kidney

The late Chuck Vernon, who owned what is thought to be the 1-X, or the very first Crocker ever built, was a recognized expert on the subject. "For more than twenty years, we've compared records of the serial numbers we received from the fellow who originally stamped those numbers, Gene Rhyne," recounts Chuck. "Our current tally tells us that only sixty-four V-twin Crockers were built, and we believe thirty complete bikes are still around today. Of those, perhaps only twenty are running."

What set the Crocker apart from all others? Chuck says, "There's nothing new about a rigid frame or sprung front girder forks. But Crocker did

The First of the Firsts

It was a Merkel. Not exactly a poetic sounding name, but while Harleys were just a glint in the eye of their makers, Joe Merkel was already selling bikes in Milwaukee, powered by a single cylinder motor in a diamond bicycle frame. By 1915, Merkel had a V-twin, mono-shock rear springing, and the trademarked name "The Flying Merkel," thanks to the rider of the legendary boardtrack racer Maldwyn Jones. This 1915 example is owned by Norm Gerlich and was restored by Shorty Tompkins.

Photo: Roy Kidney

incorporate more aluminum for lightness, including the front and rear backing plates. The gas tanks were cast aluminum, and of course they wouldn't bend. If Al Crocker had a secret, it was his wonderful combination of cam action and breathing. With the same bore and stroke of the Harley 671, the Crocker produced at least 30 percent more horsepower."

The small shop took on the likes of Harley-Davidson and Indian. Contributing to the Crocker's high desirability today is its ridability. Says Chuck, "You wouldn't want to ride a Pierce-4 or a Cyclone any distance, but with a Crocker you could. Properly set up, they could run all day at 80 to 90 mph, with a top speeding exceeding 110. They also had better breaker since they employed Indian Chief brake shoes."

Historic Isle of Man Races Take It in the Foot (and Mouth)

News from the historic thirty-seven-mile racetrack set in the cobblestone streets wriggling through this little island at the north of England was not good in the year 2001. Because of the severe medical threat associated with the outbreak of the mad cow epidemic that decimated Britain's livestock, the famous motorcycle races joined the ranks of sporting events canceled by government decree. The two-week summer festival of old and new bikes, one of the most popular in world, attracting over 40,000 spectators, was seen as a threat for spreading the disease, which attacks humans who eat infected meat. The disease has a dormancy period of up to twenty years, but once its effects take hold, forget about even remembering where your foot or mouth is. So far no cases have surfaced on the Isle of Man, but almost fifteen hundred farms on the mainland have been hit hard. There was probably more danger to riders and spectators from the racing than from the disease, since the TT (Tourist Trophy) has a history of sudden trauma; almost two hundred riders have bit the bullet since the races began in 1907. Unfortunately, many fans had both flights and hotels for the event and were planning to come anyway. One U.S. biker, who had shelled out several grand in advance, wrote the race authorities, saying, "I am starting to dislike cows in a big way."

AT AGE FIFTY-THREE, AL HAD A DREAM, TO BUILD THE FASTEST STREET MACHINE IN AMERICA, IN THE WORLD.

With Crocker, customers had a choice of engine sizes, from 61 to 90 cubic inches. While most were 61 inches, the strokers were usually 80 inches. The largest motor Al built was 86 inches, featuring his hemi-head design, and it went into the 1-X prototype. Al tested the motor in an Indian Chief frame, then refitted it into a Crocker frame, stamped with "1-X."

The first Crocker, built in 1936, evolved from successful 500-cc, single-cylinder speedway machines. Al had worked at the Thor Motorcycle Co. and was an Indian dealer on Venice Boulevard in L.A. from 1928 to 1934. While he was a visionary engineer, his foreman, Paul A. Bigsby, possessed the practical talent. At age fifty-three, Al had a dream, to build the fastest street machine in America, in the world. In his 1200-square-foot shop he built his own foundry and machine shop and began constructing his dream. Its most dramatic feature was its hemispherical combustion chambers with domed pistons.

In a 1948 interview Al explained why he'd ended production on such an incredible machine: "The war. We had the last eighty-five machines three-quarters completed but could not get the government authorization for the critical materials to finish them. We broke them up, got seventy-five dollars for the junk and an adjustment from the government to make up for the losses."

The real loss was to motorcycling history. Crocker enthusiasts still search for bits and pieces and lost New Guinea Crockers in their dedicated efforts to keep the Crocker up and running.

Historic Harley (and an Indian's Okay, Too) Hookups

This 1954 165 Hummer was restored by Mil Blair who added some custom paint and chrome, and is owned by Ellen Meagher Teresi
Photo: Doug Mazell

If you own one of those two-stroke Harley Hummers (1948–1966), contact the Harley Hummer Club at 4517 Chase Avenue, Bethesda, MD 20814. Knucklehead owners can join the Harley Knucklehead Owners Club, Rt. 1, Box 267, Seagrove, NC 27341. For the very specific oriented, owners can hook up with the 1936 Harley OHV Club at 120 Vineland Road, C-3, Winter Garden, FL 24787. And for Harley XLCR café riders, go to the XLCR Registry, 322 Attica Road, Attica, NY 14011. If you're lucky enough to own an old Indian 101 Scout, you can get the WOW newsletter, which covers 37- and 45-cubic-inch 101 Scouts (1928–1931) by writing The 101 Association, Inc., 679 Riverside Drive, Torrington, CT 06790.

Photo: Roy Kidney

World War II ended in 1945, and the GIs came home. Some managed to bring their trusty Harleys, or parts of them, back. When the WLC War Department bikes were converted for civilian use, a popular modification was a switch to what became a "standard chopper" feature, the 16-inch rear wheel.

But the venerable flathead was about to be replaced, not only on the battlefield but on the highways of America. Farewell to the flathead, hail to the new Panhead and a new America. Not to mention a new kind of American fresh from winning a war overseas, where the simple values of apple pie and Mom were not high on the menu. Things had changed, both externally and internally.

Master Restorers: So Who Fixes a 1903 Harley-Davidson?

The artisans/historians/treasure hunters/fabricators who restore antique, classic, and vintage motorcycles are a breed unto themselves. For the most part they are quiet, conservative, humble, but above all meticulous, motivated masters of their profession, one to which very few aspire these days. When all is said and done, the restorers not only restore rusting hunks of metal; they restore our vision of the past, a highly accurate vision.

Here are five representatives from that arcane profession; the Bros who mend very old metal.

Mike Smith

Photo: Paul Garson

The family of Mike Smith, including sons Mathew, Charlie, Jethro, and Jeremiah, and wife-mother Rozanne, of Oregon City, Oregon, are all dedicated to restoring antique and vintage motorcycles. Representing a unique family solidarity, each son on the occasion of his thirteenth birthday received not a shiny new bicycle or fishing rod or boom box but rather an ungift-wrapped pile of rusty metal parts that vaguely resembled a vintage motorcycle. Under their father's laser-sharp supervision, each set out to restore the machine. And not merely restore. It had to take a first place in competition.

Echoing their highest of standards and his microscopic and historically vast knowledge of pre-1915 American motorcycles, Mike's collection now holds a litany of American classics, including rare Iver-Johnson, Flying Merkel, Reading-Standard, Super-X, Henderson, Thor, Emblem, Harley-Davidson, and Indian models. While he produces bikes for a rare handful of collectors, his emphasis has been on passing on his knowledge to his sons, who have followed in his artisan's footsteps. While Mike still restores, he helps orchestrate his sons' efforts. "I've taught the boys the trade, and now they've polished their skills in many ways beyond my own. I act as technical adviser or, if we get into a trouble spot, we work through it together. Every project we have ever done has been a National First Place motorcycle. I look forward to them being the next generation of motorcycle restorer superstars. That's the legacy I can leave them."

Photo: Roy Kidney

Jeffrey Slobodian

Phoenixville, Pennsylvania, is a town forged in steel. Once it was famous for making steel cannon. Now old steel horses are given new legs thanks to Jeffrey Slobodian, a restorer who focuses on a microniche of motorcycling: antiques of pre-1912 vintage.

Jeffrey's penchant for all things old began more than thirty years ago, when he started polishing the years off antique clocks, his interest evolving through bicycles and cars, then settling on motorcycles, ultrararities like the 1896 Spiral, a do-it-yourself type of motorcycle long gone even from the history books, or a 1912 500-cc, single-cylinder New Era made in Ohio, one of only four known.

Perhaps Jeffrey's most bizarre restoration revolves around a one-wheel motorcycle, in effect a 36-inch-by-4.5-inch round motorized wheel and tire with its single seat mounted to the side. The mono-wheel is powered by a 1920 Marsh-Metz engine.

Summarizing his philosophy regarding restorations, Jeffrey says, "Once you've restored bikes produced after 1910, they become a bit ordinary, and you can almost do them with your eyes closed. But when you get something totally unknown, and you have to figure out how it comes apart, with its own unique procedurals, there's the challenge. I generally only do restorations for myself so that I have something to sell or trade for another project. I probably complete five or six bikes a year, having completed forty in the last six and a half years." (Jeffrey has since moved to Ojai, California, where he builds custom display cases and an occasional motorcycle.)

Steve Huntzinger

At age twelve, this native Californian was stuffing Briggs & Stratton lawn mower engines into bicycle frames, then tearing up the local junior high running track. Some thirty years later Steve was restoring classic Rolls-Royces, Bugattis, and Dusenbergs, but then he bought himself a 1912 Harley belt drive basket case. Now a basket case is what its name implies, a bunch of motorcycle parts in a milk crate that somebody else gave up on. "I had known about that bike since the fifth grade and had been waiting to be able to buy it," says Steve. "That was a real learning experience, and my first motorcycle restoration. In order to maintain authenticity, I called up all the old-timers I knew and was lucky enough to find an original 1913 bike that I studied microscopically for hours on end before starting my restoration. I did everything but the plating."

Photo: Paul Garson

That was twenty-five years ago, but today you'll find that same 1913 Harley in Steve's living room (his home and 3,000-square-foot redwood workshop are located about halfway between Santa Maria and San Luis Obispo, 200 miles from L.A.). Steve has restored legends, including Harleys, Indians, Hendersons, and Excelsiors, back to their pristine originality.

And, like Renaissance artists, Steve had his patrons, including Urban Hirsch, who made his work possible. And for Dale Walksler of Wheels Through Time museum fame, he restored several antique race bikes, including a 1908 Reading-Standard board-track racer, the only known example in the world. The bike was found in the basement of the Wright brothers no less, and it was in a bad state. However, Steve restored it to museum quality, an effort that qualifies him as one of the rare Master Restorers.

Steve is not content with completing world-class restorations, he feels the need for putting the old bikes back into the wind, in this case, a gale force wind and then some. In November of 2000, his team broke the existing A Vintage Gas record at El Mirage taking it away from Harley Davidson. Their 1934 Indian, sponsored by GMA All-American, cloked 127.347 mph with Rusty Lowery at the controls.

Jerry Greer

The owner of Indian Engineering in Stanton, California, Jerry is a well-known expert on Indians. In addition to restoring and selling Indian motorcycles, he manufactures some of those hard-to-find parts needed to keep these American classics on the road. Some of his specialties include grinding cam lobes and fixing pesky oil pump leaks. If you want to buy an Indian, he first recommends the 1938–1948 74-inch Chiefs and the 80-inch Chiefs (1950–1953) because of their reliability and 65 to 75 mph cruising speeds. Jerry sold T-shirts that said it all: "Ride the Son of a Bitch or Sell It to Somebody Who Will." For more info on all things Indian, call Jerry at 714-826-9940.

M. F. "Mike" Egan

Since the 1960s, the historian, writer, and restorer Mike Egan, located in Santa Paula, California, has taken on "selective, high-quality" vintage bike restorations, including antique, classic, and vintage American and English motorcycles. He specializes in rebuilding vintage Harley-Davidson 45-inch, 61-inch, 74-inch, and 80-inch overhead and side-valve twin power-plant and drive-train components, and also offers a line of NOS, used, and repro parts for the restorer, literally "tons of stuff." He was also the first "official consultant" to the Harley-Davidson Motor Co. archives when it was established in the 1980s and is still active in that capacity. He also lectures and recently published a "retrospective history" on the VIN nomenclature of Harley-Davidson motorcycles, in association with Easyriders magazine and the H-D Archives. For more info call 805-933-1557 or check out the website at www.mfegan.com.

Photo: Markus Cuff

Photo: Paul Garson

Evan Wilcox: Master Metalsmith

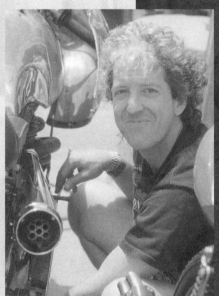

Photo: Paul Garson

A master metalsmith in the old sense, Evan Wilcox trained in the time-honored school of European craftsmanship and has become a recognized source for those who want the very best in hand-formed alloy bodywork. Evan supplies bodywork for restorations as well as one-off designs for a variety of classic, motorcycles including Harley-Davidson, Triumph, Norton, BSA, Royal Enfield, Ducati, Laverda, BMW, and Benelli. His spectrum of Harley work includes everything from XR TT to Kosman specials. You think it up, and Evan can beat it into existence. For examples of his work, log on to www.wilcoxmetal.com, or call 707-467-3993.

2

Hollister, California—July 1947: An indelible image forms of the "biker."

1947

HOLLISTER, ROSWELL, AND A BRAVE NEW BRO'S WORLD...

Let's say you're a World War II veteran and put your back-pay money in the bank, and now, with a couple years' interest, you are ready to go shopping at your local Harley-Davidson dealer. What brand spanking shiny new models would you get to ogle on the showroom floor of 1947?

The range of V-twin-powered models included bikes powered by the 45-cubic-inch (750-cc) flathead, the 61-cubic-inch (1000-cc) OHV, and the 74-cubic-inch (1200-cc) in both flathead and OHV designs. The newly introduced 61-inch OHV ran $605. Milwaukee built 4,117 of the high-compression 61-inch bikes, and 6,893 of the 74-inch hi-comp FLs. What's a nice '47 Panhead going for now . . . twenty, thirty times the original MSRP?

We all like to know our roots. The genealogy of the "bad biker" starts loosely after World War II, when U.S. servicemen returned home after taking part in a conflagration that saw over 50 million people slaughtered. It was a good war, very black-and-white, they were all considered heroes, and phrases like post-traumatic stress disorder did not exist. Yet the soldiers, after leaving their Thompson submachine guns and Mustang P-51 fighters behind and donning their civvies, were not the same guys who'd left home to see war up close and personal in the European and Pacific theaters.

Upon returning home, they found it wasn't the same. Some of them climbed on motorcycles and wandered the byways and highways of America looking for answers to unanswerable questions or teamed up with their war buddies because either they felt safer in the company of their brothers-under-arms or they didn't quite fit back into the relatively low ebb of civilian life. Motorcycles maybe gave them back the edge they needed, the adrenaline rush they had experienced so often in combat.

In any case, they were not riding into towns and burning them to the ground. That would come later. At least according to the media. And the media do like a story and often don't let the truth get in the way. They went looking for trouble and found it. In the summer of 1947, trouble found pilot Kenneth Arnold or the Booze Fighters MC. Mr. Arnold was a traveling salesman who liked to pilot his own Cessna to work. When another aircraft disappeared, he volunteered to look for it around the rugged Cascade Mountains near Seattle. He didn't find the lost plane, but he did witness nine objects flying in a V-formation against the backdrop of Mount Baker. He estimated the boomerang-shaped vehicles were clocking 1700 miles per hour, a tad faster than current military-issue aircraft. He told the media that they looked liked saucers skipping across water, hence the term *flying saucers* coined by

MOTORCYCLES MAYBE GAVE THEM BACK THE EDGE THEY NEEDED, THE ADRENALINE RUSH THEY HAD EXPERIENCED SO OFTEN IN COMBAT.

some reporter. The government experts dismissed them as a flock of birds, but that's not what the imagination of the world did.

A couple of weeks later, around July 4, at a place near Roswell, New Mexico, something crashed on Mack Brazel's cattle ranch. The local military authorities announced they had found pieces of a flying disk, yep, a spaceship, and it hit the front pages. A day later the official story changed to something more mundane: a weather balloon had crashed during a thunderstorm. And so began a controversy that's been raging for more than fifty years.

Meanwhile, not too far away, and on exactly the same day, in Hollister, California, a different kind of controversy was being conceived or perceived, depending on how you looked at it. For some it would be the seminal event heralding the "biker culture." Culture didn't quite fit the image reported and perpetuated by the press.

So what happened that infamous day in Hollister? What were the facts that led up to the fiction? Or was it fiction?

It started with the AMA deciding to bring back its popular series of races called the Gypsy Tours. As the name implies, a lot of "enthusiasts" would putt around the country enjoying the various flat-track and hill-climb venues. In those goldie oldie days of cheap gas and postwar rootlessness, it was as good a reason as any to hit the road, camping out wherever nightfall found you and your Bros, your family of motorized gypsies. Sometimes little hamlets were swamped by riders, and their infrastructure, to use a modern buzzword, was unable, or unwilling, to deal with the motley crew of what they considered "outlaws and outsiders" (the rough riders of the day liked to think of themselves pretty much that way as well). Hollister, part of the Gypsy Tour, was scheduled for a hill climb. The Harley top rider Joe Leonard would be competing. People started rolling in on a Friday night.

Back then, Hollister was called a village. And they referred to "biker gangs" as clubmen, motorcyclists who formed or joined clubs of like-minded enthusiasts. Into the apparently pleasant environment of clubmen came the so-called outlaw element. For three days these outlaws terrorized the town, creating a scene of unruliness that ultimately required the calling up of five hundred California Highway Patrol, California State Police, and local law officers to rout the lawbreakers from town. The press listed the offending clubs: the Booze Fighters, Galloping Gooses, Satan's Sinners, Satan's Daughters, and Winoes. (Yes, there was a spelling problem, but apparently women were given equal opportunity to raise hell.)

It seems some of the visitors weren't interested in the official races and were staging their own burn-outs down San Benito Street, the location of Hollister's restaurants and bars. About fifty people got busted for things like public drunkenness, indecent exposure, and resisting arrest. Not exactly the sacking of a city and the murder of its inhabitants, but it was too much for little Hollister.

What the press said happened during the July Fourth city celebrations came out like a riot, a rampage, a near rape and semipillaging of a small town by motorcycle hooligans, thugs on wheels, drunken, beer-bottle-tossing Wild Ones, all in black leather jackets and engineer boots and riding motorcycles. Somehow all the bikes became Harley-Davidsons in the mindset (which they weren't), and the equation was born. Hollister = biker

Overheard Said at Hollister

"One thing you won't find here is a single vampire," said one Bro to another.

"And why's that?" said the other, checking out a Buffy the Vampire Slayer look-alike in a skin-kissing leather outfit.

"Hollister is a garlic-growing center. Take a whiff."

NOT EXACTLY THE SACKING OF A CITY AND THE MURDER OF ITS INHABITANTS, BUT IT WAS TOO MUCH FOR LITTLE HOLLISTER.

gangs running amuck = Harley-Davidson as the incendiary fuel.

It would have been great stuff for CNN, except CNN would have been there to show the real facts, not some highly massaged nonfiction fiction set piece manufactured to sell papers and magazines. That's what Bro historians will tell you now.

The Hollister hysteria is captured by the infamous black-and-white photograph taken in front of Johnny's Bar, which appeared first in the *San Francisco Chronicle*, then on the cover of the July 21 *Life* magazine, showing an obviously seriously toasted guy on a Harley with a small mountain of beer bottles piled around his bike. Letters to the editor, including one from the actor-motorcyclist Keenan Wynn, poured into the mag deploring the exploitation of the event, pointing out that of the four thousand bike fans attending the Hollister celebration, only five hundred contributed to the trouble, the majority of the AMA members behaving with all decorum. But the indelible image in such a respected publication had its effects. The public had a new boogeyman, i.e., the bad biker. Hollister started the ball rolling and can be credited for spawning the torrent of lurid "bad biker" melodrama in so many Hollywood films and later television. And thus the stigma was born, a bad rep bikers have been trying to overcome for half a century.

The negative image was reinforced when *Life*, as part of its twenty-fifth anniversary, chose to republish the same cover in July 1972 just in case the public might have forgotten what a drunken biker hooligan looked like. And, of course, that image reminded everyone that bad bikers preferred Harleys, thus branding the bike guilty by association. Did it hurt Harley sales? Doubtful.

Cultural impact was listed somewhere near the effect of the Yucatán meteor on dinosaurs. As Harry V. Sucher, the official historian of the Harley-Davidson Owners Association, stated in his 1981 book,

A Goose Talks About Hollister

The following letter to the editor appeared in a 1972 issue of Easyriders:

Hey, I want to set the record straight about the Hollister hassle. I was one of the Galloping Gooses there, and I'm writing to tell you that *Life's* version of what happened was bullshit.

That photo of the two dudes was staged by a *Life* photographer. (I have it on good authority that the two dudes that posed for the photo were paid a visit and shown the errors of their ways.)

The bash started with the AMA (American Motorcycle Association) officials refusing to let the Gooses participate in the event unless they removed the Gooses patch from their backs. The symbol was a large fist giving the finger. AMA's demand went over with the Gooses like a fart in church, and as a result the Gooses were "outlawed" from the event. This was probably the origin of the term *outlaw,* although the AMA had no doubt outlawed other bikers and clubs from participating in other events prior to this time; however, this hassle received the most notoriety.

We had about twelve to fifteen members at that time. When we were outlawed we headed for town along with another club that was there too—the Booze Fighters. At that time I think they had about twenty-five members. It's been so long, I don't remember the other clubs that were there, although I think you were wrong about the thirteen Rebels—I think they turned AMA prior to Hollister.

Here's a photo of me and my bike at that time. It's a 1936 VLH Harley. The engine was built up to a healthy 90.98 cubic inches. It went like hell—between the times it blew up on me.

Old Goose
Los Angeles, CA

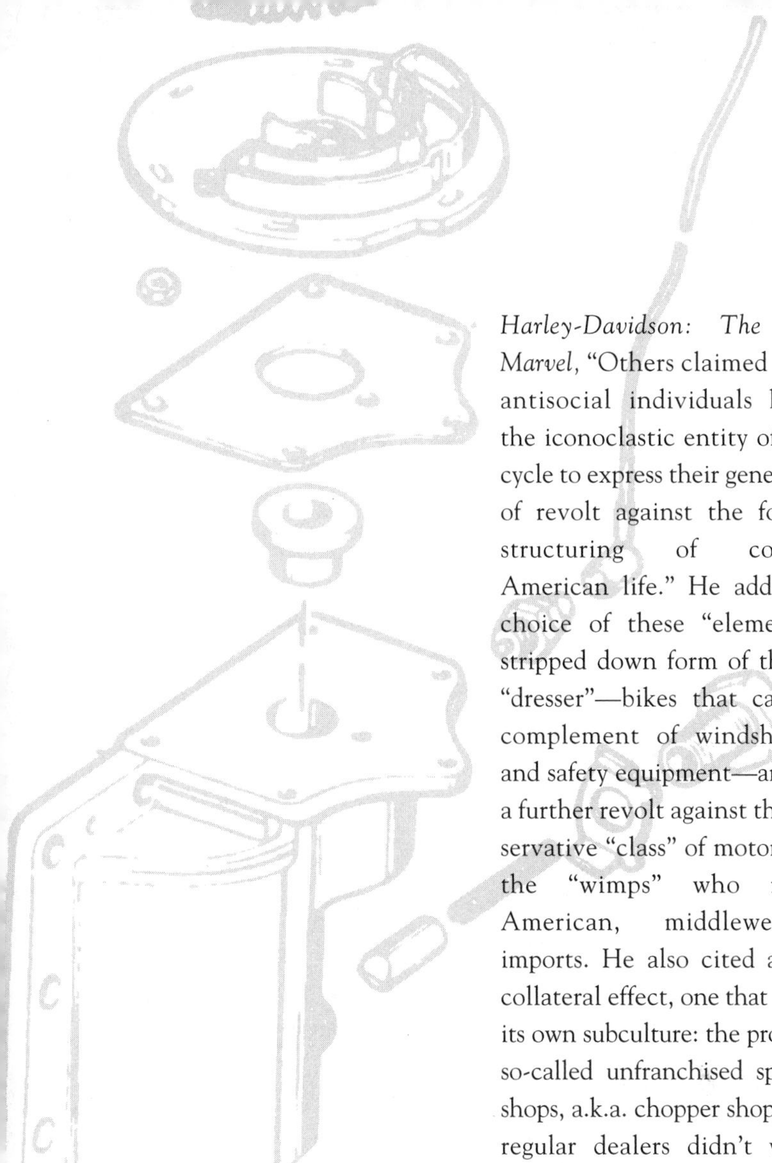

Harley-Davidson: The Milwaukee Marvel, "Others claimed that certain antisocial individuals had chosen the iconoclastic entity of the motorcycle to express their general emotions of revolt against the formal social structuring of contemporary American life." He added that the choice of these "elements" was a stripped down form of the Big Twin "dresser"—bikes that carried a full complement of windshields, bags, and safety equipment—and indicated a further revolt against the more conservative "class" of motorcyclists and the "wimps" who rode non-American, middleweight Brit imports. He also cited a significant collateral effect, one that would create its own subculture: the proliferation of so-called unfranchised specialty bike shops, a.k.a. chopper shops. Seems the regular dealers didn't want to be associated with the saddle tramp–unwashed biker element, so the so-called outlaws began opening their own shops and supporting them.

What did happen in that sleepy California town, located inland and west about halfway between Monterey and Santa Cruz (about thirty miles south of San Jose), when some guys on motorcycles came to celebrate America's Independence Day? Years later a letter penned by an eyewitness and sent to the editors of *Easyriders* magazine reportedly told it how it really was (see "A Goose Talks About Hollister").

Sex on wheels:
Vincent Black Shadow
photo: Roy Kidney

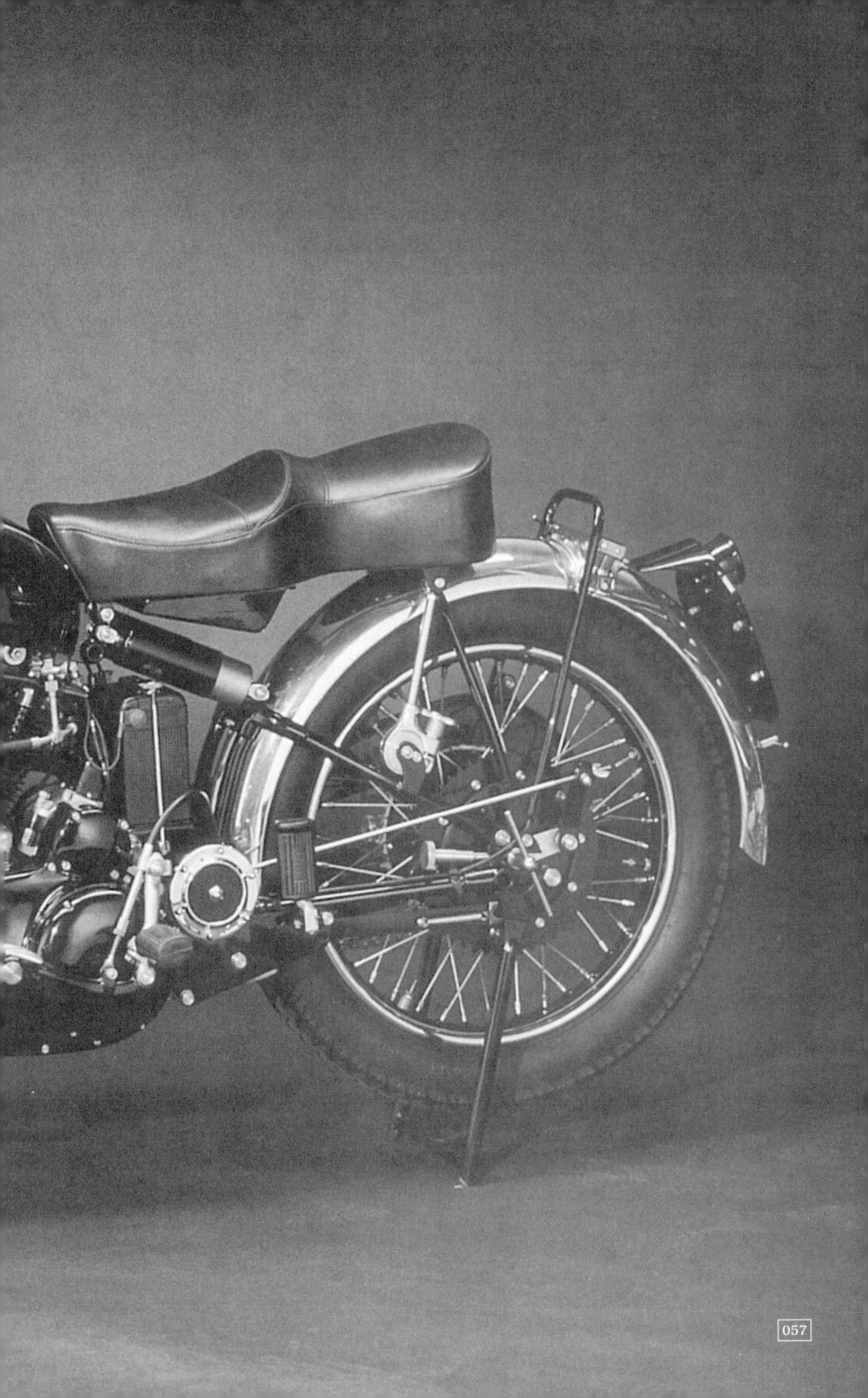

"One-Percenter"

Maybe you've seen the patch on a vest or jeans jacket: "1%." Call it a badge of honor or a refutation of the status quo, it refers to the image of the outlaw biker as being both a rarity and someone happily occupying the margin of society. The phrase was penned, not deliberately, by Lin Kuchler, then secretary of the AMA, when describing the Hollister incident: "The disreputable cyclists were possibly one percent of the total number of motorcyclists, only one percent are hoodlums and troublemakers." This sounded kinda cool to a bunch of the hardcore Bros, and they responded by accepting rather than refuting the onerous term, taking it as their own.

Years later in Japan the builders of Honda motorcycles would belatedly capitalize on this distinction when they came out with the statement "You meet the nicest people on a Honda." In Hollister, and in similar rowdy incidents occurring in its wake, you wouldn't find the nicest people, as least by society's definition back in the late 1940s. Meanwhile, a large majority of police motor officers across the country were mounted on basically stock Harley-Davidsons, which solidified the image of Harley in a positive light but also polarized the "outlaw element" on their custom bobbed fendered hot rod bikes into the other camp.

Shades of Hollister

Still not Hollister, and it's not *Then Came Bronson* either. Branson, Missouri, is that other Nashville kind of place catering to the country music set usually over the double nickel limit in age. Banners waving over the music Mecca proclaimed, "Branson Welcomes Hell's Angels USA Run 2001." Nice message, even though they added that apostrophe. (It's Hells Angels, not Hell's Angels.)

The annual gathering brought out eighty Missouri state troopers to help local authorities, making that about one officer per ten bikers at any given time. Everybody probably felt very safe, don't you think? Local merchants were grumping that attendance had dropped off, and they wanted more bikers to attend the music shows, play miniature golf, shop for souvenirs, and gum down the local chow.

So why Branson? It's in the middle of things Americana-wise and logical when people are riding in from both coasts. In any case, the hotels did okay. Two of the three large ones near downtown were filled with bikers. The third hotel was filled with state troopers. As for the mood of things, one motel clerk summed it up by saying, "They've been no trouble at all. In fact, they've been extra nice."

Hollister Fifty Years Later

Official event leaders comment: The famous *Life* photo was posed a day after the so-called riot, which was characterized as more like a beer bash gotten out of a hand. In 1997 Hollister celebrated its own fiftieth anniversary of the event, which attracted 60,000 Bros and Bro'ettes. Ellen Brown, executive director of the Hollister Independence Rally, quoted in a *New York Times* article, said, "I was more scared of the police, the SWAT teams on the roof, and the riot-patrol members." Guess what, no riot and no *Life* photographer either.

Imports vs. Homegrown in 1947: The British Invasion

Photo: Markus Cuff

In this year of UFOs and fictional biker atrocities, the Harley factory had to contend with a vexing problem. Imports. The year 1947 saw dockworkers unloading 15,073 machines, mostly ex–War Department British bikes: Ariel, Royal Enfield, BSA, and Triumph, mostly in 350-cc or small displacement. Norton, another famous English bike builder, began shipping over 500-cc, side-valve bikes, the likes of which had seen action against Rommel's Afrika Korps. The price tag, an attractive $585. They were nimble and easy to ride, with hand controls and foot-shifted

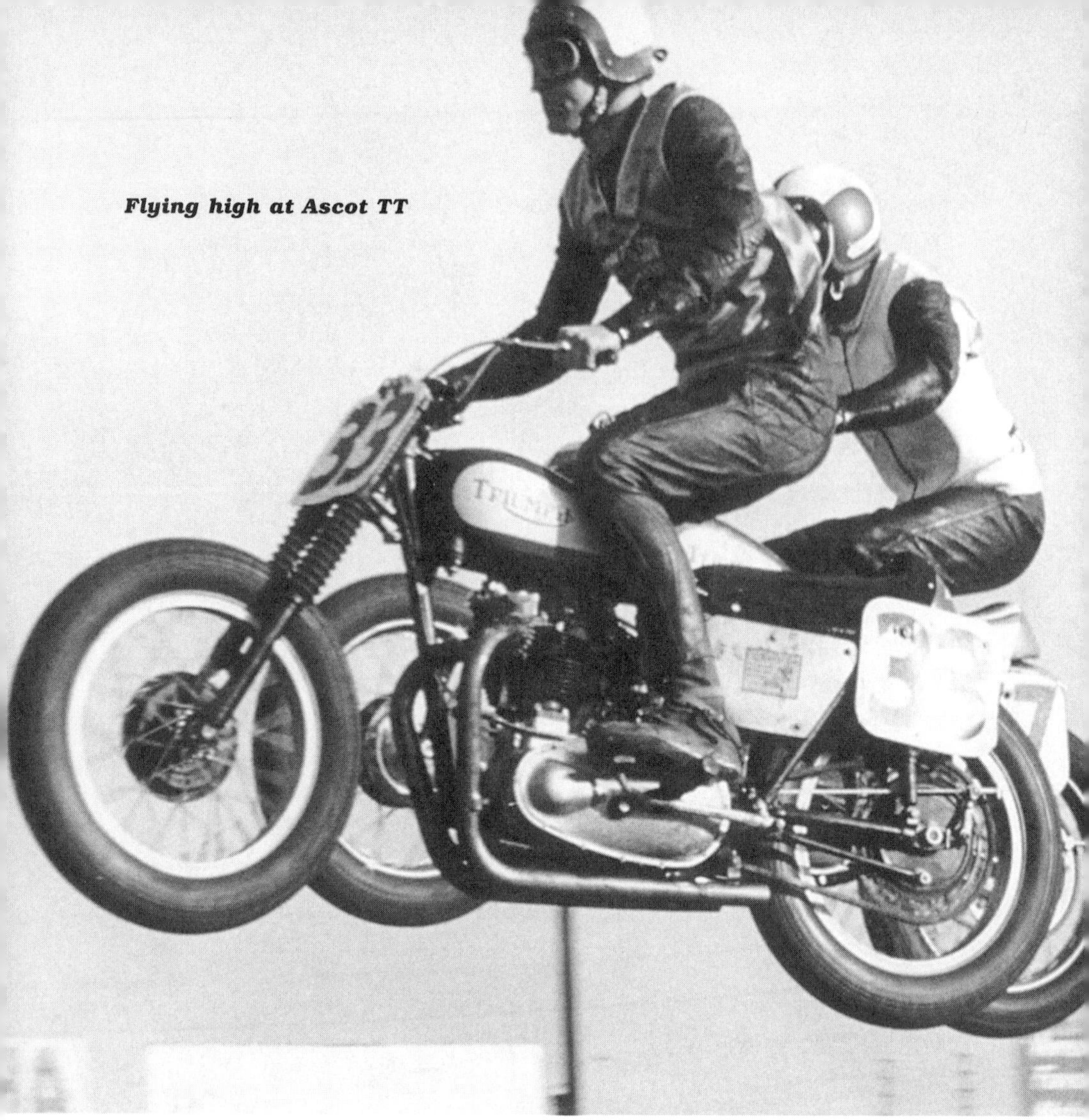

Flying high at Ascot TT

gearboxes, quite in contrast to the 700-pound U.S.-built Big Twins. American riders bought 'em and would buy lots more, especially Triumphs and Nortons, in the next two decades. Add to the brew a low 8 percent duty for the Brit imports, compared with a crushing 33 to 50 percent import duty levied against American Big Twins.

In other words, the first onslaught from abroad came across the Atlantic Ocean from Merry Olde England, a mere shadow of the two-wheeled invasion that would later storm across the Pacific from the Land of the Rising Sun. (There was some exciting news from Milwaukee in the fall of 1947; after a very hot summer in more ways than one, H-D announced its new Panhead engine design with its aluminum alloy cylinder head and hydraulically controlled lifters.)

The factory also introduced a new model, designated the S and called somewhat affectionately the Hummer. Whether the two-stroke, 125-cc single hummed along is a moot point. How it came about is another story. Seems the Germans, as part of their reparations to help make up for devastating most of Europe, forked over a bunch of prewar DKW motorcycles. We got some, the Brits and Russians did too. The Brits stuck them in Bantams, and we put them in bikes badged with the Harley name. A lot of dealers refused to sell them. They were definitely not American in pedigree or performance. But they sold fairly well, for ten years in fact.

A Gentler, Kinder Hollister . . . but Not Good Enough for the Bureaucrats

As time passed, Hollister became accustomed to hearing itself called the Birthplace of the American Biker, and that from a state where former Senator George Murphy described bikers as "the lowest form of animal." The Fourth Annual Hollister Independence Rally took place June 2 through July 5, 2000, without a single pillage or plunder disturbing a place billed as "California's Unspoiled Paradise." Unfortunately, the Gypsy Tour Motorcycle Classic, which included a bunch of cool things like burn-out contests, hill climbs, and drag races, was denied a permit by the San Benito County Board of Supervisors.

A connoisseur of Ariels
Photo: John Wycoff

However, for 2001 the permits were granted and the bikers rocked to live music, enjoyed spacious campgrounds, and ogled lots of hot motorcycles and the cool people who ride them, thousands having shown up for the event. And you could still swill a beer and bite a burger at Johnny's Bar and Grill (526 San Benito Street), where it all started back in '47.

As reported in the *New York Times*, national edition, on July 12, 2001, this was the town and the event that was the scene of the 1947 "fracas" that inspired the Marlon Brando classic bike-cult movie *The Wild One (1954)*. The article goes on to describe many of the year's events as somewhat shy of a fracas, many bikers dealing with bifocals and reading the tiny print on the arthritis relief bottles they carried in their bikes' saddlebags. Yep, the baby boomers on bikes were cranking on the years, and with them came photo albums of grandchildren rather than a collection of beer bottles. The article, penned by Timothy Egan, reports that, with H-D nearing its one hundredth anniversary, its customers are likewise reflective of vintage demographics. The average age is forty-five, with one in five Harley owners fifty-five or older.

The writer describes meeting up with a guy named Teno Star (good biker name), now fifty-two and a seasoned Bro. He and his buddies were selling skulls, knives, and leather accessories at a sidewalk stand during the Hollister gig. Teno makes a telling statement: "It's all lawyers, doctors and mcdooglers now. I prefer the old days when you had to earn your way into being a biker."

For more information on upcoming Hollister Independence Rallies, log on to the Hollister city website www.hollisterrally.com, or for Gypsy Tour information punch in www.gypsytour.com.

Also Seen at Hollister 2001

Posters for the upcoming Santa Clara County Boy Scouts Run to the Hills event. And a merchant's tally of $5 million in sales to the bikers over the weekend. Yes, Bros do have an impact on the pocketbook of America.

The A-List for Good Media Moments for Bikers

Elvis riding his Harley.

Stuff That Set the Stage for the Bro's World of 1947

Some social scientists and a lot of shade tree philosophers say that art forms are the best way to get at the gut of what's happening in the society at any particular moment. So let's see what Americans were reading, watching, and looking at in 1947. Of course, that might restrict us to those that can and like to read, go to movies besides drive-ins, and look at art other than the comic books of the time.

The books that hit the top of the must-read lists included Brit writer Malcolm Lowry's *Under the Volcano*, set in Mexico in the late 1930s and concerning the troubles of an alcoholic diplomat, played by Albert Finney in the 1984 film adaptation. As the title implies, things were simmering under the surface of the main character and the environment, and, if we stretch things, the book was reflective of an American society that looked wholesome and clean-cut on the surface but was beginning to show some patches of dark underbelly. Such was the atmosphere in which early Bros/bikers dwelled. *Under the Volcano* also elicited a sense of impending disaster, of tensions that one day might rip open the delicate fabric of polite society. America in 1947 was on the cusp between a world war and a world where nuclear Armageddon was beginning to take its sinister form.

The year 1947 also saw another blockbuster, by the American raconteur James Michener, this one titled *Tales of the South Pacific*. The book won the 1948 Pulitzer Prize for literature and recounts Michener's World War II Navy experiences in that theater of operations. Somehow it got turned into a hit stage musical called *South Pacific*, then a movie of the same name in 1958. Now here was a book Bros could get into, since many of them had been there. Exotic locations, plenty of lovely women, and plenty of adventure.

Or you could read the mystery writer Mickey Spillane's gritty novel *I, the Jury*, in which the private eye Mike Hammer hammers the people responsible for knocking off his friend. They made this one into a movie in '53, believe it or not in 3-D, then in 2-D in '82 (in case you want to view it).

ROCK AND ROLL HAD NOT YET APPEARED TO SAVE US ALL.

Also in 1947, a small book began appearing in Dutch bookstores that would eventually touch the hearts and minds of millions, *The Diary of Anne Frank*. Now we're not saying Bros were carrying these books in their saddlebags, but who knows?

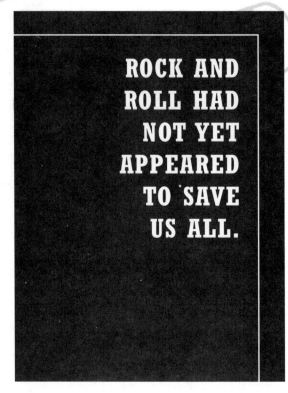

Factoid: The Original "Hell's Angels" . . . with an Apostrophe

The 1930 classic film Hell's Angels, *directed by no less than the loony genius Howard Hughes, of* Spruce Goose *fame, featured an opening scene in which the hero World War I pilots rumble around on Harleys before their death-defying mission to attack German targets.*

While Hollister was carving itself into the misinformed and disinformed history books, other events were transpiring that affected the Bro's early environment. The semihot Cold War was creating paranoid jitters, while a dozen little wars of insurgency planted the seeds for America's involvement in Indochina. Television was in its infancy, radio and movie theaters were still king. Cars were still pretty postwar ugly. The effects of World War II still scarred many a body and soul, yet America was now the most powerful country in the world, the end-of-the-rainbow place a good chunk of the rest of the world dreamt of. We were booming out babies and industry and new technologies. Nuclear mushrooms were beginning to cast ugly shadows of global fear. Rock and roll had not yet appeared to save us all. But Milwaukee had introduced the fabulous new Panhead, and every Bro wanted one.

The A-List for Other Bad Media Moments for Bikers

The year 1969 was when great American muscle cars prowled the roadways and man left litter on the Moon. But it was a bad year for bikers . . . The scene was the Altamont, California, Rolling Stones concert. The Hells Angels were contracted to handle concert security. Caught on film was a "security guard" plunging a knife in the neck of a spectator.

3 DON'T BOGART

Owner: Peter Dunkel
Photo: Roy Kidney

THAT BIKE

THE LATE 1940s

AND ON INTO THE EISENHOWER YEARS

Since we humans like to tag everything neatly with names and dates to put a little order to the seeming chaos of life in general, there's some need to pinpoint when the Harley-Davidson gained its so-called Cult Status. We don't like that word *cult*. The authorities spend millions digging up people's backyards looking for the secret underpinnings of cults.

But if you stretch out *cult* a bit, it becomes *culture*, which we kinda like. Bikers consider themselves a culture of sorts, and maybe Margaret Mead would agree that we qualify. Not that "subculture" thing, though. *Sub* is under. And Bros are not under anything. Except maybe their oil pans every couple thousand miles.

First off, we can agree that the Harley-Davidson is an American icon—hell, a global icon. So how did a motorcycle become a Holy Grail, a definite inclusion on any quilting of Americana or something that's earned its right to be etched on a gold-and-titanium plate and

Owner: Jeff Gilbert
Photo: Roy Kidney

launched into outer space along with images of Marilyn Monroe, the tunes of Jimi Hendrix, and the words of Willie G. Davidson? Well, how and why?

Staying power. A hundred years and still in production says a lot. What else have we got that can lay claim to those stats? Cars? Henry Ford formed his company in 1903, the same year H-D did, but Ford didn't starting rolling out the famous Model T until 1908 and Chevys didn't show up until 1911.

Transportation. A practical consideration. Vehicles got you from point A to point B. The motorcycle was a cost-effective alternative. Harleys were carrying solo riders and families and carting products from nearly day one. Dependable, rugged, easy to repair, they filled an expanding need. You can sum up two names as the genesis for the entire history of American transportation: Henry Ford's 15 million Model Ts and the Harley-Davidson.

YOU CAN SUM UP TWO NAMES AS THE GENESIS FOR THE ENTIRE HISTORY OF AMERICAN TRANSPORTATION: HENRY FORD'S 15 MILLION MODEL TS AND THE HARLEY-DAVIDSON.

Numbers. There are a lot of us. At least a million registered Harleys in the United States alone. And we're not alone. Harleys can probably be found in every country on the planet. Or at least some piece of them. Maybe they ride escort for the sultan of Brunei. Maybe they help irrigate a field in Baluchistan. Numbers mean longevity, survival of the species.

Fun Factor. Sheer pleasure. Excitement. Physical challenge. Adrenaline fix. Girl (or guy) catcher. Ego enhancer. All the above figure into the formula. But the Fun Factor, we argue, is the single most important factor that made the Machine an international living legend, and an integral part of the warp and woof of the American fabric. You can also call it the Cool Quotient.

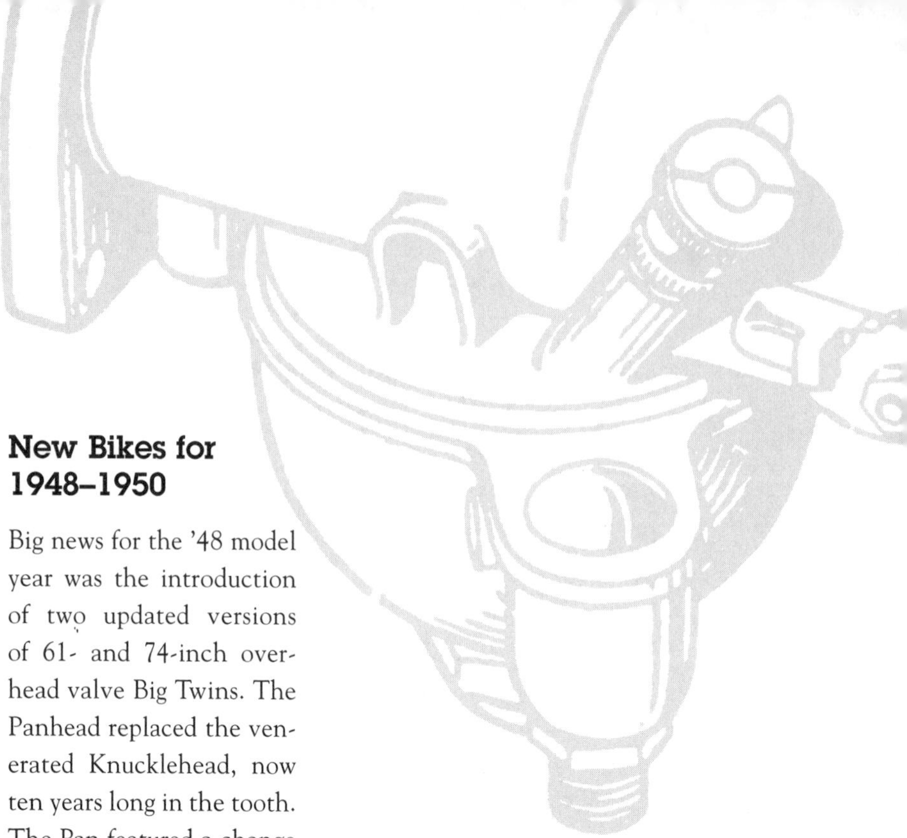

New Bikes for 1948–1950

Big news for the '48 model year was the introduction of two updated versions of 61- and 74-inch overhead valve Big Twins. The Panhead replaced the venerated Knucklehead, now ten years long in the tooth. The Pan featured a change from the Knuck's all-iron cylinder barrel and head, which had some overheating problems at high speed. For cooler running and elimination of troublesome rocker box oil leaks, the Pan got an aluminum-alloy cylinder head and hydraulically controlled lifter in the OHV mechanism. The skillet-shaped aluminum covers over the valves were the source for the nickname. Remember? We already told you that.

Engine displacement for 1948–1950 included 45, 61, and 74 cubic inches in the classic H-D V-twin configuration fitted to WL, UL, U, US, E, EL, ES, F, FL, and FS models. As for those letters you see all the time, we'll crack the code for you: WL = 45-inch flathead, high compression; UL = 74-inch flathead, high comp, four speed; U = 74-inch flathead, high comp; US = 74-inch flathead, medium compression, sidecar gearing; E = 61-inch OHV, medium comp, four speed; EL = 61 inch OHV, high comp, four speed; ES = 61-inch OHV, medium comp, sidecar gearing; F = 74-inch OHV, medium comp, four speed; FL = 74-inch OHV, high comp, four speed; FS = 74-inch OHV, medium comp, sidecar gearing. (G referred to the three-wheeled Servi-Cars. And in 1949 and 1950 a 125-cc H-D was still marketing the 1947-intro Hummer.)

In 1949 the famous Hydra-Glide 61- and 74-cubic-inch OHV was introduced. There was stunning news concerning the first suspension change in forty years. The Glide featured hydraulically damped forks, replacing the classic H-D leading link forks, hence its name, plus a larger front brake, headlamp, and redesigned handlebars. The 1950 OHV models benefited from redesigned cylinder heads for a 10 percent increase in power.

As motorcycling expanded in the United States, so did the bike mags and bike mag writers looking to make a name for themselves. Kicking Harleys was a popular pastime, the writers piling the praise on the lighter-weight, fast-handling imports from Britain and Italy. About this time Harley was the only game in town as in "Made in America," since Indian was beginning to fade from the picture. So what did the bike mag scribblers say about the H-D? Basically they called them obsolete trucks, crude, overweight and, yes, "hawg-like." Well, we liked that "hawg" thing. Big, heavy, solid, all-American. That's how we saw it, despite what the squids at the mags were saying. Oddly enough, in England and on the Continent, the bike mag guys were saying good things about the Harley.

The Motorcycle Becomes More Than a Machine

The Los Angeles resident Mike Parti is himself a benchmark. He also illustrates by word and action the depth of commitment intrinsic to being a Bro. Having honed his craft since 1950, he adheres to this philosophy: "The whole restoration is not greater than the sum of the parts. There is only one kind of restoration, and it's not an over-, under-, or in-between thing."

Photo: Paul Garson

According to Mike's purist philosophy, "The motorcycle isn't yours, nor does it belong to the current owner or restorer. It is the creation of men now long gone. Out of respect for

Owner: "Wild Bill" Eggers
Photo: Jeff Hackett

Fantasy Four

William "Wild Bill" Eggers of New York City took a clapped out basket case 1930 Indian and turned the classic four-cylinder into a retro-custom, and to hell with the purists. Even the spark plugs are chrome plated with gold caps. Forget about it, it's not for sale. Build your own.

them, you shouldn't modernize or upgrade the bike, either in engineering or cosmetics.

"Bikes didn't have layers of thickly applied clear over the base paint. The old machines were painted with enamel, first by brush. Then they changed to dipping, and finally modern spraying techniques. Telephones are black, fire engines are red. People see one of those puke green fire trucks coming, and they say, What the hell is it? When you paint, control your evil urges to stray from the correct color.

"Remember what the U.S. commander said to the Germans when they asked him to surrender during the Battle of the Bulge? He sent a letter with just one word: "Nuts!" That goes for bike restorations, too. Take for instance hardware, a bike's nuts and bolts. Always use the correct thread sizes, not something you think is better, like aircraft locknuts. Who counts threads, you might ask? A judge? No, not even a drunk one. But I know if it's right or wrong, and I have to sleep with that knowledge."

As you enter Mike Parti's workshop—with his permission, of course—you are first amazed at the number of tools filling every wall and shelf as well as much of the floor space. That includes an American Bridgeford Light Railway lathe. It's a big lathe, and Mike uses it a lot. Second, you're amazed by the orderliness, even the aesthetic arrangement, of the hundreds of hand tools, including many used by his grandfather. Perhaps the single most important restoration asset is the right tools. "An assortment of vise grips won't get you too far," says Mike as he points to a large cabinet. "Those are all taps and dies that I had made for specific applications." There is a sense of continuum, of artisanship, of history here. A 1918 Pope is up on the workstation, a roller-cam, 1750-cc Vincent engine on another.

Mike's purist approach has its practical disposition as well. "Steel is steel," he says. "And modern steel is better than older steel. It's not necessary to check the carbon content of the metal. Ties can be considered in the same light. Of course, you'll score competition points for having correct new old-stock tires. But let's say your bike is a 1934 Harley. You find 1934 tires. You put them on, and people ooh and aah. Until you blow a tire and land in a ditch with little pieces of old rubber falling like rain around you. The idea is the preservation of old bikes, not landing in a ditch. Just try to use the correct rim and tire size."

Mike Parti, like his motorcycles, is an American classic, and his heart is at the heart of what being a Bro is all about.

Mike Parti
Photo: Paul Garson

Photo: Roy Kidney

Speaking of Tires, Bros Don't Tread Lightly

Bros know that tires make the world go round, and round tires, a.k.a. doughnuts, have made the difference on the racetrack, in bad weather, or in restoration competitions. And we all know tire technology has come a long way, from roughly hewn blocks of stone through oak to solid rubber, pneumatic tires, radials, now even self-sealing, honeycombed designs. It was an Englishman, John Boyd Dunlop, who produced the first air-filled tires, although people at the time scoffed at the idea of vehicles rolling around on something as insubstantial as air. Today the jokesters are eating their dust, and Dunlop is still making tires, millions of them annually, a big chunk going to motorcycles. Other manufacturers include Avon, Goodyear, and Metzeler.

Before bikes developed shock absorber–incorporated suspensions, they were all solid or the "hardtail" design most associated with "choppers" or customized bikes. The tires themselves acted in some fashion as shock absorbers, but don't try to convince your kidneys. Whether hardtail or softail, all bikes require tires and relatively frequently, depending on one's riding style. Along with gasoline and oil, they're called consumables in bike maintenance parlance. Motorcycle shops make good money selling tires. We Bros go through a zillion of them a year.

But let's say you've got a classic, vintage, or antique bike and you want it to wear the right rubber for nostalgia's sake or to impress the concours judges. Where to go shopping? Try Coker Tire or Universal Tire. They've got every kind of old doughnut you'll need. Not unlike Indiana Jones, Corky Coker has searched the world far and wide for his own brand of treasure. "I have found original vintage tire molds in the Philippines, in Thailand, and in Uruguay as well as other countries,"

Corky informs us that the first tires were 23-inch "clinchers," but as they evolved the diameters shrank to 20- and 18-inch versions. As clinchers fell from favor, the new 28-inch drop-center designs appeared. When a tire became obsolete, tire manufacturers would ship the molds off to third world countries, where the tires were still needed—thus Corky's mold-hunting expeditions.

Today's collector demands authenticity, so Coker produces its tires from original OEM molds or molds made from the original drawings. Tooling expenses for a vintage tire can reach more than $30,000, yet customers are still surprised at the bill, as much as $300 for a reproduction tire. You want authenticity, stop complaining.

Coker Tire Company was founded in the late 1950s by Corky's father, Harold, a vintage vehicle enthusiast. When his friends kept asking him to find vintage tires for their Model A's or antique Harleys, he got into that end of tire sales. As a result, Corky, returning from college in 1974, went on the exotic trail of old tire molds. The first vintage tires, including a line of button-treaded, beaded-edged tires, were produced in 1975. The line expanded to include a variety of others as the molds and drawings were unearthed, sometimes literally. Corky, himself a Bro with a penchant for vintage bikes, now also supplies tires for late '40s, '50s, and '60s Harleys as well as other motorcycles and scooters.

Coker produces, at last count, forty-seven sizes, in white or black, of vintage motorcycle tires. Corporate headquarters are in a spread of four historic buildings in downtown Chattanooga, Tennessee. As the largest distributor of vintage tires in the world, they have some twenty-three phone lines to answer your vintage tire questions (800-251-6336).

Another major supplier of classic tire treads is Universal Tires, a company founded in 1968 by E. Ann Klein and located in Lancaster, Pennsylvania. Again the impetus was a driving need to drive on vintage tires, this time via her husband, an avid car collector always looking for the right tire. Universal was the first to redevelop the 28-by-21.5-inch clincher motorcycle tires for pre-1910 to mid-teens bikes—Harley, Indian, Excelsior, Henderson, et cetera—then developed tires for bikes built between 1920 and 1928. Universal now manufactures tires for machines built from the turn of the century through the 1930s, as well as classic airplane and car tires. Now you know where to go for a new set of treads for your Super-G racer.

But new tires are created by customer demand . . . a phone call will do it. "The last clincher tire mold we made cost Universal Tire around $14,000," says Harvey Nauss, who bought the company in 1993. Asked how one amortizes such expenses, Harvey chuckles and replies, "You try to convince the customers to order one to two hundred tires."

Harvey offers some helpful hints regarding the life span of vintage tires. "Remember, our tires, although replicating the old tires, are constructed from modern materials. Shelf life is safe at seven to eight years, probably longer before there's any deterioration. Sunlight is the

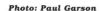

Swap Meet Magic

A motorcycle swap meet is combination treasure hunt, marathon shopping spree, junkfest, party, and reunion. Motorcycle friends gather from far and wide, often camping overnight to begin the haggling before dawn over the more prized offerings.

Photo: Paul Garson

Swap meets, big and small, are happening all year round across the country, from the parking lots of individual bike shops to vast convention halls. For many the heaps of crusty and rusty parts hold more magic than the miles of gleaming show chrome at bike shows, although often both inhabit the same venue. It's the "old gold" amateur and professional restorers come to compete over, and a swap meet is full of promise as one searches for a personal Holy Grail, that final part to complete the puzzle of pieces that went into a restoration project.

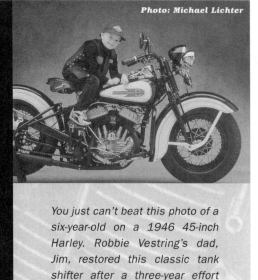

Robbie's Ride

Photo: Michael Lichter

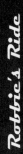

You just can't beat this photo of a six-year-old on a 1946 45-inch Harley. Robbie Vestring's dad, Jim, restored this classic tank shifter after a three-year effort from home in Cincinnati, Ohio. Robbie already has dibs on the bike when he turns sixteen.

archenemy of tires. The best way to store a tire is to leave it wrapped in the paper or plastic it comes in, then put it in a dark closet and away from electric motors that produce ozone, because it's ozone that destroys rubber.

"As far as the growth of the market," says Harvey, "the big picture is the always growing public love affair with classic bikes, and Universal will be there to keep them all rolling." For more scoop on their rubber hoops, call 800-331-7602.

The Beat Goes On

In San Francisco in 1948, the first stunt leap off the Golden Gate Bridge takes place, apparently successfully. If the guy had waited a bit longer, he'd have been seen on color television, since RCA announced its invention in 1949. Half a million steelworkers go on strike in Pittsburgh. Not because they don't have color TV. And probably not because the Harvard Law School admitted its first women students or Eugenie Anderson became the first U.S. woman ambassador (to Denmark). And probably not because Northwest Airlines became the first airline in the United States to serve booze on its flights. Maybe it was because Truman raised the minimum wage from forty to seventy-four cents per hour. A new '49 Harley FL cost around $750, which meant you had to work about 1,216 hours, figuring in the taxes taken out of your paycheck. That's about thirty workweeks, about seven and a half months, or almost three-quarters of a year's salary. Now that's something to complain about. But people, lots of people were still buying Harleys. Production in 1948–49 reached about 50,000 bikes, not counting Servi-Cars.

Frank Sinatra was still crooning away in '49, topping the charts with a little ditty called "New York, New York," which he sang in the movie *On the Town*. In November the forty-two-day-long steel strike ended, and America went back to work. In Afghanistan, the Pathan tribe establishes their own independent nation called Pushtunistan. At the other end of the spectrum, Albert Einstein introduces his generalized theory of gravitation which translates to *Keep your wheels up*.

The Custom Bike That Refreshes

Yes, it is a Coke machine, but don't look for a slot for your coins.

While this bike started life as a '94 Road King, it's no diet custom; no expense was spared to create this South Carolina "things go better with" cola-ized custom. Not only did the bike win fifteen bike shows and become one of the five bikes chosen to be in the Essen Auto Faire in Germany, but the Coke King *boasts an amazing forty-five patents pending for the components designed and fabricated specifically for it.*

Photo: Earl Austin

"Here in Atlanta," say its owners, Skip and Cathy Hoagland, "we're kind of weaned on Coca-Cola in our baby bottles, so it was natural that we went to the source to request permission to incorporate its trademarked logo for our personal use. Then we went to North Carolina, which is the home of some of the greatest engineering talent in the world, since it's NASCAR country; there we worked with Mike Stewart and Ray Owens to put the project together. Cathy came up with the Coke bottle seat, and I thought of the big bottle cap for the air cleaner, and the ideas snowballed from there. About twenty-five people worked on everything from designing parts to lathing them out, figuring out the precise Coca-Cola paint formula, and on and on."

Just like its namesake, which carefully guards its secret ingredients, the 1996 Coke King *was fabricated by the North Carolina Secret Formula Company, where Ray Owens and Mike Stewart spent three months mixing the high-caffeine cruiser. The 1996 Evo engine was filled above stock capacity, now brimming with 109 inches of stroked fluid power, so you never have to worry about the rpm fizzing out and going flat. Best yet, it doesn't require refrigeration after opening the throttle.*

4

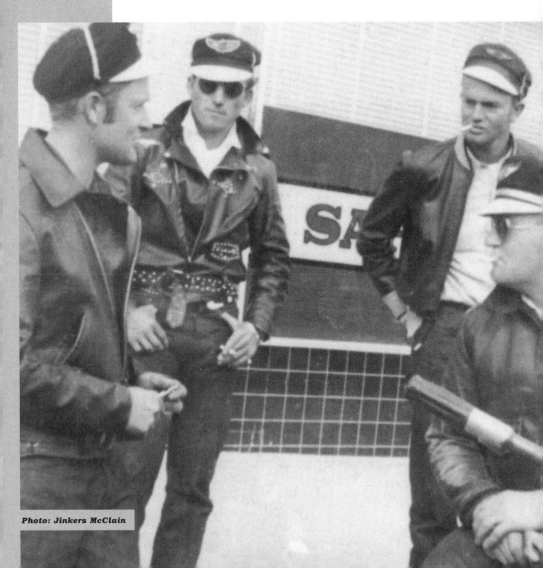

Photo: Jinkers McClain

ONE-PERCENTERS VS. THE "NICEST PEOPLE"

THE 1950s

While the Hollister Event of July 1947 forever seared the bad boy image of Harley-Davidsons into the cultural fabric, it was not so much a Shroud of Touring but of barhopping, poker runs, rallies, and local club action. More than any group we can think of, Harleys and their owners constitute the world's largest and most active mutual admiration society.

As the half-century mark rolled around, motorcyclists were splitting off into two distinct groups, the so-called One-Percenters, a.k.a. outlaw bikers, to use the AMA term. At the other end of the spectrum rolled the Nicest People category, a.k.a. mainstream riders, who were relatively clean-cut and law abiding; this term was later effectively employed by Honda to identify their demographics.

Beneath its skin of chrome and leather, the Harley-Davidson bridged the gap of the symbolic, the emblematic, and the tangible, presenting itself as the focal point and catalyst that spoke to the American character, sometimes in loud tones that disturbed the superficial status quo of the American Dream. It wasn't a bike you'd see Ozzie Nelson riding in *The Adventures of Ozzie & Harriet* but a motorcycle you would see ridden by a pack of aliens in a disturbing episode of the original *Twilight Zone*.

On a deeper if not more esoteric level, Harley-Davidsons spoke to the wheel, an integral part of the American psyche. It was oddly

Birth of the Motorcycle Cop

1925 Gastonia, NC, Police Department

Motorcycles, including Harley's Servi-Cars, were always popular with the local constabulary across the United States, from hamlets to huge metro centers, where they were used mostly in traffic control. The biggest employer of cop bikes was L.A., which formed its motor officer corps back in 1911, when six patrolmen climbed aboard their two-wheeled patrol vehicles as part of the Motorcycle Speed Squad. For the next twenty-five years, the cop bike of choice was the Indian, but Harley-Davidson eventually took over. The California Highway Patrol also utilized motorcycle officers; for example, in 1938 the CHP purchased fifty Indians. By the early 1960s the unit counted 350 men and machines responsible for 459 square miles of territory.

Reports from 1964 tell us that the Speed Squad logged 5,948,455 miles, or about 17,000 miles per officer per year. At that time an officer had to have one year under his belt in the LAPD before volunteering and then was subject to a bunch of tests, followed by intensive training in the classroom and on the pavement. If he were up to snuff, upon graduation he'd be issued a Harley-Davidson FLH 74 OHV Police Model, specially prepared by the Factory for such duties. There was also a Special Problems Enforcement Section, charged with watching over the city's freeways, checking out commercial vehicles, solving special traffic needs, and operating a new tool, the helicopter. To keep their machines purring, LAPD at that time operated a complete motorcycle maintenance facility that could totally rebuild a bike "for less than one-half of the cost of new motorcycle."

Photo: Roy Kidney

Today's CHP officers ride new police-issue BMW's, having turned in, some say reluctantly, their Kawasaki Police Specials and before that their Harley cop bikes. The new motor officers look closer to Blade Runner now, and we just wonder why in the hell American bike cops can't be riding American bikes. Can't you see bike cops riding the new V-Rod, or why not the new Buells?

P.S. The first cop bikes to use radios were those ridden by officers of the Cedar Rapids, Iowa, PD circa 1932. The radio was mounted on the rear wheel; its speaker was hooked up to the gas tank.

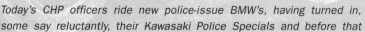

coincidental that both Harley-Davidson and the Ford Motor Company opened their doors in 1903. Henry Ford envisioned a car in every garage as an affordable and attainable transport for Every Man, a means by which he would help unify (and homogenize) the nation. Motorcycles represented the extreme opposite, yet in many ways shone a clearer, sharper light on the American penchant for risk taking, adventure, and antiauthoritarianism. And even if you were one of the civilians who disparaged motorcycles at that time, they still elicited an admixture of fear and attraction obvious to everyone. Like sex in the '50s, a Harley-Davidson was what everybody wanted but wouldn't admit to openly.

LIKE SEX IN THE '50S, A HARLEY-DAVIDSON WAS WHAT EVERYBODY WANTED BUT WOULDN'T ADMIT TO OPENLY.

Milwaukee sales were well-grounded in the family-oriented club scene, primarily in the midwestern and eastern sections of the country, while the sport-oriented riders in the West and Southwest were going over to the imports, a.k.a. Limey bikes. Harley also had a strong commitment from police departments across the country, in contrast to the "outlaw" Harley riders at the other end of the spectrum.

Meanwhile, bikers rolling through the 1950 to 1960 era felt the increasing pressures, and sometimes pleasures, created by a turbulent melange of international crises and national upheaval as social changes, like Harley-Davidsons, began speeding up. High on the list of culture modifiers was fear of imminent nuclear annihilation, the always present backdrop against which Howdy Doody entertained America's children in the decade. While Mom and apple pie were still on the menu, Howdy, like thousands of Americans, now had his own home bomb shelter.

Latest Fashion in Cop Bikes: Beemers

If you're flagged down by the motor patrol on the L.A. freeways (a contradiction in terms if we ever heard one), most likely the officer will be riding a high-tech BMW police special. Even Erik "Ponch" Estrada and Larry Wilcox of the popular CHiPs *TV series were sitting astride Beemers in the making of the TV movie* ChiPs '99.

1950: Big Bangs, Big Bikes, and Ike

The year 1950 started off with an ominous bang in the making when, in January, President Truman gave the thumbs-up for building a hydrogen nuclear bomb, something a thousand times more powerful than the A-bomb that had turned Hiroshima and Nagasaki into smoking puddles of melted human flesh.

On the home front, the right-wing politicians are still finding Commies hiding under every rug. In China, Mao is turning everything Red, much to U.S. dismay, while far, far away two countries are trying to occupy the same place, namely Vietnam, where the United States recognizes Emperor Bao Dai while the Soviets pick Ho Chi Minh, setting the stage for more carnage to come. Oddly enough, our State Department is calling for the French to back off on their colonial policies in Southeast Asia, and we are promoting the official policy of "the peaceful and democratic evolution of dependent peoples toward self-government and independence." In South Africa, the first antiapartheid riots and protests flare up.

That same kind of independence is feeling its oats back home in the U.S.A. It's called teenagers by some, motorcycle hooligans by others. And droves of both are showing up at the latest phenomenon, the drive-in theater, whose numbers double to two thousand in one year. Car interior businesses record a doubling of seat reupholstery jobs, mostly for backseats.

Nineteen fifty was the first year of the "Trail-A-Away" Hydra-Glide forks. "Smooth as flying" is how the Hydra-Glide forks were described in period sales literature. The fork's lower legs were polished on the touring Big Twins from this time forward. There was a 10 percent boost in horsepower, with the carb updated to an improved Linkert M-74B.

An adjustable trail feature was introduced to make handling on the sidecar and the three-wheeler package truck applications better.

Other Bro-affecting world news from early 1950 included the French government's call for curbing the sale of Coca-Cola. Must have been hurting wine sales. The Red Sox legend Ted Williams signs a then record contract for $125,000. Cadillac comes out with a new first, the one-piece windshield. Anything to help cage drivers to see better is a good thing in our book. Meanwhile GM reports record profits of $656.4 million. Things are booming in the United States.

People are buying "nonessential items" in the American pursuit of the good life. The Motor Co.'s 1950s range of offerings included the 74-inch Hydra-Glide (though the name didn't become official until '52), with a price tag of about $750 and production reaching about 17,000 including all models. The 1950s would see the introduction of

1950s Springer Pan Circa 1998

Yeah, they stopped making Pans more than thirty years ago, but Steve Horn of Oroville, California, a Pan Forever kinda guy, says, "There's nothing better than a rigid pan, set up with ape hangers and a springer." Steve's ridden this one, built from scratch, to Sturgis, Reno, Laughlin, et cetera. The Pan motor was pieced together from Delkron, STD, and S & S pieces and displaces 84 cubic inches. Steve says, "It's short and squat, it's bad and bitchin' and as comfortable as any softail I've ridden."

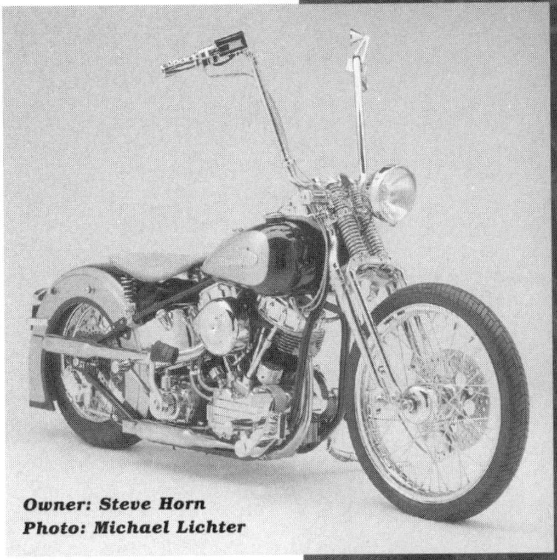

Owner: Steve Horn
Photo: Michael Lichter

telescopic front suspension and increased power, thanks to redesigned intake ports on the OHV twins. But the Motor Co. would also come out with quieter mufflers, because civilians were complaining about the noise. Of course, the "outlaws" were cutting off their mufflers altogether and further widening the gap between themselves and the "stock" riders and genteel society as a whole. A sad note came with the passing of Arthur Davidson, the last of the Founding Fathers, who died not on a bike but in a car crash. He had helped develop the first prototype H-D, built the dealer network, and promoted the company through his strong belief in advertising, and he'd brought the company through thick and thin times after World War II.

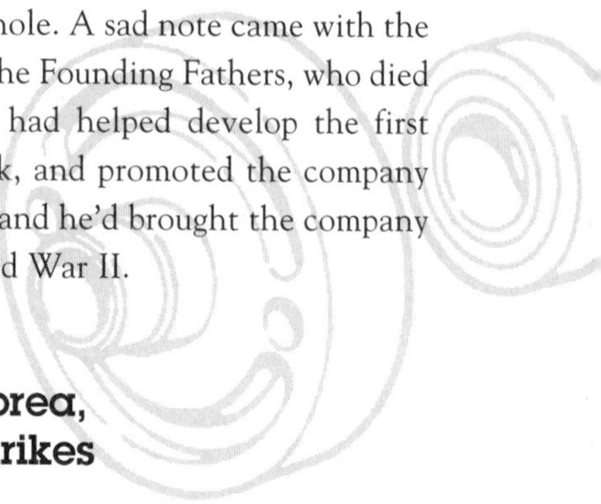

1951: Winning the War in Korea, Harley WRTT's, and Bagel Strikes

January 1951 saw the UN halting the "Red" advance in Korea, soldiers on both sides suffering in the brutal subzero winter. In the news, a bit of American audacity brings some cheer in the form of pilot Captain Charles Blair, who flies his own Mustang P-51 from New York to London in seven hours and forty-eight minutes, breaking the previous Pan Am record. Averaging 450 mph and flying at 37,000 feet, he also studies the effects of the jet stream, where the high winds could benefit airline travel. Speed is high on the list of American thinking.

Owner: Fred Lang
Photo: Roy Kidney

The Harley WRTT factory race had started getting long in the tooth, battling import bikes for dominance on the track. While World War II had placed motorcycle competition on hold, the company had gotten back into the fray in 1948, when Harley riders took home nineteen of the twenty-three American championships. In attendance at these races were both the "outlaws" and the Nicest People elements, although they mixed about as well as gasoline and water.

Notable passings include Ferdinand Porsche, designer of the VW Beetle and the sports cars bearing his name. A less well-known name, that of Charles Nessler, makes the obits as well. Nessler invented the permanent for women's hairstyles and, yes, false eyelashes.

SPEED IS HIGH ON THE LIST OF AMERICAN THINKING.

In Milwaukee tech improvements including chromed piston rings were installed with a tighter compression seal and longer life. The engine cam was improved with ramps to take up deflection in the valve gear. Meanwhile the Brits were flooding the tariff-friendly U.S. market with Triumphs, Nortons, BSA's, and Enfields, much to the chagrin of Harley-Davidson.

1952: Batista, Japan, and Hand Shifters

In 1952 Queen Elizabeth took the throne in England, where Triumph, Norton, BSA, and a bunch more cool bikes were being built and ridden. Goodyear reports $1 billion in sales, the largest ever for a rubber company. We're talking tires, and they still make them for Harleys. Down on the island of Cuba, about ninety miles from Miami, a dictator named Batista takes power by force after figuring he'd lose the normal election. A couple of years later he'd run into a lawyer named Fidel Castro. Japan is granted full sovereignty and, among other things, begins its production of motorbikes, and the handwriting is on the wall. You could say this was the official birthday of the "You Meet the Nicest People" motorcycle era. Okay, now don't start a letter-writing campaign to declare it an official holiday.

The Hand Shifter Gets the Boot . . . and Harley Goes "Sporty"

While "real Bros" rolled their own cigarettes and shifted their bikes by hand, the Factory for 1952 decided to update things a bit by offering an optional foot shifter and hand clutch control for the Big Twin models. The year also saw the end of another tradition: the classic side-valve 74 model was cut from the Milwaukee lineup. The 74s were still in use and popular in Mexico and South America, where the cops flogged them for untold years, and where today you can still occasionally snap one up for not too many pesos.

Harley also highlighted a "V-Power" sales campaign during this time to go along with the new Ford, GM, and Chrysler OHV V-8 engines. And H-D debuted the new K racing bike, replacing the WR.

But it was the K model that shook things up, and we're not talking just serious vibrations. The lightweight, sport-oriented bike, set in a low-slung frame with hydraulic forks and rear suspension, was kinda modern and set to do battle with Brit bikes like the Triumph that were selling like hotcakes. It also made the One-Percenters sit up and take notice. The K bike would eventually morph into the classic Sportster, the mount of choice for many "rebels" as well as the early customizers.

1953–54: Fifty Years of the H-D and *The Wild One*

In 1953 H-D celebrated its well-earned fiftieth anniversary, and women were breaking down barriers, some on Harleys, some, like Jacqueline Cochran, the first woman to break the sound barrier, in F-86 Sabre jets.

The Motor Co. celebrated its half-century mark with a special Golden Anniversary Model, including an awesome fiftieth-anniversary gold-colored medallion on top of the front fender plus a new two-tone paint job. H-D also tooted its horn so to

Anna Leah Smith: A Badge and a Bike

Yes, there were women bike cops, and Anna Leah Smith was one of the first. Born in 1916, the California resident, inspired by her older brother Lyle, was riding her first bike, a Henderson, at age fourteen. As a teenager she enjoyed motorcycle polo and ice racing, and for fun she and her brother were crashing their bikes through walls of fire at daredevil shows in the early 1930s. She also enjoyed long cross-country cruises, including one taking her through a blizzard. Unfortunately, both her brother and her fiancé were claimed by motorcycle accidents, but she never gave up her promise to her brother about keeping her love for motorcycling. She went to college on her bike, and when riding home for winter break often found her hair frozen and her hands frozen to the handlebars.

Anna Leah Smith—Woman Motorcycle Officer

At age twenty-four, she joined the famous Motor Maids, the first and oldest bike organization for women, and often rode with its founder and her good friend, Dot Robinson, another pioneering woman motorcyclist. During the 1940s she married and became a mother, and over the years following owned five Harleys, with never one accident. It was in 1954 that she set a precedent, graduating as no less than Top Rider from her L.A. Sheriff's Department class, joining two other women in the group to become the first female motor patrol members. She earned her sergeant's stripes and was such a competent rider that she was given the job of riding the police bikes for the new recruits back to California from Milwaukee. Summing it all up, Anna said, "It was a grand time." She passed away, at age eighty-four, in September 2000.

speak with the introduction of the now famous Jubilee horn, the chrome bell, electric diaphragm unit mounted on one side of the engine and the distinctive trumpet horn on the other. Sadly enough, it was also the end of the famous Factory tombstone-shaped taillight, but Bros did get the spiffy new detachable Royalite plastic saddlebags for dresser needs.

'Twas the last year of the EL 61-cubic-inch OHV Panhead engine. But new was a revolutionary engine offering in the form of rotating exhaust valves with caps and an improved hydraulic valve lifter installed inside the tappet body. The biggest bike event, however, took place the following year.

Portrait of an American biker
photo: T. Schisler

This is a shocking story. It could never take place in most American towns—but it did in this one. It is a public challenge not to let it happen again.

—Opening voice-over from *The Wild One*

Talk about movie milestones, this was it. A lot of people would call it a millstone instead, blaming it for besmirching the image of motorcyclists forever. In the spring of 1954, movie screens across the country were thrilled and chilled by the landmark biker film starring Marlon Brando and lots of loud, rip-roaring motorcycles and the rowdy band of "outlaws" that rode them. The seeds of Hollister '47 had again sprouted dangerous fruit. Parents were hiding their daughters and checking their boys' closets for leather jackets. Next to Commies, bikers were seen as the biggest threats to America, or so it seemed. No doubt Levi's jeans and engineer boot sales skyrocketed, and perhaps a few more motorcycles got sold as a result of the film, whose impact wouldn't be matched until some fifteen years later with the second of the two greatest ever biker films, *Easy Rider*.

Stanley Kramer's *The Wild One* is the story of a small town terrorized by a biker gang but actually more by its own paranoia (not unlike the anti-Commie mania infecting the country). Spawned by the "Hollister Event," this film gave the "outlaw" element something to identify with and the Nicest People something to complain about, so all in all it stirred up the debate, polarized sides, and got a bunch of B-grade moviemakers hustling to make a bunch of bad biker movies that further ingrained, or perhaps even created, the bad biker iconoclast. Oddly enough, the biker gang in the movie was the Black Rebels Motorcycle Club. *Black* might have referred to the color of their leather jackets and bikes,

Rebels to their general take on society. The AMA clubs grouched about the film and the bad press it gave family-oriented bike riders, even to the point of picketing some theaters. It should be noted that several of the actors in the film were actual members of so-called outlaw clubs, but no "antisocial" behavior was noted on the set.

While the film's hero, Johnny Strabler, rode a Triumph, the bad guy, Chino, played perfectly by Lee Marvin, rode a Harley, further delineating "them and us" in the public eye. Some of the heat against the film was directed at the One-Percenter inclination to "chop" valuable old Harleys, a crime that rubbed purists the wrong way. And through the film the American audience got their first look at what would become the custom bike craze, which started with bobbed fenders and cut-off mufflers. Who knew the gritty look would eventually find itself covered in sparkling chrome? Maybe the hot rod and custom car people who were already chopping and channeling Mercs and '39 Fords.

Solving the Triumph Riddle

The Triumph restorer Walt Riddle works out of his garage in Winnetka, CA, and earns his Triumph parts money working for Disney Studios. He's got about twenty-five years' experience restoring Trumpets (and an occasional Harley, Indian, and Norton). His favorite Triumph models are from 1963 through 1970. Walt upgrades his bikes with several roadworthy modifications, and also fabricates many of his own parts, including bar-end mirrors and tank racks. His restorations often rack up two hundred hours.

Photo: Paul Garson

Two Voices from Harley: A Thumbs-Up and a Thumbs-Down

"I thought *The Wild One* and the bad boy image it created was all pretty neat because I was always breaking the rules myself. I sympathized with Marlon Brando's character. All he wanted was to be understood. Just like me." These are the words of Jean Davidson, granddaughter of the Harley-Davidson founder Walter Davidson in her 2001 book *Growing Up Harley-Davidson: Memoirs of a Motorcycle Dynasty*, a very cool read. Jean was in high school when she saw the flick and recounts its effects on young people around her. She goes on to say, "My cousin Willie G.

was riding a motorcycle, and he was as clean cut as they came. Then there were the boys who were rough and tough and wore their black leather jackets and boots to school. Naturally, every boy who felt misunderstood went out and bought a black leather jacket and started walking and talking like Marlon Brando. They didn't have bikes but they wanted to look like they did. I dated a couple of them, and all they would ever talk about was the wild side of riding a Harley—and of course they pleaded with me to ask my dad to get them a bike. I used to ask my dad about the bad-boy image but he would just shake his head and say, 'Kids will be kids.'"

However, others in Milwaukee didn't share this philosophical point of view. Looking at decades of good reputation going down the media drain, H-D's then president, William H. Davidson, Willie G.'s father, was totally incensed by the film and the extreme image created by biker clubs of the time. As Jean Davidson says, "Bill Davidson fought tooth and nail for decades to retain Harley-Davidson's clean-cut image."

And censors in apparently appalled England banned the movie for, believe or not, fourteen years.

H-D Trivia That's Not So Trivial

Very popular through the '50s was the 45-cubic-inch-powered Servi-Car, a three-wheeled motorcycle introduced in 1931. The all-purpose go-getter, often equipped with a tow bar, came in various flavors for commercial and police work. All kinds of uses were made of the high-utility tri-wheelers. Eskimo Pies were hawked from them, along with fresh fish, and not a few parking tickets were hauled around in their rear trunks. After 1952 the Servi-Car became the only H-D still powered by the stout 45-inch flathead engine. A few years later, in 1959, the springer front end was replaced by Hydra-Glide forks, and then in '64 they became the Harley-Davidsons equipped with electric starters. Up until 2000, when the Sportster took the record, H-D Servi-Cars were the longest running model ever produced by Milwaukee . . . forty-two years of service. Price tag circa '55 was $1,240.

Photo: Paul Garson

It's the Limey Bros

While Harleys dominated the American scene during the 1950s (Indian expired in 1953, then was reborn more or less in 1990s), they had plenty of stiff-upper-lip competition, both on the street and on the track, in the form of excellent motorcycles of British manufacture. Many of the Nicest People (and not a few One-Percenters) rode English machines, although they were of a sportier plumage and personality than Harleys of the era, which were more cruiser in character. However, Limey bikes often rode alongside Milwaukee iron in complete harmony. Let's not forget Johnny/Marlon Brando in *The Wild One* was riding a Triumph (a Thunderbird model) and not a Harley, although people seem to get that confused.

So what's the story behind some of the best-known U.K. machines? Today we've seen a rebirth of perhaps the most famous of the Brit bikes, the Triumph, and you can buy Royal Enfield 350-cc singles banged together in India that look (and ride) exactly the way they did fifty years ago. But other famous marques, such as BSA, Vincent, Ariel, Norton, Brough-Superior, AJS, and Matchless, have faded away (although Norton made several gasps as a comeback, notably with its Wankel rotary-engined efforts). So let's make a detour to that island nation and have a look in its garage of goldie oldies.

It all started in the late 1940s, when the lighter, faster, cheaper Brit bikes started to swamp the U.S. market, much to the chagrin of Milwaukee. Later on it would be Japan's turn to hammer the H-D homegrown market. But the Brit motorcycle industry held the high ground, producing over 70,000 bikes a year during the '60s, until it lost its grip and self-imploded during the early 1970s.

Since 1896, the English had pounded out motorized two-wheelers which, in the United States, sprang out of bicycle builder workshops. Case in point, Triumph. Think Triumph, think British. Except the company was founded by two Germans, Siegfried Bettman and Mauritz Schulte. No, not the guys with the white tigers in Vegas. In 1902, after

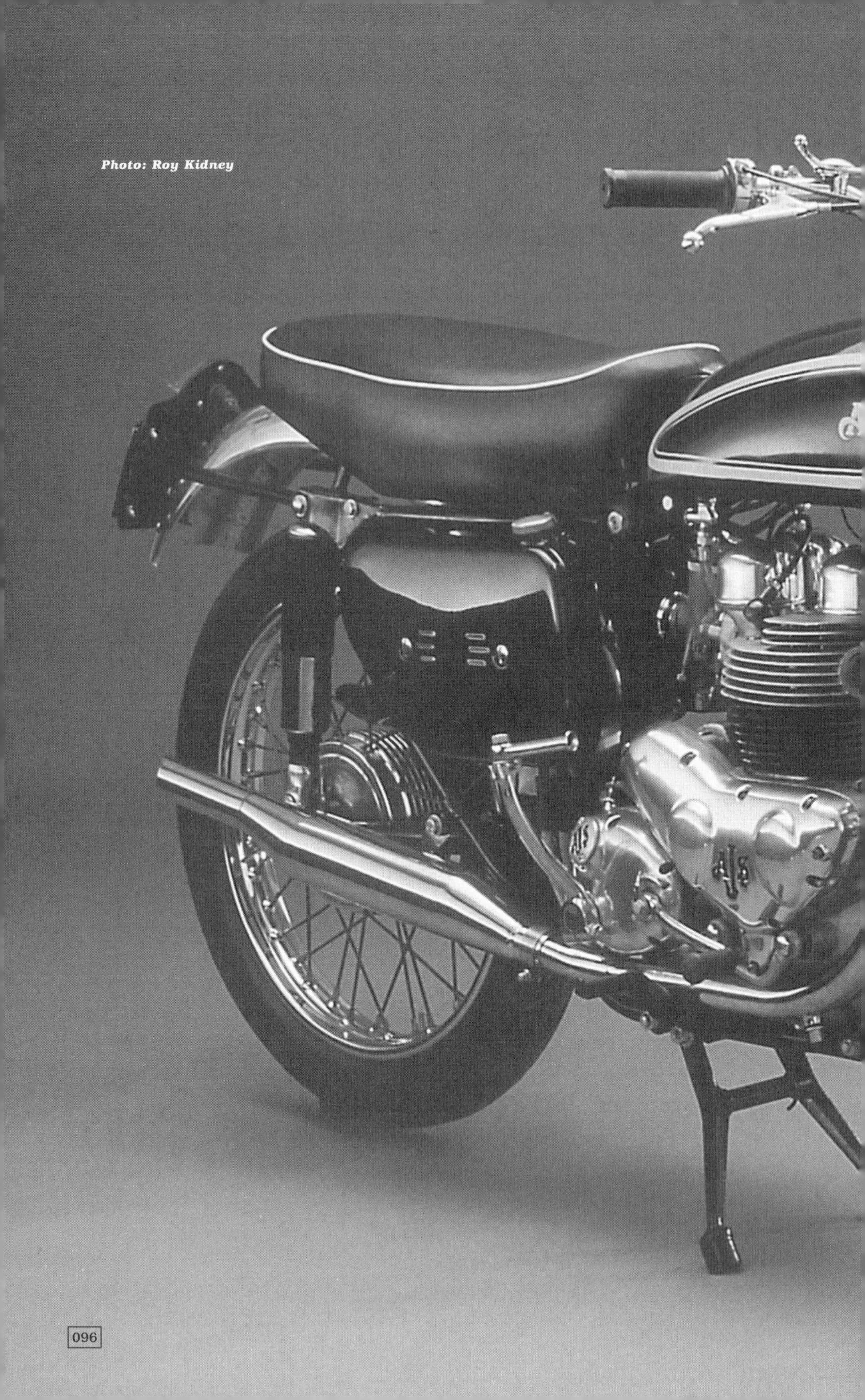

Photo: Roy Kidney

building bicycles for five years, they launched their first mc, inching out H-D by a year. Then, in 1936, they were acquired by Ariel and handed over to the brilliant and innovative engineer Edward Turner. He came up with the famous 498, say 500-cc Speed Twin, a vertical twin design that would be the ancestor of all the big Trumpets to come. It pumped out 20 hp and could hit 70 mph, a show winner back in 1937, when it wowed the world of motorcycling. The most famous Triumph was no doubt the Bonneville, unleashed in 1959 and named after the famous Salt Flats in Utah, where land speed records are made to be broken. Affectionately called the Bonnie, the classic beauty was equipped with a 649-cc, call it 650, engine good enough for 46 hp and a top speed of 110 mph.

Following several years' dormancy after the mid-1970s, Triumph was reborn in 1992 with a totally redesigned line of fine machines that earned commendation and sales success. As of the 2001 model range, you had your choice of thirteen models, including the top-of-the-line Trophy 1200 for about $12,000 and, yes, not one but two variations of a retro Bonneville running $7,000 to $8,000, testimony to the Bonnie's magic. As a prepubescent kid, this author got his first indelible impression of a '60s Triumph Bonneville with TT pipes blasting by his mother's Oldsmobile. That one image set him down the motorcycle path and resulted in the ownership of several Triumphs, with a special warm spot reserved for the 1966–1970 Bonnevilles, true beauty in motion. Blimey, they are great bikes. For more info on the new Trumpets, check out www.triumph.co.uk.

Vincent Black Prince
Owner: G. Higginbotham

Taking a look at the snortin' Nortons, you quickly see they ate up the racetrack record books for decades, in fact winning the first of the famous British TT races on the Isle of Man in 1907. Named after its founder, the chain maker James Landsdowne Norton, the company opened in 1901 and eventually created several milestone machines, notably the venerable line of 350-cc and 500-cc single-cylinder Manx racers, introduced in 1927, which would remain in production and winning races into the

Life Imitates Art: Mil's Obsession

Yes, some of us Bros border on the obsessive when it comes to the old bikes. More like totally focused and determined. Some images burn indelible impressions in the mind's memory banks. For Mil Blair of Los Angeles, it was the Panhead Harley-Davidson on the cover of the April 7, 1951, issue of the Saturday Evening Post *magazine, the illustration created by the artist Stevan Dohanos, who had searched far and wide for just the right bike to model for the assignment. The painting would percolate in Mil's unconscious for almost half a century, eventually manifesting itself in a virtual duplication of the original Post cover, which shows three young boys entranced by a customized 1950 FL Harley with "Tex" on the leather saddlebags.*

Mil was eleven years old (Bros start very young by the way), growing up in St. Paul, Minnesota, when he first saw the Post *cover. "At the time I had only ridden Cushman scooters, but I picked up on the feeling of those boys in the painting looking at the bike. I can't tell you why I liked it. It was like seeing the right curves on a girl. The massive size of the bike also got to me. And I said to myself, It takes a big man to handle it. Someday I'm going to be so tough that I can ride a bike like that." What he didn't know was that he would be talented enough to build it as well.*

In the 1950s Mil rode west on a 1947 Knucklehead to California, where his destiny as a premier custom bike builder would catch up with him big time. But it would be two hundred bikes later before he would tackle his dream machine, Tex's Pan.

Now Mil knew the names of the artist and the bike's owner, Sy "Tex" Keeler of Connecticut, but at this point in time no one knew where either could be found. For three years Mil labored on his project of projects, the genesis being a set of cases purchased rightly enough from a Texas source, the other parts tracked down from around the country to match the original image. The all-important leather saddlebags, Buco Big Berthas—all the rage in the '50s—were replicated, again in Texas.

And, to get it right, Mil needed three young boys to pose for the photograph. Two were his own, Alex and Chris, the third a neighbor, Matt Larquier. To add to the correct detailing, Mil's daughter Chris drew the airplane book cover held by one of the boys.

There's an incredible footnote to this story. Not long after its completion, Mil had brought his bike to a vintage bike show when a fellow came over, took one look, and then said, "I know somebody that would be interested in that bike." Turned out he knew a guy back in Connecticut that knew Tex and, lo and behold, in a couple days Mil was on the phone with Tex swapping stories about the bike. By the way, Tex got his name from a career in the rodeo and as a bass player in a country-western band. "Tex was seventy-one at the time and in good spirits," says Mil. "He said he was very pleased to see what I had done." Call that a happy ending.

early 1960s and beyond. The beautiful beasts could clock 140 mph, and later models featured the famous Norton Featherbed frame, still acknowledged for its fine handling. In 1948 they produced their first vertical twin, which evolved into the history-making Norton Commando in 1969. Featuring a potent 750-, then 850-cc engine, the bike stood out thanks to its innovative "isolastic" vibration-dampening frame design. So excellent was the fine-handling, 115-mph machine that the Commando was voted Machine of the Year five years straight by Britain's *Motor Cycle News* magazine. A factory racer, despite a 25-hp disadvantage to the competition, won the 1973 Formula 750 TT championship with Peter Williams aboard.

Norton joined AJS and Matchless under the Associated Motor Cycles (AMC) group in 1953; it was swallowed up by Manganese Bronze Holdings in 1966, and then Norton formed up with the Villiers and Triumph group as part of NVT, at which point things went from bad to worse; bankruptcy diminished the famous name in 1997. In the early 1980s an effort to build a new generation of Wankel rotary-engined bikes gasped and sputtered itself to oblivion.

This author has had the pleasure of experiencing a dozen Nortons over the years, his favorite being the 1969 Fastback Commando. Slip on a pair of Dunstall exhausts and just listen to the music.

Of that notable trio of BSA, Triumph, and Norton, the Birmingham Small Arms lineage of motorcycles was third in introduction, the year being 1906, but eventually it would become the largest producer of motorcycles in Britain. Along with Norton, BSA became extinct in 1973. Noted for rugged and dependable simplicity, BSA also brought us some hot dogs that still set the back of the neck all goose pimply. Considered the best of the Brit single-cylindered machines, the 110-mph BSA Gold Star rightly earned its name as a competition machine throughout the 1950s; the most famous was the DBD34. In 1962, BSA brought out their A65 Lightning, a vertical twin that, though relatively popular, paled in the shadow of its rivals, the Triumph and Norton twins. Friends and fans of the BSA's prefer to call them Beezers. This writer's favorite was the mid-'60s 650-cc Spitfire, fast, light, and agile, and with a growl close to Beeeeezzzzer! Many think BSA also had the best tank emblem going.

We can speak of AJS and Matchless in one breath, though not to diminish the shining pedigree of both; the two merged in 1931 under the aegis of Associated Motor Cycles (AMC). AJS created some serious monsters, like the 1939 Supercharged V-four, a Grand Prix racer and the first to do the ton (100 mph) on a GP track. During World War I, alongside H-D WLA's, more than 80,000 steadfast Matchless 350-cc GL thumpers served in the British armed forces. They went on to civilian use in the 1950s and were the first Brit bikes to sport telescopic forks.

SLIP ON A PAIR OF DUNSTALL EXHAUSTS AND JUST LISTEN TO THE MUSIC.

AJS's most famous racer, highly coveted today, was the 350-cc single, 110-mph 7R, often called the Boy Racer. Built from 1948 to 1962, it featured gold-painted mag-alloy engine components that, complemented by the black paint jobs, make for a most handsome set of wheels. AJS and Matchless expired in 1966, although their fans still keep the marque alive and well.

When a biker in the know hears the word Vincent, he knows they're not talking D'Onofrio or Price or van Gogh for that matter, although you could say there's a little of all three in the all-vanquishing Vincent. Dramatic, scary, and masterfully artful in execution and performance, the HRD/Vincent occupies a special seat in the pantheon of motorcycle deities. Of mythological proportions, the machines were brought to fruition by Philip Vincent, who acquired the rights to the HRD name in 1928. By 1934, in conjunction with Phil Irving, Vincent debuted their first new engine, a 500-cc single. Two years later they would plug two of the singles together and unleash the Series A Rapide, capable of 110 mph. We're talking 1936, and good enough to be called the fastest production vehicle, not just bike, on the road. However, it leaked oil like a sieve, but that was cured by the Series B, the fifty-degree V-twin becoming a stressed member of the frame. It ran effortlessly at 100 mph

The Old Toys Were the Best

No plastic fantastics here. No batteries required. The old tin toys that kids played with sixty, seventy, even eighty years ago carry the laughter and the magic with them to this day. The careful attention to detail, the unique artwork and handcrafted charm still fascinate the Bro who is always a kid at heart. Besides, these scaled-down bikes are much easier to park and maintain. And they are worth their weight in gold or plutonium. Like the cast-iron "Say It with Flowers" delivery van, a few inches long, that sold at auction for $16,000, about the price of a life-size new V-Rod Harley. Who made these miniature metal marvels? Companies called Hyubley, Champion, Kilgore, and Vindex. Yeah, Hot Wheels came later.

The vintage toys came hand-painted or lithographed in a wide spectrum of models, basically popping onto the scene at the beginning of the last century. A few years earlier toys were individually handmade by master craftsmen and thus too expensive for the average kid. Back then your uncle or grandmother maybe whittled you something or stitched together a doll. Then the industrial age and mass production made toys more affordable and abundant. Oddly enough, the first place to get into the game was Nuremberg, Germany, in 1881, so those examples are the first and considered the best and most collectible. America got things going in the 1930s, when the Louis Marx Co. produced their bike cop toys.

Many of the tin motorcycles had their own internal power source, windup spring mechanisms that sent them flying. A couple, like the Halloh from 1912 to 1941, made by E. P. Lehman, even incorporated gyroscopes to keep them tracking. After World War II, the Japanese jumped on the tin toy bandwagon and made some very popular ones that can bring in four figures today. But the real value comes in the expression they bring to a kid's face, then and today.

and did well in the handling and braking department too. In 1949 the Series C took on advanced telescopic forks. But if you say Vincent, say Black Shadow, the *T. rex* of vintage superbikes. Right out of the box, the big stand-up Smith's speedometer could peg 120 mph plus. Rollie Free in 1948 took a Black Shadow to 150 mph at the Bonneville Salt Flats wearing only a bathing suit in one of the most famous motorcycle photos of all times. The costly and beastly beautiful Vincents growled their last in 1955.

Although they went out of production during World War II, as the company switched to aircraft, the incredible Brough-Superior machines still boggle the mind, and the pocketbook. Bearing the name of their creator, W. E. Brough, the bikes first appeared in 1908. Heralded as the Rolls-Royces of motorcycles, the awesome big V-twins were a class act every inch of the way. The most famous owner of a Brough ("bruff") was T. E. Lawrence, of *Lawrence of Arabia* fame. He owned several Broughs, including an SS100 that he called George named in honor of his friend the writer George Bernard Shaw. The 100 referred to its guaranteed ability to do a hundred miles an hour . . . all day long. Unfortunately, Brough-Superiors are forever linked to Lawrence's death; he took his last ride on his SS100 in 1935. In this guy's opinion, it was perhaps the most elegant yet purposeful motorcycle ever made.

While its name kinda sounds French or Italian, the company was born in 1904 as Veloce; the first two-stroke Velocettes were actually built in 1913. The name Velocette itself inspires the sense of speed. They stopped making two-strokes early on and focused on four-stroke engine designs, the most famous examples being the 350-cc overhead cam models beginning in 1925 and built until 1950. Freddie Frith (say that five times fast) was the 1949 350-cc World Champion on a Velocette. About the most famous of the line was the revered KTT Mark 8. Around twenty years later people were raving over the Velocette Thruxton Venom. The name said it all. Actually named after an English racetrack, the powerful single won the 1967 500-cc Production TT, testimony to its prowess. Velocette did themselves in when they brought out a radical new bike, the LE, a 192-cc side-valve flat-twin with a fully enclosed bodywork. Anticipated sales appeal met disaster, although the bobbies liked its silent runny stealth for police work. Velocette switched off its lights in 1971 as the sun set on the Golden Age of British motorcycle manufacture, taking with it several other notable efforts, including Rudge, Scott, Sunbeam, Greeves, Panther, and Douglas, examples of which still ply the roads thanks to dedicated enthusiasts.

H-D WAS TOP DOG AS THE LAST SURVIVING U.S. BIKE MAKER.

1955: Harley Stands Alone

With Indian fully faded from the picture, H-D was top dog as the last surviving U.S. bike maker. Since they had pepped up the K model a year earlier, they now focused on the Fl, adding some more ponies, including manifolds cast into the heads. The new high-performance FLH was a hit, the H standing for hopped up. *Hopped-up*, by the way, apparently refers to the hops in Milwaukee's famous beer and the way mass consumption made drinkers act. In case you're writing a dictionary, *hop-heads*, by contrast, referred to drug users at the time, maybe because they were seen hopping around chasing those pink elephants.

In any case, both One-Percenters and the Nicest People—let's call them NP's because I'm tired of writing the words over and over again—could buy themselves a 60-hp FLH and for fifteen bucks more get the optional compensating sprocket to cut down on drive-line lash. The price tag in '55 for a standard FL was around $1,015; another $68 would get you the hotter FLH. In keeping with the atmosphere of impending mutual mass destruction mixed with America as number one on the planet, you could spruce up your new FLH in "atomic blue with champion yellow side panels."

1956: There Are Two Kings Now: Elvis and the FLH

Things continue to speed up, including new fuel-injected Chevys and Elvis's hips and hits ("Love Me Tender," "Hound Dog," "Heartbreak Hotel"). In America workers are taking home an average of $74 per week; the minimum wage has been raised to $1.00 an hour. That means if you work about 1,200 hours you can buy yourself a new Harley. The beatnik poet Allen Ginsberg publishes *Howl*, in which he writes, "I have seen the best minds of my generation destroyed by madness." Maybe it's because they got a look at the new French starlet . . . Brigitte Bardot. And in the see-saw battle of the Cold War era Olympics, this year's games in Melbourne, Australia, see the USSR coming out on top with the most medals.

Daytona: The Classic Race

The Daytona 200, America's "premier motorcycle race," began on the hard-packed sands of Daytona Beach, Florida, in 1937 and continues to this day, albeit on a modern racetrack since 1961; the banked turns at the Daytona International Speedway have resounded with the roars of all kinds of single-, twin-, triple-, and four-cylinder engines. Winning at Daytona is the dream of every pro and amateur competitor. Liken it to scaling Mount Everest or getting a date with Julia Roberts. Since 1937 Daytona has seen 1,700 racers from around the planet gather to test their mettle and metal. While it was "Iron Man" Ed Kretz, Sr., who won the first race aboard an Indian 750 Scout, both Harley-Davidsons and Brit bikes have taken their share of wins, but the lion's share now rests with Japanese superbikes.

Taking a look at the years 1937 to 1959, we see an interesting and hard-fought mix. While racing went on hiatus during the World War II years, we can see the battle for first place was often a duel between H-D and the snortin' Nortons of England.

Ed "Iron Man" Kretz

Harley-Davidson took home the gold in 1938, 1939, 1940, 1953, and 1955 through 1959, thanks to 750 WLDR's and then 750 KR's, with the rider Brad Andres chalking up three Daytona championships: '55, '59, and '60. Archrival Norton won in 1941 and swept 1949 through 1952, the bikes being Norton 500-cc, single-cylinder Manx racers. The Norton champion Dick Klamforth had the distinction of winning Daytona three times: '49, '51, and '52. BSA topped the record books with a grand slam 1-2-3-4-5 win 500 A7 in 1954. Indian took its last two victories in 1947 and 1948, the latter piloted by Floyd Emde, whose son Don Emde would follow in his father's tire treads to win the 1972 Daytona 200 aboard a Yamaha. Times, and bikes, do change, but the courage and skill remain the same.

By 1990, years after Harley and the Brits had left the arena, H-D still held the record for most wins by brand: sixteen. Norton had chalked up five, Triumph three, and BSA two.

Photo: Nate Ulrich

Bros are often into both two wheels and four, and see tire-melting action on both official and "outlaw" tracks across the country. An estimated 350,000 "hot rodders" flock to the sport, with over a million spectators filling the bleachers. Drag racing is also recognized as a major moneymaking venture, and sponsors start lining up as what was once anti-social behavior gets socially accepted via the cash register.

The first recognized Harley drag racer of note was one Mike Tucker, who campaigned a basically stock FLH that had been stripped and treated to some tuning tweaks. Other racers that dragged Harley to the quarter-mile in Pomona, California, were Joe Smith, Ken Tipton, and Bob George, the last building a monster double-engined H-D called the Beast.

While One-Percenters were influenced by what they saw, and felt, at the drag strip, other less outlawish Bros were feeling the custom fever. The outlaw bikers had generally chopped off extra weight to make their bikes go faster; now designers were manufacturing and selling lightweight components-gas tanks, seats, oil tanks—the legitimizing of choppers would lead to a Golden Age of custom motorcycles. The basis for a "custom" bike was the Harley, although Triumphs, and later even Japanese bikes, were treated to the individualistic treatment.

The One-Percenters now were forming organized clubs, with political clout gaining momentum. They even became legally incorporated and were prepared to sue publications and journalists that criticized their doings. The times they were a-changing . . .

Meanwhile the Motor Co. refused to acknowledge the chopper movement, and authorized dealers still wouldn't put a wrench to an "outlaw" bike, i.e., a chopper.

Of the total sales of 11,906 Harleys in '56, the largest single number was the FHLF at 2,315, a measure of its popularity. Introduced in '53, these Big Twin OHV 74's featured foot shifters, thus the F designation. Price: $1,123.

Snortin' Norton

Photo: Paul Garson

Raced by the American George Kerker of Kerker exhaust fame, this Norton features a 1963 Slimline Featherbed frame revered for its handling prowess. Nickel plated, it's matched to a set of Ceriani road race forks. Somehow the bike, raced during the 1972–73 season, got converted to street legal status. This veteran classic is capable of 120 mph, according to its owner, Brian Abure.

1957: *Sputnik*, Sportsters, and Sideburns

Nineteen fifty-seven was a pivotal year for the Bro's world, for rock 'n' roll, and for Harley-Davidson. While the Soviets take the cake for placing the first artificial satellite (187 pounds) into Earth orbit as the Space Race heats up the Cold War, Milwaukee launches its own sensation: the XL, better known as the Sportster, better known as the Sporty. Made to meet the threat of Brit sport bikes, built upon the back of the "underwhelming" K model, the 883-cc V-twin tipped the scales at 495 pounds and blasted across the American psyche at just over 100 mph, all for $1,103. The Sportster figured into the current American hot rod fever, the Horsepower Wars signaled by Detroit's V-8 power plants. The short-stroke Sporty engine, albeit with only 40 hp, was Harley's hot rod motorcycle, a relative term when compared with the FL movable couches. The first Sporties, dressed out in pepper red and black, carried the proven ironheads, though heavy, buckhorn handlebars, and biggish fuel tanks, so they ranked somewhere in the sport-touring class, although One-Percenters and NP's were quick to look for more ponies through tuning tweaking. Hearing the clamor for more steam, Milwaukee cooked up higher-compression models a few years down the road.

The famous peanut gas tank would soon replace the bigger tank, while the new for '58 XLCH, a rip-snorting "Competition Hot" model turned heads . . . away from the Brit bikes. Those in the know thought the 1962

Panheads Forever!
Photo: Roy Kidney

Sportster was the fastest of them all, and it often appeared at drag strips. In fact, not until 1972 would any other stock motorcycle keep pace with the hard-charging '62 Sporty. In 1967, Sportster got electric starts; by '68 there was no more kicker starter, a tearful moment for the purists and One-Percenters who thought real bikes had to be kicked over. But by '68 the 40 hp had jumped to 58, relatively fearsome for the day. Such was the panache of the Sporty that it was chosen as the ride for a new TV show called *Then Came Bronson* starring Michael Parks in 1969.

By '71, the engine had grown to 1000-cc, but the feds started making things difficult, imposing all kind of restrictions that affected both style and performance. Yet the Sportster carried on, and customizers retro-fixed most of those annoyances. In 1977 Willie G. would create a controversial version, the limited edition XLCR or Café Racer, all dressed out in black "ultramodern" styling. This gamble got mixed reviews, and sales were not setting the bean counters on fire back in Milwaukee. Produced for only two model years, fewer than 3,400 CR's were built. Now of course they're worth their weight in gold as people have finally

1932 Indian Police Bike

The L.A. resident Paul Greenstein learned a lot about cop bikes while working in the LAPD archives, eventually building his very own Indian cop bike. The photogenic pursuit vehicle has appeared in a half dozen movies.

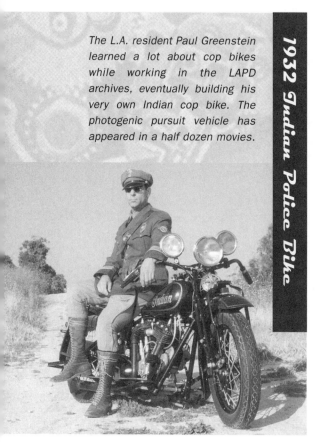

Owner: Paul Greenstein

1957 FLH
All Original

Dale Walksler's unrestored beauty resides in his Wheels Through Time museum and features all the options popular at the time of its appearance, including fishtail pipes, leather bags attached to the chrome fender plate, and the "cheese grater" bumpers.

Owner: Dale Walkster
Photo: Roy Kidney

figured out what incredibly cool bikes they were. This writer was fortunate to own one and loved the gnarly beast; I would certainly like to see the CR design replicated with the new Twin Cam or even V-Rod engine.

Then there was the 1983 XR1000, a.k.a. AMA Battle of the Twins road racing model, with dual Dell'Orto pumpers, XR750 pipes, and aluminum heads. You could say the fearsome road burner lived up to the original intention of the first XL's, pumping out 70 hp and boasting styling with real attitude . . . but you couldn't give these bikes away when they appeared in dealer showrooms, or so it seemed. Twenty-some years later and they're "historic collectibles." Time heals all sales wounds, especially with Harleys.

The Sportster was a gamble for H-D, a bold one, and a surprise . . . something the Motor Co. would keep giving the motorcycling world for decades to come. It would become a living legend, an internationally recognized motorcycle icon, and an awesome success story for H-D.

TV Ads and Tobacco Take Hits in '57

In 1957, in addition to Sportsters and *Sputnik*, the country was all incensed over sideburns—the One-Percenters, a.k.a. outlaws, hooligans, hoodlums, et cetera, going for the hairy thing, the NP's still close-cropped, yet the boundaries are starting to blur. A twenty-year-old

University of Pennsylvania track star resigns from the team rather than shave off his Elvis-inspired sideburns. He says, "It doesn't make you a hoodlum just wearing sideburns." The athlete is also studying acting. His name is Bruce Dern . . . ring any bells? Speaking of "outlaw" influences, the ducktail haircut or DA, a.k.a. duck's ass, can get you canned in high school. Echoing the prevalent "rebel" attitude in a different way, Henry Fonda portrays a dissenting juror seeking justice in the classic film *12 Angry Men*, which seems to characterize the times in which Bros find themselves.

The government cracks down on "false advertising," citing several supposed arthritis ointments, while a report establishes a link between smoking and lung cancer, which of course the cig syndicate denies for decades to come. While the Nicest People listen to Pat Boone croon, the One-Percenters prefer the new Alan Freed Rock 'n' Roll prime-time TV network specials, and the Everly Brothers have a hit with "Wake Up Little Susie."

1957 XL Sportster: First of a Breed

For many XL stands for excellent, though not extral large. For those less disposed to it, it's the "other" Harley as opposed to the Big Twin Models. Introduced when hot rodding was hot in Detroit and car fins were getting bigger and sharper, the 40-hp Sportster was the Motor Co.'s idea of a middleweight (495-pound) sport tourer. Not exactly the road rocket the public wanted, it still looked way cool and was way popular, and the Sportster was here to stay. In '58, a high-compression model showed up to fill the need for more performance. Affectionately known as Sporty, the XL has been a mainstay of H-D and over the years, appearing in a variety of manifestations from no-frills economy models to the sleek, if not well-recieved, cafe–racer 1977–78 XLCR to various anniversary issues. For many thousands the Sportster was their first Harley, and for many it still is.

Looking for British Parts?

If you've got old English iron, here are a couple places that can help big time. Try British Cycle Supply Co. in Wolfville, Nova Scotia, Canada at 902-542-7478; fax 902-542-7479. Or call Bill Getty in SoCal at J.R.C. Engineering at 909-940-5411 or www.jrceng.com; British Only Motorcycles and Parts, Inc., at www.britishonly.com; Baxter Cycle at www.baxtercycle.com; British Motorcycle Parts Autojumble (index of used Brit mc parts) at www.btinternet.com/~hawkshaw.motorcycles/scoop; Old Britts Norton Restoration (Seattle) at www.oldbritts.com; British Parts Chicago at www.britishpartschicago.com; the WWW Motor Directory at www.moto-directory.com/oem-nos/british. Or just type in "British motorcycle parts" on your web search and over thirty thousand sites will pop up, which means you should be able to find that impossible to find part . . . maybe.

But the real skinny on finding Brit parts, according to Bill Getty, is that you should establish a relationship with one of the old-line British bike dealers, where you'll find the last repositories of OEM parts still in wrappers. For example, Engle Motors in Kansas City, Missouri, or Gonzalez Cycle in Tacoma, Washington. You'd be amazed what they have sitting in their basements. And for the ultimate, it's British Only, says Bill, who adds that not even in England will you find a treasure trove in the massive amounts available at the Garden City, Michigan, location. Phone: 734-421-0303; fax 734-422-9253.

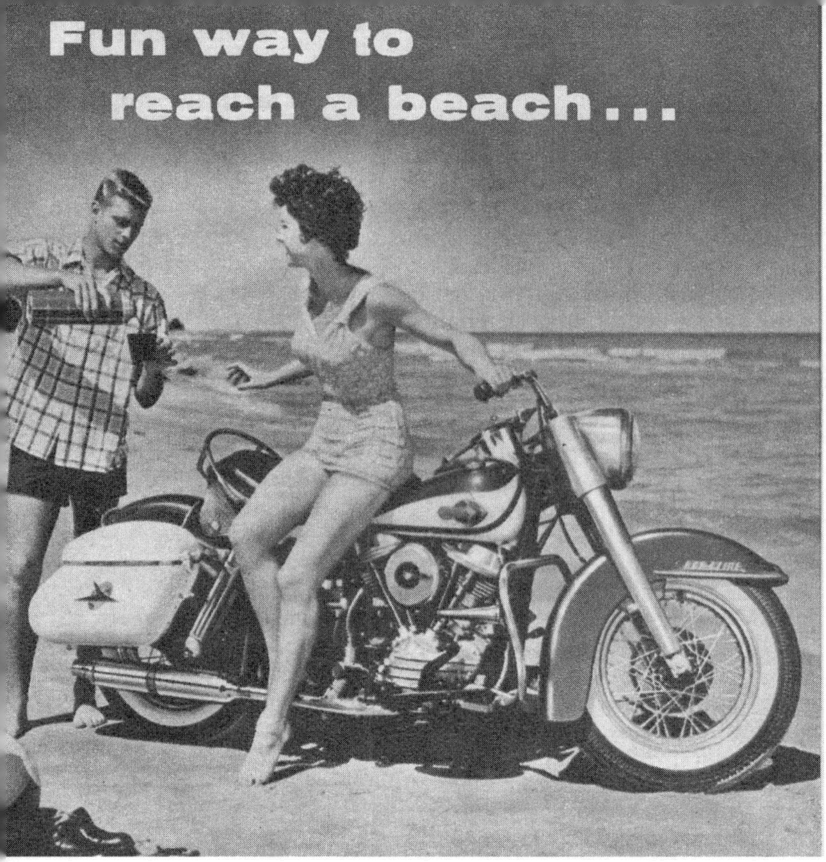

on a HARLEY-DAVIDSON Duo-Glide

al, a beach and a Duo-Glide — the perfect combination for a ect day. But then any destina- *is more fun getting to* on a ley-Davidson Duo-Glide.

'ou travel in style when you go -Glide — gleaming headlight elle and twin-flare paneling d into a bold new look. Once he saddle, you'll like the way big 74 OHV engine flattens out , flashes you ahead of traffic. lt for comfort, too! Duo-Glide oint suspension smooths out ps — floating comfort for riding both solo or double.

Be proud in the saddle — test-ride the exciting new Duo-Glides (both standard FL and super-powered FLH models) at your Harley-Davidson dealer today. Or mail handy coupon for colorful, new folder.

HARLEY-DAVIDSON MOTOR CO.

Send me more facts on the luxury cruiser of motorcycles, the Harley-Davidson Duo-Glide.

Name..Age..............

Address..

....

HARLEY-
DAVIDSON
Motorcycles

Announci
HARLEY-

NOW! Get
Harley-David
as little as $1

Here's the newest tw road . . . perfect tran and play. It's the b it's packed with fam ty features.

Economical—100 to ride than walk. fortable, handles li will teach you to r parks anywhere . . . faster. Harley-Da everywhere. See th today . . . and ask a write for free liter

Seems the sinners are getting the upper hand. A report states, "The problem of juvenile delinquency has reached epidemic proportions throughout the world. Experts have traced the crisis to worldwide breakdown of order that followed in the wake of World War II, and point out that the juvenile delinquent most often lacks a suitable home environment." A lot of these "disaffected youth" form gangs minus motorcycles.

1958: U.S Gets Spaced, Lima Beans Nixon, and Harley Debuts the Duo-Glide

Vanguard rockets are placing U.S. satellites into orbit, Richard Nixon gets booed big time while on his "Goodwill Tour" to Lima, Peru, and Milwaukee adds rear suspension to the Hydra-Glide, renaming it the Duo-Glide . . . duo as in two shock absorbers or a duet of front hydraulic–rear hydraulic shock suspension, take your pick. Nineteen fifty-eight was also the first year you get those new cool whitewall tires. H-D was now selling 12,000 bikes a year with hand shifters edging out tank shifters. Gone were the hardtail factory frame, comfort being the new watchword as more riders were coming onboard. Naturally customizers and the One-Percenters were chopping the new Duo-Glides, much to the horror of the NP element.

Honda Benly
Photo: Paul Garson

1959: Foreboding Announcement from the Land of the Rising Sun

The Soviets are soaring past the Moon with probes while Buddy Holly, the "Big Bopper," and Ritchie "La Bamba" Valens go the other way in a plane crash that leaves Bros of all categories stunned.

IT WAS FROM SOME COMPANY NAMED AFTER SOME GUY NAMED HONDA. THE FIRST MACHINES WERE LITERALLY SOLD OFF A TRUCK AT A STREET CORNER IN LOS ANGELES.

In 1959 the deluxe Duo-Glides were the unequaled champions of the road, the FL's and FLH's lauded as the most luxurious and most popular road machines in America. "One ride and you'll decide it's a Harley-Davidson for you" read the '59 factory ad.

It was late in the year, November to be exact, when a small announcement first appeared in Floyd Clymer's *Cycle* magazine. Though mostly unnoticed, it would shake up the Bro's world like no other. The ad mentioned the availability of a 50-cc moped-like bike from Japan, the Honda Cub. It also spotlighted the 250-cc and 300-cc Dream, good for 84 mph and 91 mph respectively. Proclaimed "the most dependable motorcycle," the Hondas featured electric start. Just push a button and you could trundle away on a cute little-smooth running . . . motorcycle, a machine the NP's could cuddle with in their garage and even let their daughters ride. It was from some company named after some guy named Honda. The first machines were literally sold off a truck at a street corner in Los Angeles.

The ad was in many respects the trumpet blare announcing a whole new era in motorcycling that would both harm and ultimately help Harley-Davidson and certainly rock the Bro's world . . . that of the One-Percenters and the NP's and everybody in between.

In his book *A Treasury of the Motorcycles of the World*, published in 1965, Floyd Clymer describes how it all came down, and we quote (and hope we don't get a bunch of lawyers bugging us) from the original because it captures the flavor of the times and because we like to hear Floyd's voice, an important one in the history of motorcycling:

The first we heard of the Japanese Honda was when a U.S. Air Force Captain stationed in Japan sent us some interesting photos and a short story about Mr. S. Honda and his motorcycle factory. This was about 1955. Through correspondence, in the fall of 1958, arrangements were made for the company to send the first Honda to come into the United States to Cycle *magazine for a road test which appeared in the December, 1958 issue. The machine attracted a great deal of attention and had some unique features. Honda then started their advertising campaign, which was to become a fantastic one, by using twelve full-page ads in* Cycle *magazine. As a result of interest created and the letters and telegrams from U.S. dealers and enthusiasts, Honda decided to open a U.S. branch. Mr. K. Kawashima, who was to become the Managing Director in the United States, came from Japan. Mr. William Hunt, who had been in the Air Force in Japan, was with him, and in our first talk they announced plans for entering the U.S. market. At the time their sales promotions ideas seemed fantastic and seemingly unobtainable. They first considered having their main offices in Houston, Texas, apparently because the port facilities there seemed most desirable. I suggested, however, that Houston was a long distance from the major markets in the United States and they should locate either on the East or West Coast or Chicago or Detroit. Their decision later was to locate in Los Angeles where they started and later built a very fine building in nearby Gardena where U.S. Honda business is handled today.*

At first there appeared to be some resentment among many U.S. dealers feeling that Honda would cut into their business. What actually happened was that Honda, through their advertising and promotional efforts, helped to create a new interest in motorcycle business which resulted in increased business for motorcycle importers and dealers in competitive makes.

At the end of what are called the Fabulous Fifties, Bros were enjoying the benefits of Velcro, Metrecal, and the first Sony transistor TV sets. Now what could the '60s do to beat all that?

5

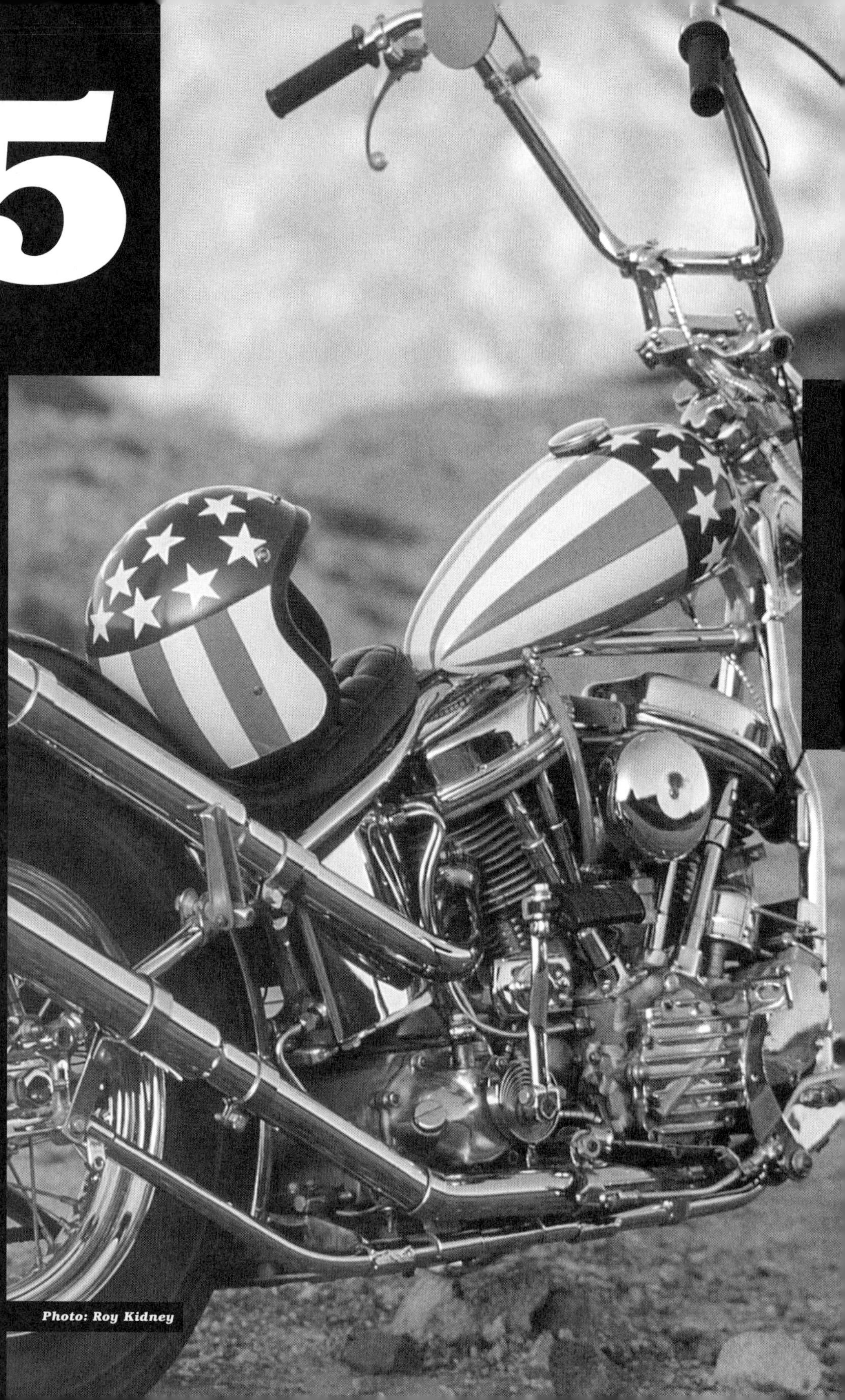

Photo: Roy Kidney

THE 1960s

DRESSERS vs. CHOPPERS

If you survived the 1960s—like made it through high school or college or Nam—you know it was the greatest, or the most disastrous, decade ever. Of course people that survived the 1930s, 1940s, 1950s, and so on thought the same thing. But the baby boomer Bros who navigated through the radical '60s had more than LSD, the Beatles, and the Vietcong to deal with—although those three would be enough for any mortal man. We also felt the impact of assassins' bullets, the first footfall on the Moon, and a movie called *Easy Rider*. We'll never be the same again. Along the way we'll spotlight some choppers and dressers that may not be exactly "typical."

1960

We got the first artificial kidney, which was good news for those of us majoring in Smirnoff 101 at school. Alan "Rock 'n' Roll" Freed went to court on charges of "payola." The U-2 spy plane was shot down over the USSR, with Francis Gary Powers surviving. He didn't take his cyanide pill, and Ike was really embarrassed, since it was at the start of the Big Four summit.

We had a good reason now not to take a shower, thanks to Anthony Perkins and *Psycho*. Those of use who were teenagers when JFK came on the scene need no history lessons. Some called it Camelot; some called it a dynasty. Any way you looked at it, it was a very bright light that penetrated deep into the American psyche and heart. JFK was voted into the presidency at the end of the year, and the rest, as they say, is history.

Are You Dressed or Are You Chopped?

Some divide the 1960s Bro's world into two halves: the dressers and the choppers, maybe envisioning one side wearing polyester and bow ties and the other decked out in tattoos and steel-toed boots. But in a 1960s world, where black and white were going down the tube in more ways than one, the split in the Bro's world was not so much a breakup as a diversification. One thing held them together stronger even than DNA or Super Glue, and that was the Milwaukee motorcycle.

In the simplest terms a dresser is a motorcycle all gussied up with saddlebags to carry road gear, a windshield to keep the bugs out of your teeth, a radio/CD/CB/DVD/MP3/BVD (you name it) to bring your tunes along, and untold other doodads and creature comforts to make the long haul seem shorter. Also called baggers because of their assortment of homemade and manufactured luggage, dressers were there from before the proliferation of cars and trucks, and were used to carry whole families about, to go shopping, to tote things. That includes sidecars to transport additional passengers or goods. It was later that they got "dressed up," and sometimes not exactly by Christian Dior.

During the '50s and '60s, it was not uncommon to spot a dresser festooned with more lights than the Christmas tree at Rockefeller Center. Not to mention enough chrome ornamentation to cover the Moon, which during the '60s Americans would fix as a target. These brightly lit dressers, somewhere between living room furniture and avant-garde works of art, brought their owners attention and, as rolling billboards for the sport, helped spread the charisma of motorcycling. As they say, beauty is in the eye of the beholder and taste is in the mouth, but in America, along with freedom of speech, there was freedom of motorcycle.

> **DURING THE '50S AND '60S, IT WAS NOT UNCOMMON TO SPOT A DRESSER FESTOONED WITH MORE LIGHTS THAN THE CHRISTMAS TREE AT ROCKEFELLER CENTER.**

And so it was with those that walked the chopper path. As their name implies, and first seen in the hands of so-called outlaws, these variations on the motorcycling theme had, in sharp contrast to the dressers, all the extraneous factory doodads trash-canned and stripped away. In the '60s the chopper was rapidly morphing into the custom bike as social trends and economics had their effects on both language and concepts. A custom bike or chopper was a personal statement made by its owner, in effect an extension of his character if not another part of his body, but definitely a thing of heart and mind, all wrenched together by passion, often of a unique and extreme kind.

While a Bro could have and enjoy both a dresser and a chopper/custom bike, often the two split off into some kind of symbolic dichotomy during the wild and crazy '60s. But when you attend a major event like Sturgis or Daytona or even a Motor Co. anniversary, you'll see a vast number of dressers. Among them you'll find your custom bikes, machines usually built for short runs to fun, although some Bros take their choppers on the long haul as well.

In a way you could paint custom bikes into the vibrant palette of the 1960s counterculture phenomena, with its paramount theme of individualism. They were part and parcel of the custom trend in bikes as Bros "painted" up their own individualistic masterpieces. It would all lead to the creation of a new American art form which, like jazz and rock 'n' roll, would take over the world's imagination.

A leader motorcycle historian, restorer, and collector (and friend of Von Dutch), the Southern Californian M. F. Egan sums up neatly the beginnings of the custom bike movement from the pages of *Easyriders*:

Back to the Future Chopper: Milwaukee Iron's Homage to History

While choppers were being chopped decades before this bike was born from the fertile imagination of Milwaukee Iron's Randy Simpson of Lynchburg, Virginia, this bike blends the best of the past and present. Randy, a builder of many show winners, went back to the JD years of 1921–1929 for his inspiration, then orchestrated the fabrication of many of its unique pieces, including the brake rotors, rocker boxes, caliper brackets, street-sweeper pipes, top motor mount, and gas caps. The 1920s-style tank holds oil, gas, and electrics, while the frame was built to handle a '70s Shovelhead engine, in this case an '82 complete with electric start. As the photo shows, this masterpiece can easily be identified as a blast from the past, a consummate New Age vintage chopper that makes a nostalgic yet dramatic statement and in so doing bridges both ends of the custom bike phenomena. In other words, we like the hell out of it. You can reach Milwaukee Iron at 804-845-7688 or log on to www.milwaukeeironinc.com.

Photo: Bill Ellis

Beatniks joined the bikers in exhibiting their anti-establishment dress and behavior in the late '50s. The choppers of this period were stripped-down stock Harleys and Indians with chopped fenders and wide tires. No custom aftermarket parts had surfaced, so the riders individualized their bikes with simple changes that included using XA forks, shortening fenders, or removing excess dresser parts.

In the middle of this activity was a little-known pinstriper in Southern California painting cars, trucks, and motorcycles in an all but forgotten art form. He was a pinstriper, painter, cartoonist, machinist, and customizer. His medium was guns, knives, hot rods, and motorcycles. His striping became so popular that it was referred to as Dutched.

Formally untrained, Von Dutch's father, an Old World craftsman, taught him to letter and paint from the time he could walk. He did not socialize as a child. He buried himself in reading about, and manufacturing, explosives. Self-taught as a gunsmith, he was in great demand by gun shops while still attending high school. He was entrusted with a brand-new black Gullwing Mercedes when he saw the Mercedes covered in vertical red and yellow flames from front to back. The flame job was an immediate success with hot rodders and motorcyclists. This leap from the conventional started a whole new direction for the antiestablishment-minded.

At what point in time did custom choppers explode on the scene and eclipse stock machines in popularity? When motorcycling as a sport was trying so hard to mainstream, the 1960s radical custom chopper came along to serve

Time Out to Get Bagged Big Time: "King of the Hill" Dresser

There are thousands of baggers out in there in Bro-land—stockers lugging luggage—but there are also custom dressers, or baggers that have been taken to the extreme. Case in point, Tim Schmidt's 1994 FLHTCU built by The Bike Shop/Murray Kennedy. A resident of King City, Ontario, decided he wanted to push the envelope on baggers, so he gave the job to one of Canada's hottest artists, Murray Kennedy. Voilà, as they say in parts of Canada, and a mere three years later Tim got his ultimate "King of the Hill" bagger.

And it cost only $150,000, which should get the guys at Guinness to start phoning Tim if they haven't already. There are enough high-tech electronics in this bike to bring the ICBM computer system of the ex–Soviet Union up to par thanks to the voltage whiz Chris Boutzezis, who plumbed enough wiring into this 45-amp leviathan to handle, among other very extreme bells and whistles, a set of video cameras that scan the road behind and the road ahead. The circuit also fires up the 200-watt Alpine sound system complete with six-CD player. Did we mention the radio–TV screen monitor? Or the hydraulic rear-end-lift mechanism that raises or lowers the bike and its integrated jack stand? It's amazing what you can get for 150 G's. Push a button, the saddlebags open or the riding pegs motor out from their recesses.

Powering this maximum overdrive custom is a trusty 113-inch S & S engine that gets an extra kick via an NOS nitrous oxide injection system. And that color by the way is Orgasmic Orange, sprayed also by Murray Kennedy of The Bike Shop, who hand-fabricated the long list of one-off components.

When Tim Schmidt goes for a long ride, he knows he can take the kitchen sink with him on this, quite possibly the ultimate Bagger of All Times.

as the icon vehicle for the rowdy youth of the day to alienate straight society. Maybe defining choppers will help.

What most nonmotorcycle people envision a chopper to be is an unsafe, stripped-down Harley-Davidson that strikes fear in the hearts of cage drivers and purple-haired old ladies wearing Coke bottle glasses. In reality, a chopper is a long, wide-forked, low profile, ape-hangered, dual-piped, noisy Big Twin Harley. Take the front fender off of a springer fork or Wide Glide, and you've got a wider looking front end. Replace the saddle tanks with a peanut tank, bolt up two extralong straight pipes, and top the forks with sky-high handlebars, and you have a nonconforming, confrontational, stripped-down, noisy chopper. Add to the recipe a wild-eyed, tattooed Tasmanian devil, weaving down peaceful city streets at high speeds, and you have a chain-spinning custom chopper ridden by an outlaw biker.

Names like Ed Roth, Von Dutch, Gary Littlejohn, C. B. Clauson, Ron Paugh, Gary Bang, and Bill Carter were synonymous with the movers and shakers of the custom chopper era. The aforementioned contributed to innovating the flame-painted, extended-fork, chrome-plated terror on two wheels. When did the novelty start? Choppers evolved for twenty years following The Wild One. Lots of talented artists, new aftermarket dealers, foreign manufacturers, film and TV producers, Vietnam vets, and outlaw bikers contributed to solidifying the resulting crazy and barbaric image and new reality. An entire new motorcycle fashion industry was born with the advent of the custom chopper, and over thirty-five years later it is a multibillion-dollar industry that is still growing. The chopper's popularity grew with the youth of the day, who identified with

AN ENTIRE NEW MOTORCYCLE FASHION INDUSTRY WAS BORN WITH THE ADVENT OF THE CUSTOM CHOPPER, AND OVER THIRTY-FIVE YEARS LATER IT IS A MULTIBILLION-DOLLAR INDUSTRY THAT IS STILL GROWING.

all that was wrong with American postwar culture. The baby boomers, born after World War II, were making their rite of passage into adulthood and wanted to be heard.

When did the extended fork craze come into fashion, turning the bobber from its racing origins into the flamboyant, uncivilized, flamed-out chopper of Easy Rider *fame—complete with ape hangers, narrow front wheels, nonbrake hubs, straight pipes, and the reemergence of the rigid frame?*

The start of the new craze of long front forks was related to this writer by Von Dutch in the 1960s. The story goes like this. Custom auto and motorcycle shows were started informally by loosely knit clubs in the early 1950s. Custom car magazines, like Car Craft *and* Hot Rod, *were just coming into their own. Custom cycle magazines had not started yet. Ed Roth started the first chopper magazine in 1965. Bobbed Harleys with 2-inch-longer military XA springer forks would be photographed at the car shows and printed later in custom car magazines. Photographers found that a low shot of a bike always appears more dynamic than a straight-on or downward-looking shot. When a photographer positioned himself real low for a two-thirds front-angle shot, the 2-inch-longer front forks invariably looked longer in the distorted photo.*

According to Dutch, this photo optical illusion gave birth to the extended fork craze. It wasn't long before builders picked up on the fictional style and began to adapt the extended look to their next creations by making the forks longer.

The extended-fork chopper in profile looked cool, thus fanning the flames of popularity, and encouraged builders to keep making the forks longer and longer until handling was hampered. They discovered early on that the longer they created the fork, the higher the bike grew at its midsection. There was a point where the front end became so long that the frame neck needed to be kicked out to rake and allow the motorcycle to get back down for a rider's feet to be able to touch the ground. Handling suffered horribly on the radically extended forks. The front wheel no longer turned as on a conventional length fork but flopped from side to side, causing a braking action as opposed to turning smoothly through an arc. Of course, some bikes had no internals in the engine because they were just outrageous show machines. But once the magazine featured one and hit the newsstand, readers had to have one for the street. The stylish craze developed with little concern for roadability.

Early custom builders had to fabricate the longer forks themselves. There were no aftermarket custom suppliers in the early stages. The Harley springer-fork rear leg had a special wedged taper and about the same shape and taper as a Model A Ford suspension wishbone, which was twice as long and perfect for extending the rear springer legs. Builders combed the junkyards and found relatively inexpensive Model A wishbone replacements for lengthening the originals. Buchanan's in Monterey Park, California, performed this work, using the Model A wishbones for years, until suppliers began to make the complete extended springer forks available. The front legs were round tubing that was readily available.

THE STYLISH CRAZE DEVELOPED WITH LITTLE CONCERN FOR ROADABILITY.

Extending the glide fork tubes took a different turn. In the beginning a simple device known as a slug was used. It was threaded into the upper end of the stock-length fork tube, extending its length by however long the slug was. The learning curve was violent; when the fork bounced and bottomed in the first pothole, it stuck. The builder realized he had to lengthen the fork coil spring as well or put a spacer inside the tube to take up the extended length to tension the internal coil spring. The slugs proved dangerous when hitting obstacles or railroad tracks and would bend or break off, leaving the pilot in a lurch or tossed unceremoniously to the ground. Longer fork tubes and coil springs were the answers that eventually superseded the slugs.

Dick Allen was one of the first in the L.A. area to manufacture and market a successful, high-quality, custom-extended chrome springer fork that bolted right on the Harley of your choice. Earl Durfee in Stanton, California, was the first to make an extended Indian girder fork for custom Harleys. There were lots of knockoff builders making extended forks that posed perils to the rider. The low-buck custom springers were made out of cheap thin-wall tubing with little concern for the load that it would be bearing. Many of the gypo brand springer forks collapsed at the first RR crossing, wrecking the chopper and seriously injuring the rider. Likely as not, the rider's next ride was to the cemetery, where he never got a chance to complain about the inferior quality of the product. Some of the early chopper aftermarket distributor and dealer sales and marketing ethics were as wild and unregulated as the Old West. If legal problems arose from inferior products, the manufacturer folded up his tent, changed his name, and moved on.

Sturgis's Best-Kept Secret: The Cole Motorcycle Museum

Even if you've been to ten Sturgis rallies, you might just have ridden right past one of the event's best-kept secrets, one helluvan interesting vintage and antique motorcycle museum. And it's not like it's the Lost Dutchman's Mine or harder to find than an original Furby; the place is smack dab in the heart of Sturgis, located at Main Street and Second no less. The creation of E. G. Cole, a motorcycle enthusiast who calls Peach Blossom, Georgia, his stomping grounds, the Sturgis museum is the result of over twenty years of collecting that's taken E.G. all over the country looking for his particular brand of iron ore treasure. "I was visiting Sturgis and liked the old buildings and their high ceilings, and found one that seemed just right. I said to myself, Hey, man, a bunch of old bikes would look good in this place," he says. After a year and half's work, the building he purchased was ready for its new occupants, over sixty original or beautifully restored motorcycles representing the high points in the history of motorized two-wheel wonders.

Photo: Michael Lichter

The bikes range from 1900 to 1966, and some are seldom seen in public. Each bike is a bit of history to be savored. For example, among the Harleys, Indians, Crockers, and many other marques, you'll enjoy the sight of consecutive-year Panheads minted from 1948 to 1965 and as nice as the day they set foot in a showroom. Other Harleys span the spectrum from rare vintage hill climbers to a fire-breathing XR750. Custom bikes are also represented, for instance, the totally chromed and intricately engraved Harley dresser that the original owner spent seventeen years building, which amassed over two hundred trophies. You can find it and a mouthwatering, brain-stimulating collection of classic motorcycle artwork, toys, and vintage signs, all adding to the rarefied atmosphere of the Cole Museum.

Next time you're in Sturgis, look it up. For the five-buck entry fee, you'll enjoy a break from the partying.

Through the evolving history of the cut-down to bobber to custom chopper, the theme remained the same to the threshold of a new millennium in 1999. Stock engines were replaced by high-performance, blueprinted engines putting out tire-smoking ponies to the back wheel. The application of custom metal and paintwork was to enrich and individualize the styling, chassis upgrades were to improve control and handling, and all of these factors have

Bike Feature: How Do You Spell Chopppppppppppppper? Long Bike to the Extreme

The Bro that built this bike and a slew of other retro-hyper choppers just calls himself Chica of Chica Custom Cycles in Huntington Beach, California. He builds machines that harken back to the original long bikes, the extreme machines that many identify with the classic chopper. The essential element of this downright full-blown digger bike is the six-inch stretched Denver's Choppers rigid frame with a forty-five-degree rake and a way, way out there 40-inch extended springer front end, also from Denver's. The bike measures an amazing 11.5 feet.

The owner, Don Milhouse, gets his ponies from a classic 1939 Knucklehead motor rebuilt to 80 cubic inches and an equally classic carb in the form of an English SU from the guys at Rivera Engineering. Meanwhile Chica Custom Cycles created the stretched-out pipes and mufflers, handlebars, risers, fenders, pegs, coffin gas tank, seat, gotta-have-it sissybar, and hubs.

Owner: Don Millhouse
Photo: David Goldner

By the way, the Al Martinez paint job is called Lava, with special Vreeble Crackle paint. If you think you can handle the hot stuff, give Chica a hoot at 714-842-9587 or check out their website at www.chicacustom.com.

remained consistent goals. The idea of personalizing and individualizing the motorcycle to reflect a rider's tastes goes back to the teens.

Let's not overlook the constant rider compulsion to upgrade and improve motorcycle superiority, whether it's in the acceleration or the braking department. The joke about braking on early motorcycles was that the rider had better plan his stops well in advance of execution because there was no such thing as an emergency stop. The rider may have ended up hitting whatever he was trying to avoid, whether it be a fence, ditch, or some other immovable object. When the outrageous extended-fork choppers came along in the early '60s, the front brake was quickly abandoned for style's sake, only to discover the 600-pound bike wouldn't stop well without one. Small, stylish custom front brakes were installed, didn't do the job, and were called, appropriately enough, hill holders. Sixty years after the pioneers resolved braking problems by installing a front brake for fashion's sake, the rider was confronted with the same dangerous uncertain ability to stop. The need for a front brake was even more critical for the big modern Harley-Davidsons, which now outweighed their early-model counterparts by several hundred pounds.

That's basically how bikes evolved from bobber to chopper. They were developed by backyard performance enthusiasts looming into nationally known street rod custom shops. The learning curve was shared from coast to coast. It was spread by the chopper magazine media, spawned by the blossoming custom motorcycle industry. Easyriders *has evolved along with the rest of the custom industry and remains a major player in the custom motorcycle world.*

P.S. About the Mercedes-Benz 300SL Gullwing that Dutch flamed. This writer knows the full story behind that custom-painted car, because he knows its original owner, a story unto himself. His name is Earle Bruce, and as we write this book Earle's clocked ninety-four years on the odometer of life and is still blasting strong. In the 1940s he acted in films with Bogart, crooned in posh nightclubs, courted starlets by the dozens, and raced cars on the street and at Bonneville. His Gullwing, the first in California, was brand new when it got a scratch on the front end. Earle took it his friend Von Dutch, for he was one of Dutch's few friends and very much like him. When he returned to pick up his car with the little nick prepped back to stock, he found something quite different. Dutch had completely flamed the car. Earle, after his initial shock, smiled, and kept it just the way it was. Earle today still drives the '40 Ford he bought new in September 1939 and customized right off the showroom floor, complete with a blown flathead engine. And he still drinks a six-pack of Bud for breakfast.

Harley Throws a Party: The Ninety-fifth Anniversary

If there was an event that canceled out the hogwash surrounding the infamous '47 Hollister debacle, it was Harley-Davidson's celebration in 1998. 100,000 bikers dispelled the negative stereotyping that had plagued Bros for fifty years. But where was Life *magazine to shoot the photos? The Motor Co., its steadfastness through thick and thin times, its true American Grit, and its loyal riders had survived and outlived them all.*

Call it a reunion.

From June 8 to 15, 1998, Bros and Bro'ettes, in the words of Easyriders' *Editor Dave "Phantom" Nichols, "came from every state in the union and every province and country on Earth. They rode with pride and honor for their shared heritage. They rode to Milwaukee to see where their baby was born and to feel the thunder of over 100,000 Harleys roaring in unison. Harley-Davidson's Ninety-fifth Anniversary Reunion was the biggest birthday party ever staged, with every kind of entertainment imaginable for two-wheeled enthusiasts.*

Rides departed from Harley dealerships all across the United States. Rendezvous points along the way, such as the gigantic tailgate party at Lambeau Field in Green Bay, Wisconsin, got brothers and sisters in the mood for the main event on Saturday, June 13.

Torrents of cold rain pelted riders for the first few days, and every hotel and motel in the Milwaukee area was packed to overflowing. More than 4,000 brave souls camped out during the week of festivities at Harley's only authorized camping site, the Easyriders*-sponsored Riders Ranch. The 100-acre party at the Waukesha County Expo Center gave everyone a chance to dry off and check out the vendors, pick up a trophy at the* Easyriders *Bike Show and Tattoo Contest, enjoy the Biker Film Festival, or listen to live bands every night on the two dedicated stages.*

The Harley Owners Group (HOG) celebrated its fifteenth anniversary with nonstop events at the Wisconsin State Fair Park, including the Road Home Historical Show, the world's toughest rodeo, rockin' tunes by Rare Earth, Badfinger, and more.

Harley's historian, Dr. Martin J. Rosenblum, was on hand to show off some of the Motor Company's most prized antiques. An exhibit covering ninety-five years of legendary Harley motorcycles was on display all week at the Milwaukee Public Museum. Harley staged abbreviated tours of their various plants, including the Sportster power trains at the Capitol Drive facility.

Milwaukee rocked all week with nonstop street parties and parades, but the big draw was the ultimate ride, as more than 50,000 riders lined up Saturday morning at 5:30 for the Ninety-fifth Anniversary Parade, which took off at 8:00 A.M. sharp. The route began at County Stadium and roared down East I-94 and along Memorial Drive to the Summerfest grounds at Henry Maier Festival Park. All of Milwaukee turned out to welcome the riders home. Even the hardest heart was touched by this incredible outpouring of emotion as dignitaries including Jay Leno, Peter Fonda, and Willie G. Davidson led the parade.

The Summerfest grounds hosted a free street party that stretched along the lakefront and included music by Lynyrd Skynyrd, while over at Veteran's Park 20,000 attended a free concert by the Wallflowers. As night fell, the Ninety-fifth logo could be seen downtown in a dazzling laser light show reflected on landmark buildings. Downtown was clogged with Harleys, making cars useless. The entire city became a biker haven, reportedly bringing in more than $140 million to the city's coffers during the week.

As riders began trickling out of the city on Sunday, all knew that they had been a part of something phenomenal. The entire city of 601,839 went Hog wild, opening their homes and hearts to riders from all walks of life, every race and creed. Over 100,000 bikers proved that they could party for a solid week with nothing but good attitudes. The roar of Harley thunder symbolized the roar of a proud people brought together to celebrate a company that defines the American dream.

Hey, if this was the ninety-fifth, can you imagine what the hundredth blowout will be like?"

"The Decade of Disaster and Triumph" Rolls On

1961: Ham and Nam—Ham, the chimp astronaut, gets paid an apple for an eighteen-minute ride in space. The Berlin Wall goes up; a new folk singer, Bob Dylan, attracts attention; we're dancing the twist. The first Yank is KIA in Nam. His name is James Davis.

Milwaukee: The Duo-Glide was now called the Aristocrat of Motorcycles, and the Motor Co. described it as "making a clean break with the past." There was even new Harley-speak for its styling: Astro-flite.

1962: We Go Cuckoo—The Academy Award winner *Lawrence of Arabia* tells the life of T. E. Lawrence, who besides winning World War I in Arabia rode Brough-Superior motorcycles. Ken Kesey's *One Flew Over the Cuckoo's Nest* says it all.

Milwaukee: Not much new except a new paint choice, but Duo-Glide still rode the cruiser crest as King of the Highway. Price tag for a '62 FLH was $1,400.

> **THE DUO-GLIDE WAS NOW CALLE THE ARISTOCRAT OF MOTORCYCLE AND THE MOTOR CO. DESCRIBED IT AS "MAKING A CLEAN BREAK WITH THE PAST.**

1963: Death doesn't take a holiday: A Buddhist monk torches himself in Saigon. November 22, 1963, happens in Dallas.

Milwaukee: This year's model, among other improvements/changes, saw the appearance of what Bros called the fudgecycle pedal, a one-piece rubber kicker, which replaced the bicycle-style pedal that had been a Harley fixture since the teens.

1964: At the Bonneville Salt Flats, Craig Breedlove becomes the first man to pass 500 mph on land. In Milwaukee, the Factory decided not to mess with a good thing, so H-D just added an improved front chain oil system, new ignition key, and new two-tone paint panel.

1965: Two-wheeling takes on new meaning with the introduction of the skateboard. In Milwaukee, it was a landmark year for Harley and its Electra-Glide Panhead model. The 6-volt system jumped to 12 to spin the new Delco electric starter motor, from which the Electra name was derived. But this was also the last year for the Pan as Harley was shoveling in a whole new engine.

1966: Over 100,000 U.S. troops are in Nam. In Milwaukee, another milestone in the evolution of the Milwaukee Marvel . . . the new Shovelhead engine took its place in the Harley lineage. New cylinders, new aluminum cylinder heads, Sportster-style rocker boxes. New, New, New. A top-of-the-line FLH now hit $1,610.

Restorer: Dave Royal; Photo: Roy Kidney

1967: Elvis marries Priscilla in Vegas while the Beatles debut *Sgt. Pepper's Lonely Hearts Club Band.* In Milwaukee, the Sportster got its own electric start, and America's leg muscles started to shrink.

1968: Flower power is growing, lots of it planted in San Francisco's Haight-Ashbury, while we learn a new war term: Tet Offensive. In Milwaukee, the FL Electra-Glide benefited from a redesigned wet clutch, and the XL rode better thanks to longer travel front forks.

1969: Apollo Soars, *Easy Rider* Cruises—*Apollo 11* astronauts set foot on the Moon. In Milwaukee there were no major changes except for stacked mufflers on the Sporty.

The Movie: *Easy Rider* Becomes the Ultimate Bro's Film

What were you driving or riding on or in when in 1969 *Easy Rider* blasted across movie screens from coast to coast, spanning states and states of mind just like the odyssey captured by the film? Peter Fonda, Dennis Hopper, Jack Nicholson. Icons, legends, heroes, outlaws, pilgrims, black sheep, outcasts, sacrificial lambs . . . there are as many interpretations as there were spokes on Captain America and Billy's bike.

Peter Fonda aboard Captain America
Photo: Markus Cuff

How many times have you seen it? Do you have the video? Do you have the DVD? Are you watching it on high-definition cable? A timeless classic, *Easy Rider* set the stage for both an inner and an outer revolution that spun the rpm's of the custom bike movement past redline, maybe even kick-started a whole new age of motorcycling (certainly the name for the most famous biker magazine of all, *Easyriders*, born two years later, in 1971). The film put the life in lifestyle. More than that, it cut to the bone and cleaved the heart, evoking many of the emotions felt, and endured, by Americans, no matter if they rode or not, in a decade that shattered values, morals, innocence, and bodies like no other.

If you haven't seen the movie then you're probably less than ten years old, have been cryogenically frozen for the past thirty years, or are late arriving from Zeta Reticuli. The story, written by Hopper, Fonda, and Terry Southern, involves two bikers named Wyatt and Billy, played by Fonda and Hopper, who need to ride their choppers to New Orleans for Mardi Gras to do a drug deal, with ten grand stuffed in Captain America's peanut gas tank. Along the way they pick up a passenger in the form of the gin-soaked lawyer George Hanson, played by Nicholson. Sex, drugs, violent death fill out the rest of the story. But star billing is also taken by Wyatt's bike, always known as the Captain America bike.

. . . GREED, CRIME, CRUELTY, COMPASSION, POETRY . . .

The film goes after the double-standard moral thing in a big way . . . greed, crime, cruelty, compassion, poetry, all mixed up in a melting pot we call America. It also puts you In the Wind, conjuring up the magic of riding long distances and seeing the country's vast physical beauty. Hopper edited several versions, including a four-hour opus with a lot more traveling footage, but finally decided on the ninety-four-minute version to reach the widest audience.

Dennis Hopper directed the film and would gain his own fame as a radical actor-person himself as the years rolled by. Fonda would become an acclaimed actor as well as an ambassador for motorcycling, often leading major events as the grand marshal. Nicholson, well, he gets to sit in the front row at Lakers' games. Lest we forget, Jack Nicholson's role in *ER* was not his first biker flick. The unknown young thespian had shown up as an outlaw biker in the '67 flopper called *Hell's Angels on Wheels*. Fortunately, a lot of people forgot that one.

A number of films with biker themes flowed out of various sources before the '69 release of *Easy Rider* and deserve their due as well, at least historically speaking. The famous B-movie maker Roger Corman's 1966 *The Wild Angels* unleashed the bad biker (and bad biker actors) film in general. Oddly enough, Peter Fonda was in this flick, too, and maybe he got a bit typecast. Other soon to be celebrities include Bruce Dern (yeah, the sideburn guy), Nancy "These Boots Are Made for Walkin' " Sinatra, and Michael J. *Bonnie and Clyde* Pollard, all members

Factory Donates $100,000 to Vietnam Vet Initiatives

Harley-Davidson Motor Company supported two Vietnam veterans' initiatives with a hundred-thousand-dollar donation made at the culmination of the Summer 2001 Rolling Thunder XIV motorcycle rally in Washington, D.C. A fifty-thousand-dollar contribution was made to the American Battle Monuments Commission to help fund a congressionally authorized memorial plaque at the Vietnam Veterans Memorial in Washington, D.C., honoring veterans who died after their service in the Vietnam War but as a direct result of that service. Another fifty-thousand-dollar contribution was made to the Vietnam Veterans Memorial Fund to help support the Traveling Wall, a half-scale replica of the Vietnam Veterans Memorial, and the Wall That Heals, traveling museum and information center, which visit communities throughout the United States. "On behalf of Harley-Davidson and our many employees, dealers, and customers, we are proud to support these noble efforts honoring the service of Vietnam veterans," said Jim McCaslin, president of Harley-Davidson Motor Company.

of a California mc club/gang. There are some stereotypical raping and pillaging, gang and police battles, drugs, booze, an orgy, a funeral, and enough sinning to get the NP's really incensed. But, as fate would have it, the movie critics got it selected as the official American entry in the 1966 Venice Film Festival. Yeah, there was a lot of weed and LSD around then. Corman was so happy with the film, he remade it a year later and called it *Devil's Angels*, with no less a great actor to be than John Cassavetes as leader of the Skulls MC. Recommendation: Pass and skip to the popcorn.

Francis Ford Coppola's Biker Flick

A little rain must fall on every aspiring actor's career, including that of James Caan, who would later play the loose cannon Sonny in *The Godfather*. In this biker film, called *The Rain People*, he plays Kilgannon, a brain-injured football player who of course rides a chopper with the most bizarre "trumpet" exhaust system this side of a slide trombone. Another famous-face-to-be in this way bad '69 flick is Robert Duvall.

First there was a ninety-eight-minute movie version of *Then Came Bronson*, then, with the backing of the Motor Co., TV saddled up a series starring the custom Sportster and the actor Michael Parks. The show attracted a loyal following. Parks's character, James Bronson, is a frustrated writer who rolls across the country on his bike looking for adventure and writing material. While some critics generally called the big screen's story line "vacuous" and the dialogue "pointless," it did have a Harley and a guy who liked riding it, which is more than you can say for the dweeb critics.

Biker Pilgrimages: Sturgis et al.

Bikers have been gathering in twos and threes around a campfire or a bottle of Jack Daniel's for decades. Eventually these gatherings became "organized," drawing hundreds, then thousands of riders. Some of these annual events have become sacred goals of pilgrimage over the years and in more ways than one the rallying points for the Biker Generation.

Whether you ride a chopper or a dresser, there are some rides you just must take. These include the annual Sturgis Rally, Daytona Beach, Laconia, the Love Ride, Myrtle Beach, Arizona Bike Week, the Ride to the Wall, and a host of others on national, regional, and local levels. Something of the spark that lights all Bros' fires exists in even the smallest gathering, be it a town's Toy Run during the Christmas holidays or a poker run set up by a local dealership. Camaraderie, socializing, bragging rights, mechanical skill, generosity, patriotism—they're all part of the picture.

Photo: Michael Lichter

Sturgis: The Black Hills Gleam with Chrome

In August a gleaming chromed city sprouts in the Black Hills of South Dakota. It surpasses even Woodstock, since that was a single event and the Black Hills Motor Classic is an annual thing. Most everybody will agree that Sturgis is *the* Bro event of the year . . . any year.

Ironically, Sturgis started as an Indian motorcycle inspiration created by Clarence J. C. "Pappy" Hoel and his Jack Pine Gypsies buddies in 1938, one year after the first Daytona Beach bike race, which coincidentally was won by an Indian. Back then the scene was pretty clean-cut in AMA Nicest People tradition, with official H-D presence located in Rapid City and the One-Percenter contingent setting up in historic Deadwood, about ten miles down the road. The first Sturgis also had racing and stunt riding over a ten-day period. In the last few years, the twenty-four-hour partying was fed by about 125 different planned events and plenty of beer, not to mention literally miles of motorcycles from all over the planet: dressers, choppers, radical customs, drag racers, vintage bikes . . . you'll find it all at Sturgis.

Photo: Michael Lichter

In 2003 Sturgis will be part of the one hundredth anniversary of the Motor Company and should set new attendance records, the past

Chopper Circa 2001: Perewitz Goes Rigid

As industry icons go, Dave Perewitz is a very relaxed guy, but he went extremely rigid when a customer walked through the door of his Brockton, Massachusetts, Cycle Fab shop with a notebook full of "homework." Clark Khourey of Yarmouth ("Yawmuth," according to Dave) had a hankering for a custom bike and had spent considerable time perusing the catalogs, bike mags, and custom parts websites, piecing together what he considered his dream machine. Dave appraised his new client, saying, "I told him, 'Yeah, I'll build you a bike, as long as you don't get sticker shock.' Clark didn't blink an eye, and showed up with the cash deposit. I have very few customers that give me the quality input he did. He really, really did his homework, and knew what he wanted, and together we worked up a package that satisfied both his concepts and my experience in the real work, and several months and several dollars later, Clark had himself his chopper that he's now pounding around the planet having a great time."

Photo: Dino Petrocelli

The heart of any chopper is the frame (not to mention those serious ape hangers reaching for the skies), and Dave and Clark selected the Daytec Rigid. Since a GMA drive-side brake was part of the plan, Dave had to widen the left side of the frame, adding a three-out and a two-up stretch with a thirty-six-degree rake. A further engineering challenge was massaging the bottom of the frame to accommodate another ingredient in Clark's specifications, a Karata 4-inch belt drive. While the bodywork was in progress, Dave ordered up a 113-inch TP engine and the Mikuni HSR42 to go with it. "As far as the aesthetics, Clark wanted something very simple and clean looking," Dave says. "He didn't want any graphics or that kind of stuff, just a rich, deep color. So we brewed up a tasty mix that was finished off with several coats of clear. Call the color Vintage Rich Brandywine."

For more information on Cycle Fab's wide spectrum of custom parts, call Dave at 508-586-2511, or log on to www.perewitz.com.

figures having reached to as many as 600,000 people. Yeah, try renting a motel room if you started in 1990.

If You're Thinking of Going to Sturgis for the Hundredth Anniversary . . .

Here are the stats for attendance at Sturgis from 1991 through 2001. Square foot for square foot, more Harleys than anywhere at any time on the planet.

1991	100,000
1992	120,000
1993	150,000
1994	200,000
1995	215,000
1996	175,000
1997	220,000
1998	225,000
1999	250,000
2000	600,000—whoa!
2001	250,000
2002	Don't know, hasn't happened as we write this thing.
2003	August 4–10. One hundred years of Harleys . . . should be a record setter.

Daytona: 2001 Saw the Sixtieth Anniversary

Daytona Beach, Florida, celebrated its sixtieth Bike Week in 2001. Call it Sturgis with sun and surf, call both of them the cathode and anode that continually recharge the Bro's battery. But whatever you call it, you got to do that by experiencing it yourself. You can actually experience Bike Week in two flavors.

He Who Has the Most Toys: Motorcycle Museums

There is a general rule in Bro thinking. More is better. More bikes. More bike parts. More bike books. It's not greed or compulsion. Call it a form of conservation. Classic bikes being in the category of endangered species, it's up to each Bro to save as many as possible. And to support those who take that thought to the max, the collectors create museums for the rest of us to enjoy. While some people may travel hundreds of miles to see the World's Largest Lint Ball or spend hours waiting in line for a thirty-second chance to hurl their prefabricated lunch, a Bro heads for a bike museum, and there are a few very, very nice ones that must be visited at least once every few years to maintain one's sense of history. If you want your Bro passport to carry any weight, it has to carry the stamps attesting to the following pilgrimages.

There's the renowned Bike Week extravaganza in March, but in the last several years there's also been Biketoberfest taking place in October at the same location. Its crowd is a bit smaller than Bike Week's but growing every year. A lot of people like it just because it's not as crowded as Bike Week, when your own belly button is hard-pressed to make it through the door of any of the watering holes and shops lining Main Street.

Photo: Michael Lichter

In a nutshell, Daytona is an event in praise of life itself. There's plenty of testosterone, posturing, displays of power, and sex—lots of sexiness everywhere—and the overlying and underlying rumble and thunder of V-twin engines. It's tribal, hedonistic, charged with chemistry, a gathering of humans to celebrate not only their machines but the essence of life itself: raw, loud, intense, exciting. In one voice, several hundred thousand people literally shout, "Hear me roar."

Situated on the eastern coastline of the Sunshine State, Daytona Beach was early on a host to car racers, thanks to its hard-packed white beaches that stretch for twelve miles. It saw bike racing from 1937 to

Photo: Michael Lichter

Photo: Michael Lichter

1960 that drew the crowds but, as the Japanese bikes began dominating the inland racetrack, the beachside turned into a Harley gathering point, a Mecca for Milwaukee enthusiasts from around the world.

A benchmark year in the evolution of Daytona was 1973, the advent of the famous Rats Hole motorcycle show, at which builders began showing off their latest custom creations. The cops expected about 5,000 spectators; 15,000 crowded the show. In 1976 the Motor Co., realizing Daytona was the place to be, set up an exhibition in a local hotel with Harley drag racing nearby drawing more crowds. Vendors were flocking to what you might call Milwaukee's Florida home. You could now choose from about 3 million different kinds of T-shirts.

A black shadow eclipsed the scene in the late 1970s as the result of motorcycle gang violence coupled with police antibiker tactics and the feeling that local businesses were overcharging for almost everything. Daytona was about to become history, it seemed. But a new police chief worked things out, and Bike Week was reinstated, although some thought it was now too structured and still way commercialized. Be that as it may, Bike Week took off again as the Party Place to Be, and upwards of 500,000 have been known to make their way to the annual event.

For the latest info about upcoming Daytona events, log on to www.officialbikeweek.com, or call 800-854-1234, ext. 510.

The Love Ride: Ribs, Rubbies, and Rolling Thunder

What's it like to attend a Love Ride? Here's one eyewitness account.

Well, we survived the seventeenth Love Ride. If you haven't been to this L.A. area biker event, mark it on your must-do calendar. It's a good excuse to visit SoCal, and you won't be scratching your head for things to do—Disneyland, Universal Studios, Venice Beach, the Hollywood Bowl, Bartel's H-D dealership, Fatburgers for grub—all the reasons worth living, all right in your grasp.

According to Guinness the Love Ride is the largest fund-raising single-day event in the world. It's also got great gobs of sunshine, several square miles of polished billet aluminum, and enough leather to upholster the moons of Jupiter. RUBs (rich urban bikers) rubbed shoulders with patch-wearing club members and families with strollers. The Love Ride's a truly universal event that, although predominately Harley-Davidson, does not exclude other brands.

Purple Hearts and Art: Chicago's National Vietnam Vets Museum

If you're ever in Chicago, you'll want to visit a particular art gallery that doesn't have a single Picasso, Monet, or Rembrandt. In fact, you'll probably not recognize the names of the 128 (and growing) artists unless you happen to have served in the Vietnam War. The Chicago National Vietnam Veterans Art Museum houses works in all media, the only requirement that an artist has to have been "in country." Artists from any country, on both sides of the conflict, are welcome to contribute. Museum President Ned Broderick is always looking for new work, and all it takes is a few slides of your artwork sent in to the museum.

One of the most awesome pieces is a work consisting of 58,220 individually made dog tags inscribed with the names of those U.S. personnel who fell in Vietnam. The sculpture, called Above and Beyond, *hangs in the museum's atrium and seems a solid mass of metal, which, with a mere puff of breath, begins to ripple like a feather, symbolic in many ways of the power and fragility of life. Designed as a center for healing and understanding, the museum is not funded by the government in any way and survives, and thrives, through public support. For more information, call 800-476-8808 or visit the website at www.nvvam.org.*

Fast Forward Chopper: Bare Bones in the Old Tradition

Now if you still think Jesse James shot the sheriff, you haven't been watching the Discovery Channel, because the cable network has now aired not one but two "choppumentaries" about Master Builder Jesse James of West Coast Choppers (Long Beach, California).

The media has latched on to Jesse as the embodiment of all things custom/chopper and chronicled his fast-lane life and times as he builds and rides some outstanding machines. Jesse believes in the no-frills, all-thrills approach to biking and says if you can't carry it in your pockets then leave it home, and whatever doesn't make the bike go or stop faster, leave that at home, too.

Photo: Michael Lichter

The Love Ride traces its roots back to 1981 and something called the Biker's Carnival, a fund-raiser put together by Oliver Shokouh, owner of the then new Harley-Davidson of Glendale dealership. Oliver held the first event behind his shop in conjunction with the H-D Motor Company, who had become the official corporate sponsor for the Muscular Dystrophy Association. The event raised $1,500 for MDA. Jump to 1984 and the Love Ride was born, with Peter Fonda and Willie G. showing up. Since then the gathering of eagles has raised over $12 million, this year's proceeds going to MDA and the *L.A. Times'* Reading by 9 literacy initiative.

The Author and Arlen Ness
Photo: Markus Cuff

The Sunday morning kickoff featured Jay Leno as the grand marshal and Peter Fonda as the honorary grand marshal (this town ain't big enough for two marshals), while John Kay and Steppenwolf got up god-awful early Sunday morning to play "Born to Be Wild" at Harley-Davidson of Glendale for the thousands who turned up to take part in the 50-mile "motorcycle caravan" that chugged along L.A. freeways to Castaic Lake Recreation Center in Santa Clarita.

And whereas about everybody uses an Evo or Twin Cam (not forgetting Merch; Delkron; Eagle Motor Co.; Patrick Racing, who makes Jesse's heads; Zippers; TP; and other engine masters), Jesse chose an S & S Shovelhead to power his take on your BBC from WCC . . . that's Basic Black Chopper from West Coast Choppers, except nothing's basic about it. The Shovel is hard-core; Jesse is hard-core. So it's a personality match. The motor came along with a project in the works that wasn't working for Jesse's bro Paul Cavalo. Jesse kept the motor, then stuffed it into a Choppers for Life hardtail frame, and then proceeded to beat the hell out of the metal sheets until some very tidy parts emerged, including the classic peanut gas tank, snug-hugging fenders, and swooping side pipes. And you don't press a button to start this one, you kick it to life.

One gander at the photos, and you think, Less is best. You want to talk to Jesse? Wait in line, but if you get by his pit bulls and shark tank, call him at 562-983-6666. Yeah, 666 is in there. If that's too scary for you, log on to www.westcoastchoppers.com.

Otis Chandler May Have the Most Toys: Cars, Bikes, and Animal Heads

Visiting Otis Chandler's museum, located about an hour north of Los Angeles in Oxnard, California, can be a time-altering experience. Mr. Chandler, by the way, is from the L.A. Times *newspaper-owning family, and he later took charge of the entire Times Mirror Company and thirty-five other publishing-related companies, so he has had his finger on very newsworthy and note-worthy machines, both four-wheeled and two-wheeled. Otis is an accomplished athlete, race car driver, hunter (conservation-related), and also a bike guy big time. His first ride was a used hundred-dollar '47 Knucklehead that he rode to college. His 45,000-square-foot museum has the best of both wheeled worlds. Officially the place is called the Vintage Museum of Transportation and Wildlife because there are a lot of big, and not so big, game trophies occupying the same building, along with hemi-cudas and Cleveland Fours, not to mention a very extensive collection of historic Harleys. It's a mindblower. For more information call 805-486-0666.*

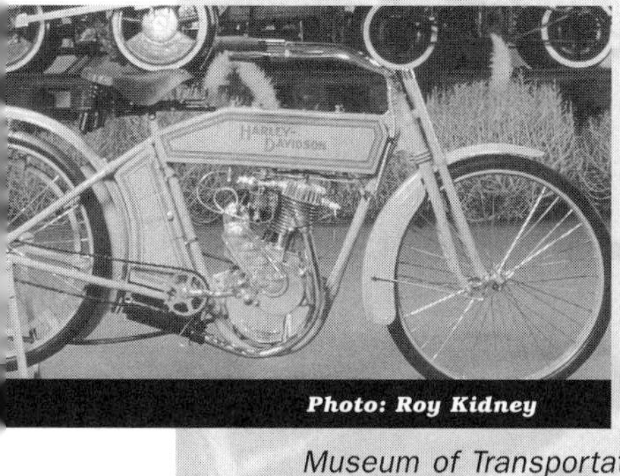

Photo: Roy Kidney

Photos: Markus Cuff

And, yes, there were a lot of "graybeards" in attendance (median age 43.6 years) who could definitely identify with the classic tunes, like "Who'll Stop the Rain," played onstage at Castaic by Creedence. It must have worked because the day, though starting off coolish, warmed up bright and sunny for stellar weather. Later in the day, Blood, Sweat & Tears played their golden hits, like "Spinning Wheel" and "God Bless the Child."

You could walk, ride, or even drive away with some big-buck giveaway items. For a two-hundred-dollar donation you also got a ticket for a drawing that could land you a new Harley-Davidson Deuce or a 2001 Ford–Harley-Davidson special edition truck, or a Love Ride 17 commemorative guitar by Fender.

Helmets and hats off to Oliver Shokouh for continuing a history-making tradition and to all the thousands of riders who braved cool temperatures and a traffic jam that must have earned a Guinness Book of Records rating.

For information about Love Ride 18, call the hotline at 818-246-5618, ext. 7, or check out the website at www.loveride.org.

Loving Laconia: The Other Bike Week

While even people who wouldn't know a Panhead from a pancake know about Sturgis and Daytona Bike Week, fewer can give you a thumbs-up about Laconia. It used to shine up there with the other bike

Photo: Michael Lichter

gatherings, and it shares some of the same history. Started in 1923, Laconia Bike Week, staged in the city of the same name in New Hampshire, usually takes place in June. AMA-sponsored racing was introduced in the 1930s, and in 1990 the New Hampshire International Speedway Stadium was constructed in nearby Loudon to handle modern racers. Here starts some of the confusion about Laconia, because it's also called Loudon, which tends to dilute things. Then there's the famous hill-climb action at Mount Belknap, which gets lumped under Laconia, too.

Photo: Michael Lichter

But if you're looking at the map, you'll find an area in the small town of Laconia called Weirs Beach. It's like a smaller version of Daytona Beach and attracts the densest concentrations of bikers. There were some breaches of decorum, a.k.a. rioting, there back in the 1960s, and the police backlash, particularly in the 1990s, seriously diminished the event. But, once again, cooler heads prevailed, and the event has taken on new life in the last couple of years, with something like 200,000 attending the summer fest.

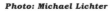

Photo: Michael Lichter

The Victor McLaglen Motor Corps

This famous stunt team adds new meaning to the concept of maintaining a balanced life thanks to their incredible mass formations aboard Harleys ridden in ways not described in any handbook from Milwaukee. Founded in 1935 with the help of the famous movie star of that era whose name they bear, the group began competing in world events, taking the 1936 World Championship Trophy. With both men and women on the team, and ages ranging from teenagers to over seventy, the precision drill team champions both motorcycling appreciation and safety across the country. Headquartered in La Palma, California, they're always looking for new members who have the practice time, a well-running Harley, and the inclination to get radically inclined. For more info and event schedules, log on to their website www.thevmmc.com.

Photo: Sam Jones

Laughlin River Run

For another perspective on bike events, we turn the microphone over to Clean Dean, a.k.a. Dean Shawler, longtime editor of *Biker* magazine, for his own take on this very popular Nevada event as held in 2001. As they say, it's printed in its entirety and uncensored.

The Laughlin River Run has grown to be the largest motorcycle event on the West Coast as claimed by the promoters, Dal-Con Promotions. I don't know about you, but bein' 350 miles inland from any Pacific beach, and ridin' through 300 miles of desert to get there, just doesn't seem like West Coast to me. 'Course what else couldja call it: the largest Middle of the Fuckin' Desert event? Largest somewhere between the West Coast and the Midwest event? Biggest west side of the Colorado River event?

Nevertheless, the official Laughlin count was around 70,000, with about that many motorcycles. The police department's news release reported that

Bike Feature: A Family Affair Dresser

It all started when Pierre Boucher spotted an ad in the paper for a used Harley FLHTC. His other bike was a 1200 Sportster, and now his wife, Diane, was asking for something more comfortable because she had a back problem. "So together we went to look at the FLH," Pierre explained. "It was a nightmare. The fenders were all dented, the seat torn apart, the motor aluminum pitted, the outer faking cracked, the mufflers rusted, the tires bald. It had spent its winters parked outside in a snowbank. But I wanted that bike. I wanted comfort, and an Electra-Glide is like gliding long distances on a couch. I knew I could fix it. My wife was not as enthusiastic. I told her I'd make it nice, just clean it up a little—maybe a few pieces of bolt-on chrome and a paint job. That 'little' turned into a lot. Every summer we rode it, and then worked on it bit by bit over the winters.

Photo: Michael Lichter

"I call this bike a Family Affair because my wife and I gave our input together, making it a mutual effort. For example, she picked out the two-tone paint scheme, GM Burnt Wood and Cream. My wife wanted an Indian woman and wolves, her grandmother being a Native American. The freedom theme is there again, Indians living a nomadic lifestyle with no barriers to their freedom. I used to drive my truck through the Southwest desert and wanted desert scenes, so we put both themes together. Martin (the painter) said to come back in two months. Awesome was the only word we could think when we picked up the bike."

We sadly must report that Pierre won't be making that ride to Laconia. He passed away in 2000, but we knew Pierre and how much he loved his bike and all that it meant, so this one's for Pierre, a true Bro in the best sense of the word.

the crowds were extremely well behaved, and any problems in the crowd were dealt with quickly.

It seems there's a new sheriff in town (Lieutenant Tom Smitley), who told his men that he wanted this to be a better event, and that the people be treated nice, like customers. And I guess they did just that because there were warning tickets given in place of the moneymakers in many cases, and if riders had their helmets on their bikes and not their heads, they were politely asked to put them on.

There were three major traffic accidents involving motorcycles this year. A man got killed on Needles Highway northbound near mile-marker six, when he lost control and slid across into the path of a group of bikes heading south. On Highway 95, between Railroad Pass and Searchlight, a couple was immediately snuffed when an SUV with a flat tire took 'em out. Another incident on Casino Drive sent a couple people to the hospital when some dipshit lost control of his scooter and ended up in the crowd.

Ten motorcycles were reported stolen from various locations in Laughlin. A task force was on hand to check vehicle identification numbers, and they towed eight bikes that had altered VINs. They claimed some of these bikes had stolen parts, identified through NCIC, that'd been stolen in previous years from different locations around the U.S. The bikes confiscated will get further investigation from the Las Vegas Metropolitan Police Department's Auto Theft Detail.

TEN MOTORCYCLES WERE REPORTED STOLEN FROM VARIOUS LOCATIONS IN LAUGHLIN.

Here's some more statistics ya might find interesting: felony arrests, 7; accidents, 4; gross misdemeanors, 6; misdemeanors, 35; juvenile curfew cites, 12; misdemeanor cites, 2; juvenile criminal arrests, 7; DUI arrests, 8; controlled substance arrests, 5; traffic citations, 297; domestic violence arrests, 4; traffic arrests, 11; lewd conduct arrests, 6; disorderly conduct arrests, 8; weapons violations, 5; and warrant arrests, 12. Not too bad when you consider the thousands and thousands of scooter folk that clogged this event.

There were some new things happenin' this year that were reportedly very successful. One was the First Annual Ride & Slide at the Needles Aquatic Center. The admission was $5 and girls got in 2-for-1. It was the right weather for it! The Bikers Bench Press Championship at the River Palms went over well. I missed the Hawaiian Tropic Bikini Contest at the Colorado Belle, but I did make it to the First Annual Ladies at Laughlin River Run Conference and Luncheon.

The Ladies at Laughlin luncheon at Harrah's was pretty cool, actually. It's interesting hearing women talk about riding with the same passion for it as men, but they have their own set of obstacles to overcome. Christine Ravazzolo, a pretty little lady of barely 5 feet and not much over 100 pounds, explained and demonstrated how to pick up a motorcycle after droppin' it. When she asked the crowd, "What's the first thing you do when you drop your bike?" a meek little voice broke the silence with "Cry?" Randy Twells was the organizer of the luncheon, with prominent ladies in motorcycling celebrities sharing the podium. There was $16,500 raised for the Susan G. Komen Breast Cancer Foundation. Some of the sponsors present were the Motor Maids, and Worn Wheels, and Friction Zone magazines. A Ride for the Cure was held after the luncheon.

Photo: Stan Miles

The Styx concert at the Flamingo was great. The Jimmie Van Zant Band opened for Foghat at River Palms. The Riverside Resort had the Marshall Tucker Band bastin' the biker tunes, and comedian Howie Mandel had 'em in stitches at Harrah's.

Aftermarket vendors were there in full force. Artist Eric Herrmann was laboring over his new work-in-progress painting called Gettin' Lucky, showin' a fella with the chick and the money hookin' it outa town. At MB & Strings' booth I met Bill Morgan with RideTek; his new product is a black vinyl top that straps to hard saddlebag lids that give ya more room for strappin' on stuff. Joe Teresi's Dyno Drag

The Wall

Etched upon the gleaming black stone of the Wall are over fifty thousand names. Many Bros visit the monument during the annual Rolling Thunder event to pay their respects.

truck was gettin' a lot of attention in front of the Edgewater as crowds watched wild drag racing action. Motorcycle demo rides were held all over town, and a bike show was held by Dal Con, across from the Golden Nugget, on Saturday with a good turnout of every style of bike imaginable.

The Avi Casino, between Laughlin and Needles, had the Fryed Brothers performin' there again. If you've never heard them, you should. The Run Whatcha Brung drag races went well, and $12,500 was collected for children's charities.

In a nutshell, the Laughlin River Run isn't for everyone because it gets costly, it's usually hotter than shit, and there's no tits. Still, the events are happenin', the casinos are full, and it's hard to find any place to park. I guess that makes this run right for the 70,000 people that keep comin' back. You're just gonna hafta witness it yourself.

—Clean Dean Easyriders, *August 2001*

For more info on the event, log on to www.laughlinriverrun.com.

Red River Run

Yep, another river. In 2002 the run celebrated its own twentieth anniversary. Centering on Red River, New Mexico, over the Memorial Day weekend, the event, besides being a ride through some superscenic country, is also a matter of respect. Respect for the men and women who made it possible to ride our bikes to Red River, or any other river for that matter. There are also a lot of fun activities at Brandenburg Park, including various cash prize competitions like the Strong Man, Strong Lady, Longest Ponytail, slow ride, $100 prize, Farthest Distance Traveled prize, 50/50 Poker Run, Balloon Toss, and contest for the Most Tattoos. More information at www.redrivernm.com.

Let's Get Unorganized: Riding for the Sake of Riding

Today, everything, even rallies and runs, is computerized down to the last Porta Potti. But there are some Bros who still toss a toothbrush into a saddlebag and head out for points unknown. It's something like back in the '60s when Bros were jumping on their bikes and riding a thousand miles because they hankered after a particular bowl of chili or the taste of a local beer. Here's a road story written by a rider who you could say is a throwback to those freewheelin' days, a Bro who spends more or or less most of his life on the road . . . and what a long, strange road it's been. Some call him a vagabond, some call him a Pilgrim. While his legal name is Scotty Kerekes, he just calls himself Scooter Tramp Scotty. This piece appeared in the August 2001 issue of *ER*. It sums up what the Bro thing is all about.

Breakdown in Yuma

The late December weather was dry and the air warm (eat your hearts out you Northern boys) as we blew across the lonely desert highway on my old FLT. I had dragged the beautiful and talented Miss Adrienne from the sanctity of her home in the mountains of Southern California only days earlier.

Palm Springs was behind us now, but the memory of the friends we'd made there was still fresh in my mind. And the romance blooming between Adrienne and I had been amplified to explosive proportions as we lounged in the luxury of the huge, 102-degree, hot-springs-fed hot tubs at the local Indian casino. Our steamy dip had mellowed our minds and melted our bodies together.

Even though the FLT's motor is rubber mounted, I could still feel its power course through my body as we approached the Arizona state line. We wanted to spend another week traveling together before Adrienne had to return to the grind. Where we were headed and our destination was unknown. We were just traveling, one might say, because life is too short not to.

Photo: Scotty Kerekes

After a day riding in the sun and into the night, it was just after 11:00 P.M. that we found ourselves cruising the small streets of Yuma. A local dude had told us of a bar with a live band that he promised would be our salvation. As midnight approached, with its promise of New Year's cheer, I laid into the throttle. Dropping the heavy motorcycle into gear, I pulled away from a stoplight only to have my heart sink as the FLT's motor broke into a deafening racket. Pulling quickly to the curb, I dismounted to stick my ear against the idling engine. Yep, Betsy had a serious motor knock. Shut the bitch off! (Ever notice how a bike's stature quickly deteriorates from sweety, baby, love of my life, to bitch just as soon as the motor breaks?)

A beautiful display of New Year's fireworks lit the sky as we pushed the "2-ton" beast through dimly lit side streets. A half mile later, as both of us gasped for air, we arrived in front of a closed coffee shop. After pushing the dead machine behind the building, I laid my foam pad and sleeping bags onto the well-hidden cement walkway.

Friends have asked these questions of me a hundred times over the years: Have you ever broken down out there? Do you worry about it? And what do you do when it happens? The answer has always been the same: "Have a little faith, man."

If a man travels alone, often, and on limited funds, time and experience will eventually lead him to live by little else. Breakdowns on the road can many times lead to meeting some of the coolest people and having the most interesting times, if only you let them. Besides, shit always seems to work itself out better if I leave it alone than if I'd planned it. If there is in reality any truth to this philosophy, a man can spend his days almost as free as the birds themselves if he so chooses. With that in mind, I crawled into bed to squeeze on Adrienne for a while before we finally zonked out.

The sun approached the noon hour the following day as, wrench in hand, I sat in the small parking lot and tried to make heads or tails of our dilemma. The java joint's doors were now open, and one of its curiosity seekers, being a biker himself, wandered out to inquire about the broken Harley-Davidson.

"What's the matter with your scooter, man?"

"Not sure. I'm thinkin' maybe a broken lifter. Know of any shops around that are open?"

"Not on New Year's Day." He shrugged. He stood there, obviously

Trev Deeley's Two-Wheeled Time Capsule

For this one, you'll need to pack your camera's widest lens. Located in Richmond, British Columbia, the Trev Deeley Museum transcends all borders with its massive collection of all manner and breed of motorcycle. It all started back in 1914, when Fred Deeley, Sr., sensing the business opportunities in North America, sailed from England to Vancouver to sell bicycles, then Brit bikes like Triumph, BSA, and Ariel. He did well to say the least. Today his grandson Trev Deeley is the exclusive distributor for Harley-Davidson in Canada, with over a hundred dealerships. He did well, too. In fact, Trev was the first non-American as well as the first person outside of the Milwaukee Factory to sit at the Harley-Davidson board of directors table.

Stepping into the 16,000-square-foot environs of the Deeley Museum can leave you stunned for a moment. It is way big, featuring a main floor and a mezzanine. Forty-five years ago Trev thought he'd stash a few old bikes in the basement. Things can get out of hand. While the official museum was opened in the late 1940s, this magnum opus opened its doors on May 18, 1993.

You'll find over fifty makes and somewhere near three hundred bikes all told, with several more always in the restorer's hands. Naturally, there are a few tons of Harleys, the oldest being a 1913 model. Trev will also point out a 1952 KR and 1949 WR, two Harley racers from his own racing career, which included the 1948, 1950, and 1953 Daytona 200s.

You can reach the museum at 604-273-5421. Open Monday through Friday, 10:00 A.M. to 4:00 P.M. Admission is free.

Trev Deeley Museum

contemplating something for a moment before saying, "I've got an idea! Don't y'all go nowhere now, I'll be right back."

"Okay," I said. "We'll wait right here." I certainly wasn't going nowhere.

Upon his return I stood to make the acquaintance of the two exceptionally rough-looking biker dudes who'd arrived with him on a pair of equally rough Shovelheads. "Name's Scotty," I said, reachin' out my hand.

"Chuck," replied the tall, dark, bearded figure as he looked into my eyes and took hold of my hand. "This here's Jim."

Wheels Through Time Museum: Dale Walksler's Homage to History

Considered one of the best public displays anywhere, the museum first opened its doors in March 1993 when located in Mt. Vernon, Illinois. While the museum features literally hundreds of the rarest of American motorcycles and equally unique paraphernalia spanning almost a hundred years of history, perhaps its most intriguing and interesting aspect is Dale Walksler himself. You won't find a more personable, down-to-earth, and incredibly well-informed old bike Bro on either side of Milwaukee. And don't ask Dale if the 1912 Harley board-track racer displayed on the wall runs. Because he'll grab it down and fire it up and ride it right out of the doors of the museum and down the road.

Photo: Roy Kidney

While he keeps busy restoring motorcycles in the museum's workrooms, Dale is always happy to show visitors around. You can spend days (and this writer has) in the museum because there is so much to see and enjoy. You'll find an eclectic brew of bikes, from Evel Knievel's 1970 XR750 to a Harley-powered airplane. In March 2002, Dale relocated the museum to its new 46-acre home in Maggie Valley, North Carolina, featuring over 200 motorcycles and even more history between its walls. For more info log on to www.wheelsthroughtime.com or call 828-926-6266.

"Glad to meet yuh," said the other man. "What's the problem with your FLT?"

"Got a nasty motor knock."

"Start it up and let's have a listen," Chuck said.

I did.

"Yup. You wasn't lying about that knock. Bike got a lota miles on it?"

"A hundred and ninety thousand," I told him.

"That's a lot. Tell you what, Scotty. I'm the owner of Southwest Scooters, and my shop is only three blocks away. Why don't you bring it over, and we'll get a better look at it there."

CHUCK LIVED IN AN OLD RV THAT SPENT ITS DAYS PARKED JUST OUTSIDE THE BAY DOORS ON A CONCRETE SLAB.

The little two-story shop stood proudly facing the small secondary street. The lot next door and the entire backyard was guarded by a wooden fence with a sliding chain-link gate. When Chuck removed the lock, I brought the crippled machine around to the back. Jim swung open the bay doors to reveal a shop that was well equipped with all the necessary tools of the trade. I promptly pushed the bitch through the doors before leaning her onto the kickstand.

Chuck lived in an old RV that spent its days parked just outside the bay doors on a concrete slab. We talked for a while, and I told him I knew my way around a wrench fairly well. He said he'd figured on that, then offered the use of his shop and tools for as long as I needed. Just as I was thinkin' what a cool mother-flicker this guy is, Chuck pointed to the second story above the shop and said, "Top story's an apartment, Scotty. A buddy of mine who's outa town at the moment usually stays up there. Hell, the place is just sittin' anyway, and I know he won't mind, so's you two are plenty welcome to use the place for as long as you need, if you're so inclined." Even as I was expressing my undying gratitude to this guy the thought Well, thank you, God kept racing through my mind.

After moving into our new apartment, I tore into the bike. It turned out that the cause of all that racket had been a broken lifter roller. The disintegrated roller bearings had fallen into the cam cavity and destroyed the cam. Having *never attempted this kind of a repair before, I would have to learn as I went. In other words, this job was gonna take a while.*

After a few days Adrienne, having to return to her grind, jumped a Greyhound home and was gone.

On the fourth night, and feeling like one of the three bears returning home, my new apartment's actual occupant walked in, only to find that I had eaten all the porridge and was now sleeping on his couch. The dude's name was Tramp, and he was one of those crazy bastards who had experienced just the right amount of knife fights, drugs, bike wrecks, and I suspect was probably dropped on his head as a baby, to produce the kind of insanity that you just can't help but like.

Chuck had rented a new building on the main drag that offered his shop a much better location, and before long bikers began to crawl from the woodwork, bringing with them old Panheads and pickup trucks. They worked like a swarm of bees and, piece by piece, the shop began to disappear from around me, only to be reassembled again at the new location. When not wrenching on my own bike, I would offer up my elbow grease and join the boys in their combined efforts of moving the shop.

The new place needed much work, and as I stood in the center of the front room next to Chuck, I watched men carry equipment through the door, patch the cracks in the walls, and paint the ceiling. Turning to the Boss Man, I said, "I know you ain't got a lotta money at the moment, Chuck, so tell me, how can you afford to pay all these guys?"

"I'm not payin' these boys, Scotty, they're just helpin' out cuz they're my bros." The old-time biker differs (obviously) in many ways from the average citizen. Besides his seeming inability to back down from trouble, one common quality he possesses is the depths and bonds of his friendships. I have seen men repeatedly come—sometimes in force—to eagerly aid their fellows in times of need so bad that almost no sober citizen would take the time nor make the effort to help, just declare sympathy and walk away. Flowers, cards, and visitors may be showered on the hospital bed of a downed brother while, beyond the walls of his confinement, poker runs and other fundraisers are being organized in an effort to help supplement his hospital costs. I have seen men use money out of their own pockets and labor tirelessly in the secrecy of a garage to resurrect their brother's wrecked bike from the dead, reaping only the man's surprised look and undying gratitude as their

So You Want a Really Different Road Trip Destination, Do Ya?

Tired of Sturgis, Bike Week, or the Iron Butt Run and want something a bit different for the summer trip slide show routine? Well, we've got some places that you won't find listed at the travel agent's . . . for a variety of reasons. Now remember, these are real places, and you can find them on the map or by bike.

How about a visit to Embarrass, Minnesota? This town is situated about 200 miles north of St. Paul and has the distinction of being rated the coldest piece of real estate in the continental United States; the weatherman there often posts midwinter temperatures cracking the thermometer at –60 degrees F. Even in June it's been known to snow, so if you want to freeze your ass off during the summer, here's your place. Hey, maybe that's where they really got the name for the town. Supposedly the name comes from the early French settlers, the word meaning "obstacles," and referred to just living there. In any case the French left for warmer climes, and the Finnish moved in . . . –60 degrees F felt more like home to them we guess.

Now if you're cruisin' out west and find yourself in the Lone Star State, get yourself a bowl and ride on over to Noodle, a town bursting at the seams with a total population of forty. Located near Abilene, this speck on the map got its name during Old West times when noodle *was often used to mean absolutely nothing. It'd be nice to get a Noodle, Texas, road pin, right?*

Last but not least, we'd like to send you to Hell . . . Hell, Michigan, that is. The town celebrates its name with a summer Satan's Holiday festival and road race called the Run to Hell. That's a foot race, not a bike race, by the way. The town, a swamp of a place in southeast Michigan, got its moniker in 1841, when a settler was asked what it should be called. The guy replied, "I don't care. You can name it Hell if you want to." And they did.

reward when he returns from the hospital and finds his scooter sparkling in the garage once again.

Southwest Scooters dealt primarily with older bikes, and their supply of Evo stuff was limited, so Tramp chauffeured me to and from the Yuma dealership in his pickup for the parts I needed. John (the lead mechanic there) sold me a stock, used cam for cheap, then installed four new wheels on my lifters. In the end, with parts, gaskets, labor, and all, I had spent a grand total of $125 of hard-earned cash at Yuma Harley-Davidson.

Once back at Southwest Scooters, and with the bike finally reassembled, I fired her up. The knock had left me, but now in its place was a nasty—or should I say gushing—oil leak. Part of the standard procedure required for this repair had been to pull the oil pump and remove the metal particles from its internals. This job was easier said than done; I had obviously destroyed the delicate little bastard of an oil pump gasket upon reassembly.

I rode the bitch to the dealership. By now the boys at Yuma H-D knew of my predicament and, after inspecting the Exxon Valdez, John said, "Go get a new gasket from the parts counter. These oil pumps can be real tricky to reassemble, so why don't you pull the thing apart in the back room over there? That way if you have any trouble we'll be right here."

"But I didn't bring any tools, John."

"That's okay, you can use mine."

"Are you sure?"

"Just shut up and do it, Scotty."

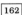

The job was a nightmare. Nothing went right. Even with the talented help of John and Bob (the shop owner and a veteran H-D mechanic of over forty years), we ruined three gaskets before the thing was finally back together, then it didn't wanna pump oil. In the end, the bitch finally lost the battle and was once again the roadworthy machine I knew *and loved. The parts counter would only accept payment for one of the four gaskets that they had given me, and John and Bob just shook my hand and wished me luck. I could never have finished this job without the assistance of these two guys, and couldn't help but wonder how many dealerships were left in the world who'd go to such lengths to aid a stranded traveler.*

As I rode the lonely desert highway west, leaving Yuma behind, my mind wandered back to the events of the week past. I'd broken down in a strange land. Two strangers had shown up to supply me tools and refuge. Then, a Harley-Davidson dealership had all but insisted on loaning me tools and talent needed complete a job that I myself was incapable of.

If there really are angels, could some of them be bearded men who ride Hogs? Regardless of how you see it, and just like a hundred times before, Fate had once again supplied the mode and the means for one man's journey free and easy.

Until next time, ride long and prosper.

Now, as we head into the 1970s, it's a time for breaking the mold in more ways than one . . . Harley's domination of the U.S. marketplace is seemingly lost to the Japanese. What gives, Bro? But we might learn something from the Beatles. In 1970 they were thinking of splitting up to go their separate ways. All things must change. That goes for Harley-Davidson, too. And, like they say, that which doesn't kill you, makes you stronger.

Let's Get Organized: For Bros Who Want the Whole Tour Enchilada

While Bros sometimes like to go solo, sometimes it's also cool to go along with a group of like-minded souls who want to explore a specific area of the country, this or another. Several companies provide full package deals, from soups to chromed nuts, in which everything is nicely organized, especially helpful when you're thinking of visiting a place where language, currencies, and customs vary from Made in the USA. A professional tour is a good way to get the most out of your vacation time and dollars.

The following companies (and, yes, there are others) offer organized motorcycle tours in the United States, abroad, or both. Rates, schedules, and details vary widely (and they are "subject to change"), so contact them for the latest information.

Photo: Michael Lichter

Domestic Tours
ADAC Reise GmbH

Despite its very Germanic name, ADAC Reise offers a number of tours this year in the United States (California/Southwest, Northwest, Alaska, and Route 66) in addition to the Canadian and Alaska Highways.

ADAC Reise GmbH
Motarradreisen
81361 Munich
Germany
Phone: 011-49-89-767-64931;
fax: 01149-89-743-9153

America Bound Tours

With tours predominantly of the Southwest, America Bound can fix you up with a guide or you can go on your own.

America Bound Tours
2100 North Sepulveda Blvd., Suite 20
Manhattan Beach, CA 90266
Phone: 310-545-5439;
fax: 310-545-2458

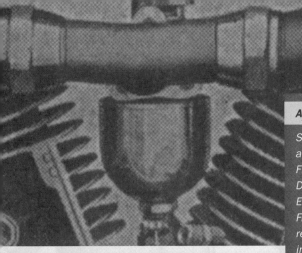

American Freedom Riders, Inc.

Six-, eight-, and fourteen-day tours are available through the West, Florida (including Bike Week in Daytona Beach), the Blue Ridge, New England, and Canada. American Freedom Riders will ship your bike or rent you one. Optional excursions include hot-air ballooning, trout fishing, and helicopter tours.

American Freedom Riders, Inc.
1371 Jerusalem Ave.
North Merrick, NY 11566
Phone: 800-482-6654;
fax: 516-292-1195

Dutch Country Motorcycle Tours

If you're starting small, with day trips, Dutch Country offers various basic four- and eight-hour guided tours that include Amish farmland, covered bridges, and a coal mine.

Dutch Country Motorcycle Tours
P.O. Box Box 34
Smoketown, PA 17576
Phone: 717-656-6885

Freedom Tours

Harleys are available for ten-day Saguaros and Sombreros Tours in October. Otherwise, ride your own or rent another brand for six- and nine-day Colorado tours, and sixteen-day Southwest tours.

Freedom Tours
P.O. Box 848
Longmont, CO 80502
Phone: 800-643-2109
or 303-682-9482

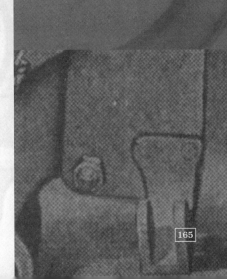

Iron Horse Rentals

This company used to run tours but has since gotten solely into the Harley rental business. If you want to arrange your own tour, they can rent you a Harley from Los Angeles, Orlando, Tampa, Fort Lauderdale, or North Egremont, Massachusetts.

Iron Horse Rentals
380 L.B. McLeod Rd.
Orlando, FL 32811
Phone: 407-426-7091;
fax: 407-426-9390

Vermont Motorcycle Tours

They don't rent bikes, but these folks provide ten five-day tours of Vermont. Ride your motorcycle and follow their guide to tours and recommended motels.

Vermont Motorcycle Tours
P.O. Box 1326
Stowe, VT 05672-1326
Phone: 800-814-1117;
fax: 802-253-4028

Western States Motorcycle Tours

Take your pick of self-guided or guided tours around the scenic Southwest.

Western States Motorcycle Tours
1823 West Seldon Ln.
Phoenix, AZ 85021
Phone and fax: 602-943-9030

International Tours
AMA Tours

If you're a member of the American Motorcyclist Association (AMA), you can head for Nova Scotia, Newfoundland, New Zealand, England, Wales, or the Isle of Man for three weeks for the Grand Prix races.

American Motorcyclist Association
P.O. Box 6114
Westerville, OH 43081
Phone: 614-891-2425;
fax: 614-891-5012

Bosenberg Motorcycle Excursions

With seven- ten- and twelve-day tours, Bosenberg Motorcycle Excursions visits Germany, Switzerland, Italy, Austria, France, and Luxembourg.

Bosenberg Motorcycle Excursions
Mainzer Strasse 54
55545 Bad Kreuznach, Germany
Phone: 011-49-671-67312;
fax: 011-49-671-67153;
website: www.Bosenberg.com

Edelweiss Bike Travel

An offshoot of Edelweiss Bike Travel, V-Twin Victory Tours, offers tours to Daytona Beach and Sturgis, plus overseas tours that include Europe, Great Britain, and New Zealand.

Phone (West): 800-582-2263;
phone (East): 800-877-2784

The Great Canadian Motor Corporation

From Toronto take a fourteen-day, nonguided "Cities and Nature" tour that includes Ontario, Quebec, Ottawa, and Montreal. From Vancouver, tours range from weekends to fourteen days, and include Alaska. Snowmobile and Jeep tours are also available.

The Great Canadian Motor Corp.
P.O. Box 239
Revelstoke, BC V0E 2S0 Canada
Phone: 800-667-8865;
fax: 250-837-6577

Lotus Tours

Conducting tours since 1982, Lotus offers adventures to a number of exotic locales, including Turkey, Tuscany, Corsica and Sardinia, and the former Eastern Bloc countries, such as Hungary, Poland, and Slovenia, as well as Australia, Peru, India, Mongolia, China, the Isle of Man, and even Tibet and Nepal. (To help prepare you for your ride, Lotus also offers a Freddie Spencer High Performance Riding School package and Gary LaPlant Ride-in Ranch Dirt Bike Clinics.)

Lotus Tours
1723 North Fern St.
Chicago, IL 60614-5714
Phone: 312-951-0031;
fax: 312-951-7313;
website: www.lotustours.com

MHS Motorradtouren GmbH

In addition to tours in the United States, MHS offers thirteen- and twenty-four-day tours in Baja, South Africa, and India.

MHS Motorradtouren GmbH
Donnersbergerstr 32
D-806343 Munich, Germany
Phone: 011-49-89-168-4888;
fax: 011-49-89-166-5549

Motorcycle Adventures Australia

Here's an eighteen-day tour of Australia that will take you to both cities and the outback.

Motorcycle Adventures Australia
264 Warrandyte Rd.
Langwarrin, Victoria 3910 Australia
Phone: 011-613-977-65114;
fax: 011-613-977-65364

Pancho Villa Moto-Tours

If you ride with Pancho, you usually ride your own bike; they don't rent Harleys. The company concentrates on Mexico and Panama. Off-road expedition tours include Tierra del Fuego and Peru. Custom group tours are also available.

Pancho Villa Moto-Tours
4510 Highway 281 North, No. 3
Spring Branch, TX 78070
Phone: 800-233-0564;
website: www panchovilla.com

Von Thielmann Tours

These tours visit Europe, Baja, Thailand, and New Zealand, running twelve times per year. Custom group tours also available.

Von Thielmann Tours
P.O. Box 87764
San Diego, CA 92138-7764
Phone: 619-463-7788

6

THE 1970s

TORA! TORA! TORA!

In 1970 a film called *Tora! Tora! Tora!* exploded across movie screens, chronicling the events leading up to Pearl Harbor and winning the Academy Award for special effects. It echoes what many called the Japanese invasion of the U.S. motorcycle market, a multipronged attack that seriously threatens the life blood of Harley-Davidson. It isn't exactly a sneak attack, but it's just as devastating. Milwaukee fights back, but it's a matter of numbers.

This is also the year Nixon creates the Council on Environmental Quality in order to fight water and air pollution. Can you spell catalytic converter? Somewhere in there is noise pollution, and who's the most visible violator, the archenemy of peace and quiet? And the least politically connected? Yep, the Bros.

But hippies are taking plenty of heat, too, described as "drug-age Bedouins," the flower children roam the country seeking . . . insight? Sometimes bikers and hippies rub more than shoulders, although the countercultures have much in common besides a fed report that estimates there are 8 million American marijuana users. Flower Power grows some righteous herb. Two bumper stickers characterize the opposite poles of the day: "Pot: Hobby Not Habit" and "If You Don't Like the Police, Next Time You're in Trouble Call a Hippie."

New social trends include the massive proliferation of massage parlors, and the shattering of mores, as when *Penthouse* in its April issue becomes the first national mag to show pubic hair. Speaking of hair, high schools are changing their dress codes to accommodate all the "long hairs," and we're talking males.

Bullets are flying Stateside as well when National Guardsmen "overreact" at Kent State and radical groups drop their own bombs in a wave of domestic terrorism. The police get a new derogatory name, "pig," but Hog or Hawg is still reserved for Harleys. Four commercial jetliners are hijacked by Arab commandos. They all land. Call it practice.

Under control of the American Machine and Foundry Company (AMF), who officially took over Harley-Davidson on January 7, 1969 (for about $22 million), the team at Harley-Davidson entered the new decade with a lineup of 883-cc Sportsters, including the optional "boat-tail" model and the now alternator- vs. generator-equipped 1200-cc FL's in various trims. There was also the 750-cc flathead Servi-Car, not to mention the Italian-built Aermacchi two-stroke, small displacement singles.

SPEAKING OF HAIR, HIGH SCHOOLS ARE CHANGING THEIR DRESS CODES TO ACCOMMODATE ALL THE "LONG HAIRS," AND WE'RE TALKING MALES.

The Shovelhead-powered FL's were so popular that in 1970 something like 150,000 held out their money, but nobody was taking it since demand had outstripped supply. It would seem selling 150 K more bikes would have brought some serious economic benefits to the company, but they just couldn't come up with the product.

The Not So Hostile Takeover: H-D Becomes AMF

We should say a word about the so-called takeover of H-D by AMF. It seemed a function of the economic climate of the times, companies being swallowed up by ravenous conglomerates. It was in 1965 that the company went public after having an accounting firm "guestimate" that each share of the stock the family members held was worth twenty dollars. The figure was

Motorcyclist to the Rescue of Monarch Butterflies

In the good deed category, enter the motorcycle-riding American expatriate who, in January 1975, stumbled on the massive trail of dead butterflies and thus became the first outsider to discover the nesting sites of the famous monarch butterflies and thereby shed light on their amazing 3,000-mile migration to Mexico from the United States.

established after some shareholders wanted to sell in order to invest their money in other enterprises. But in the late 1960s H-D's top management watched sales figures hover around the same numbers. Though sales were not quite stagnant, the head honchos thought they could kindle hotter sales by joining a larger organization with more capital and more advertising oomph. There was some real worry about bankruptcy and H-D becoming another extinct motorcycle manufacturer statistic. So in 1967–68, the Company started making "we want to merge" sounds.

The blood in the water attracted three large conglomerates. The first was Bangor Punta, associated with railroads and sugar companies in Cuba as well as pleasure boats, camping equipment, fashion fabrics, jewelry, guns, you name it. Apparently B-P's main interest in H-D was its line of golf carts, at that time 18 percent of H-D's production. H-D itself wanted to sell to the Outboard Marine Co. (OMC), which built Johnsons and Evinrudes (the founder was a friend of Arthur Davidson), but OMC turned down the twenty-three-dollar-a-share price, saying it didn't want to be associated with a company whose customers were nasty bikers.

The other player in the competition to own H-D, which turned fiercely contested and controversial, was AMF, a company that started out making railroad cars but also made yachts, and later a wide assortment of products including electrical components, bakery equipment, recreational products such as billiard tables, and, yes, bowling equipment, that last becoming sarcastically synonymous with AMF for most people.

It should be noted that the president of AMF, Rodney C. Gott, was a serious Harley rider himself (the Harley museum was later named after him) and wanted to add H-D to his company's line of "leisure time products."

As Jean Davidson, Walter Davidson's granddaughter, recalls in her book, *Growing Up Harley-Davidson*, "I remember going to the stockholder meetings and listening to the arguments for and against the sale. There was a lot of yelling and much sadness. I remember thinking that

Jeff Decker: Cast in Bronze

Jeff Decker can be found hard at work banging on bronze at his Hippodrome Studio located in Springville, Utah. Subjects for his bronzes include famous marques such as the Cyclone, Excelsior, Indian, Harley-Davidson, and the Flying Merkel. A particularly monumental project was the life-size bronze sculpture of the Joe Petrali Harley streamline that set the record in 1937, a work commissioned by Bob Dron.

Says Jeff, "I've sculpted race cars, World Cup speedboats, and Thomas Cup race planes. All fascinate me as much as motorcycles, but these make for weaker subjects in my mind because the jewel of the vehicle is hid beneath the hood and the pilot at best is cut off at the waist in the cockpit. A motorcycle lends itself more gracefully to a piece of fine Western art, where the cowboy is astride his steed. People today love their bikes as much as cowboys loved their horses over a century ago. This is what I wanted to show when I sculpted Maldwyn Jones in the teens on a Flying Merkel so far from stock you know he built it just the way he wanted, or the image of Rollie Free in the late '40s doing over 150 mph almost naked at the Bonneville Salt Flats. These guys were every bit as colorful as the Buffalo Bill Codys of another era. That's what I hope to capture in my work—the glory of the Golden Age of American Motorcycle Racing—and to pay homage to these men and their machines. Every tapping valve is exposed, and the jockey is contorted on his new mechanical beast, pushing it to its limit."

Photo: courtesy of Jeff Decker

Jeff keeps pushing his bronze bike art to the limit as well, and to see more of it or to acquire a piece of your own, you can call 801-489-5285.

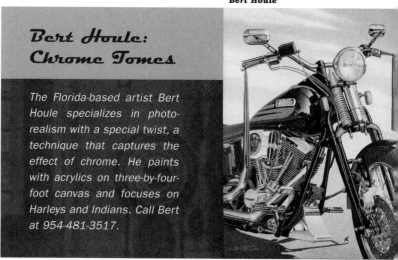

Bert Houle: Chrome Tomes

The Florida-based artist Bert Houle specializes in photo-realism with a special twist, a technique that captures the effect of chrome. He paints with acrylics on three-by-four-foot canvas and focuses on Harleys and Indians. Call Bert at 954-481-3517.

Photo: courtesy of Bert Houle

I was glad my father did not live to see this: he would be sick just being a part of the family arguments." She goes on, "Through this whole process, Harley-Davidson President William H. Davidson thought the family was turning on him. He did not want to sell out the company to anyone. The family members who were not working at Harley-Davidson wanted to liquidate their stock."

AMF came out on top and assimilated H-D but made no big changes to the Milwaukee management; they even began a major ad campaign spotlighting H-D products. According to AMF, one of the real reasons they bought H-D was as a tax shelter, since they had made so much money in the previous couple of years. In any case, after the acquisition H-D stock suddenly rose in value.

Rather than rehash a well-hashed chapter in the Company's complex history, suffice it to say that a lot of Harley people felt betrayed, pissed off, confused, or a combination of all three when a traditional family-owned company went corporate with a capital C. Some say AMF nearly killed H-D, while others say AMF actually kept Harley above water in order for it to make its next evolutionary leap. The facts showed that, despite the country's strong economic state and growing motorcycle sales, the Motor Co. was still in a long decline. Things were looking bleak, and H-D, wanting to know why, called for an in-depth analysis.

Several factors contributed to the poor state of affairs, including the Civil War level of production, insufficient floor space, and the habit of family members sitting around and making decisions, a situation that

Michael Lichter: Photographer Extraordinaire

You've seen hundreds, hey, thousands, of his photos in the pages of Easyriders *and its sister publications (and plenty in this book), so they speak for themselves as to Michael's talent and artistry. He's been photographing the Bro's world for* Easyriders *since 1980 and began chronicling Sturgis annually in 1981, often from the saddle of his own Harley.*

Michael has published more than six hundred stories on motorcycles and the biker lifestyle; he also exhibits and sells prints of his work. Michael, his wife, Catherine, and children, Kiera and Sean, reside near Boulder, Colorado. To contact Michael with questions regarding motorcycle photography, commercial photography, stock photography, print purchases, postcard books, or comments about his website, you can call toll free 877-595-9819 or log on to www.lichterphoto.com for more information and a way cool assortment of photos covering all aspects of the Bro's world.

deteriorated as the original founders passed away. Most important, the company was out of touch with the consumer and the marketplace. It's said that it was the AMF Sales and Marketing Department that encouraged Willie G. to hit the road and mingle with the masses of Harley fans, thereby gaining an insight into their needs.

In any case, the custom bike scene was an ever-growing industry, with builders slicing off the bulky Electra-Glide front ends and bolting on whatever wild and woolly custom forks they could find, one school of thought being to push that front wheel out as far as possible, and then go even farther. Several Southwest and West Coast dealers, hit hard by declining sales like the rest of the dealer network, also get credit for putting together custom-styled bikes based on older machines or ex-cop bikes.

Those who complain about the AMF era should take into account that AMF immediately doubled H-D's output of bikes, but the price tags also increased, further disturbing dealers already in a tough spot. A new Harley Big Twin carried the same heat as a new Chevy sedan. Also, when they pushed more bikes through the antiquated assembly line, you could say quality control lost control. Worse yet, some of the veteran workers were calling it quits. Bikes were arriving at the dealers with pieces missing, literally. Warranty problems became a nightmare. Dealers were freaking.

In any case, AMF did come up with the "#1" logo and the slogan "The All American Freedom Machine" and more or less hooked up with the "biker" culture image H-D had long disavowed.

1971 and the Debut of FX: A Harley That Created a Special Effect

Now, as 1971 took over the calendar, enter a Willie G. Davidson design milestone . . . call it a brilliant one. It came in the form of a design H-D labeled the Super Glide and designated the FX. And it was superlative in all areas. It should be noted that the Super Glide was also the first major output of the now AMF-owned company. Apparently, AMF, more comfortable with bowling balls, scratched their corporate head when it came to the H-D Styling Department and more or less let Willie G. go his own way as long as he didn't redesign the bowling alley. So he did a bit of surgical transplanting, the organ donor being the Sportster, in particular its cool aluminum front forks. Not only did they look good but they worked marvelously. To make the whole stand out visually, Willie G. then designed the famous or infamous boat-tail seat and tail section. The FX held a list of significant "firsts." Besides being the first new design under the AMF corporate logo, it was the first Factory custom period.

The Naked Truth About Biker Jackets: Langlitz

VQ magazine Editor Dick Teresi needed a new bike jacket. The last time he had gone shopping was about thirty years ago. More than styles had changed.

For guidance about bikewear, we went to the crème de la crème of jacket makers: Langlitz Leathers, which operates out of a small Division Street shop in Portland, Oregon. It was at Langlitz that the motorcycle jacket was, if not invented, at least refined into the classic hybrid of style and utility that it is today.

Ross Langlitz was a mechanic specializing in Harley-Davidsons, who as a racer won forty-seven trophies from 1938 to 1954, a remarkable feat considering that he lost his right leg in a motorcycle accident when he was only seventeen. The hospital staff told him he would never ride again. So as soon as Langlitz reached home, he got on his bike, rode back to the hospital, and hobbled in to show his doctors they were wrong.

A glove cutter during World War II, Langlitz found all the extant jackets wanting, so he built his own. (Motorcycle jackets, by the way, are always built, never made.) Langlitz died in 1989, and Langlitz Leathers is now run by Dave Hansen, the founder's son-in-law, who continues to build that original 1947 jacket.

"He didn't invent the motorcycle jacket," says Hansen of his late father-in-law. "He turned it into what it is today.This is one of the most backward businesses in America," he told us. "You don't want to follow our example." Hansen also said publicity didn't help Langlitz sell more product. Its thirteen employees can make only six jackets per day. "To make more, I'd have to hire more people, because none of us likes to work late or on weekends. Then

I'd have to find a bigger building. And I like this building." All publicity does is make the waiting time for custom jackets longer. At this writing, the average wait is seven months.

Russ Langlitz wearing his first leather jacket, circa 1947.

Their Columbia model (about $575, stripped down) is essentially the same jacket Ross Langlitz built in the 1940s. It was black, and as rugged and elegantly simple as an old Harley rigid Panhead—and almost as heavy. Quilted pads on the shoulders and sleeves add an aesthetic touch, and protect the rider from road rash, that distinctive epidermal pattern one gets from skidding along the pavement sans bike.

The first thing to look for in a good jacket, says Hansen, is an offset front zipper. The zipper begins at center bottom and slants toward the right shoulder. This gives an extra flap of leather beneath the zipper that keeps the wind off your chest. In summer the zipper can be lowered, and the flaps become lapels that can be laid flat.

The second thing is the cut of the sleeves. A strictly fashion jacket, as Hansen calls it, is cut to look good on a model whose arms are dropped at his sides. A real motorcycle jacket's sleeves cant forward. They are designed for a biker, whose arms, reasonably enough, spend a lot of time out in front of him to reach the handlebars. Gussets in the armpits allow for free motion. Traditional zippers on the wrists keep the jacket airtight.

The trunk of the jacket is designed for a person in a sitting position, again for obvious reasons. The front should be shorter than the back, because otherwise, when you sit on a bike, your legs would buckle the front of the jacket. The back is slightly longer to cover the otherwise exposed part of your pants. There should be lots of pockets, because motorcycles don't have glove compartments for your maps and tools.

The Langlitz Columbia has all of these features, and so should any jacket you buy. Other differences are more subtle. For example, a jacket should resist rain. "Especially important in Oregon," points out Hansen. The traditional zippered pockets, he says, are obvious leakage points. So the Langlitz jacket has a weld above and below each zipper. A weld is a strip of leather folded over, like a skinny hillock. "The idea," says Hansen, "is to make the water jump from one weld to another." Gussets under the zipper catch any moisture that gets through.

And lots of seams, no matter how decorative, says Hansen, mean smaller pieces of leather were used. Thus a weaker design and more water leakage. The thinner, more stylish belt means weaker belt loops. The Columbia loops are mounted with four layers of leather, which is one reason motorcycle cops love the jacket. It easily holds a gun and holster. Some "bargain" jackets have neat, fine, aesthetic stitching. Wrong, says Hansen. This perforates the leather, makes it rip-prone. The Columbia uses heavy, carpetlike thread with the holes far apart. It is hard to sew leather this way, but such stitching makes a jacket stronger, drier. Seams on the Columbia are double-stitched.

As for the leather itself, both jackets were made from good old American leather, an important feature. "U.S. cows are big," says Hansen. "The leather tans well, doesn't smell or bleed." Hansen is distrustful of foreign leather, some of which he claims is prone to smell or bleed in the rain.

The cheapest jacket Langlitz sells is $475. The Columbia with all the bells and whistles (goatskin, fringe, thermal lining, fur collar, epaulets, lined pockets) runs to $995, though Hansen says he's never built one for over $900. You can buy one off the rack at the Portland shop, but it makes more sense to get a custom jacket. Twelve different measurements are required. Sixty-inch chest? No problem. Langlitz will build a jacket for you.

Of course, the Columbia is the ultimate—Hansen says that if he could figure out a way to make a more expensive jacket, he would—but it's the standard you can use to evaluate a more reasonably priced (and more easily available) motorcycle jacket. Keep in mind that you might want to stay away from colorful jackets, which denote a person who rides bikes of foreign origin. "We're more likely to sell a jacket to a Harley rider," says Hansen. Riders of Japanese bikes prefer brighter, more flamboyant designs.

Hansen told us about one more test for a motorcycle jacket. One of his regular customers was browsing a leather shop when a salesman, trying to sell a "fashion motorcycle jacket" to another customer, spotted the Langlitz man and recognized the Columbia jacket. "What's so great about that coat," taunted the salesman, "that it should cost $300 more than this one?"

The Langlitz man removed his jacket, threw it on the floor, and put his foot on the shoulder. He grabbed the sleeve with both hands and pulled with all his weight. Nothing happened. He then threw the salesman's jacket on the floor, assumed the same position, and ripped the sleeve completely from the shoulder. Point made.

The Xcellent XR750

Owner: Mike Bowen
Photo: Paul Garson

Replacing the KR 750 flathead, the XR750 appeared in 1970 to better battle the Brit and Japanese dirt-track racers. The engine featured iron cylinders until 1972, when the alloy modification took hold. The bike weighed 100 pounds less than a stock Sportster and had 10 more horsepower, which translates to fast. The XR750 raced for more than a quarter century and gained a reputation as the all-time durability champ among production racing bikes. The L.A. resident, bike fan, and actor Mike Bowen built himself a street version after being inspired by watching XR750 racing at the Ascot half mile and San Jose mile. The legendary Mert Lawwill built up the motor that's fed by dual 38-mm Del Orto pumper carbs, while Marzocchi forks and a Champion swing-arm fine-tune the handling.

Before its introduction, no other bike company had paid so much serious heed to what customers were complaining about or asking for. You got whatever the manufacturer dished out, then you fixed it. Not anymore. And H-D kept the FX squarely in the family; it was an evolutionary hybrid that brought together some of the best features of two already existing models. Blood and tradition still held firm. Both Sporty riders and FL fans could appreciate its family lineage.

The FX, a truly daring though well-thought-out move, was H-D's first "cruiser" set to fan the lust of a new riding public that saw a stock bike in the showroom with enough custom tweakness to satisfy the innate custom cravings. It also was the progenitor of a long line of famous Harleys, the Fat Bob, the Wide Glide, the Super Glide II . . . Harley history repeating itself for sure, but always with a new twist and not just on the throttle. The dealers liked it; the buying customers liked it. It looked great, started easy, ran fast, handled well (70 pounds lighter than an FL). What was not to like? As David K. Wright says in his history of the company, "It was the perfect bike at the perfect time. Somehow Willie G. had created something that was as outrageous as a Yippee and as conservative as an Orange County cop in one master stroke."

And where were you in 1971, when the first "Have a Nice Day!" yellow smiley buttons showed up? Some people didn't take too kindly to them, thinking they looked a lot like the guys in black pajamas we were fighting in Nam. Millions of others thought otherwise, taking up the chant that we still hear today.

Lovable bigots get a boost with the debut of Archie Bunker in TV's *All in the Family*. Nam blazes on. At home, a lot of pickup trucks are carrying "America: Love It or Leave It" bumper stickers, while a lot of VW bumpers counter with "Vietnam: Love It or Leave It." pointing out the wide diversity of American tastes in more ways than one.

In an act that affects motorcycle sales, and about everything else, Prez Nix orders a ninety-day wage-price-rent freeze and, very significant, a 10 percent surcharge on foreign imports . . . and that definitely includes products with the names Honda and Yamaha. You can hear the cheering from Milwaukee all the way to the custom shops in California.

AMF and the original Harley people were growing increasingly at odds. Some say there was even deliberate sabotage on the Factory assembly

From Pinballs to Panheads: Dan Hughes

Growing up in Chicago, Dan Hughes would sit by his father and watch him paint refrigerators for a living. Robert Dan Hughes worked as a commercial artist creating hand drawings for retail store newspaper ads. These were the days before computers, when artists were called upon to draw everything from the latest DeSoto to the newest Frigidaire and newspapers were, in a way, foldable art galleries. "When I was three," says Dan, "I was already drawing highly elaborate scenes of battleships and frogmen, the result of watching my father at his profession." Back in the '70s, Dan earned his bread drawing lawn mowers and refrigerators full of food.

Photo: courtesy of Dave Hughes

Dan eventually moved to Milwaukee and drew ads for the likes of Miller beer, boat engines for Johnson and Evinrude, and lots of pinball machines. "Commercial art was always work, while motorcycling was something I always enjoyed doing, so I made one of those career changes, and spent several years working at bike shops. Then that little voice came back, telling me it was time to get back into my art, but this time I wanted to merge both passions."

As a result Dan spends his days painting motorcycles on his farm nestled near Springfield, Illinois, mostly working in acrylics, though he's also a talented airbrusher. He says, "For me, airbrushing was tedious because I really enjoy brushstrokes and being able to look at a painting and being able to tell it's a real painting. Photo-realistic work leaves me a little cold; I like to see the detail and subtle nuances created that make it so unique. I spent a summer getting back in the painting groove, and then sent out a few photos of my paintings. Lo and behold, Dave Nichols from Easyriders *calls me. It was a great boost and a jump start, his support coming just at the right time.*

"I have a special affinity for Harley-Davidsons because a Harley is art. There something about a Harley . . . it's just really interesting visually, something the other manufacturers have lost touch with. You can really appreciate the mechanical qualities. Everything's there to see, like the exposed push rods and distinctively shaped cases and finning."

While both the originals and prints of his work are available, Dan is now taking individual assignments from bike owners who want their custom on canvas. You can see more of Dan's work at www.hdart.com or call 217-947-2587.

More Salt, Please: Indians Can Go Fast, Too

In a case of déjà Indian vu, in August 2000, Indian Motorcycles hired Dave "Huggy Bear" Hansen, owner of The Shop (Ventura, California), to break a record set by Indian in 1926. Dave, a past master on Indians, rose to the challenge and with Don Smith put together a '37 Indian chassis and a '47 80-cubic-inch Indian side-valve motor taken from Dave's 30,000-mile street bike, the engine tuned by Kurt Morrow. When all was said and done, the Indian, piloted by Vance Breese, broke the old record and established a new Indian speed record at Bonneville, clocking 122.948 mph.

Photo: courtesy of Dave Hansen

line. The line had been drawn. It was AMF on one side, H-D on the other. Some dealers even rubbed off the AMF logo from their bikes, so deep was their distrust and dislike of the situation. It got more depressing when William J. Harley died on August 23, 1971, at age fifty-nine, a guiding H-D light gone out. Then Walter Davidson, Jr., resigned as VP and sales manager. He had strongly promoted Harley brand loyalty but at the same time peeved the dealers, who thought he was out touch with marketplace reality.

1972 and "Selective Deletions"

The beginning of 1972 saw a magazine sales record when the first issue of the feminist magazine Ms. sold all 300,000 copies in nine days. In some kind of rebuttal, Burt Reynolds shows up naked in *Cosmopolitan* magazine. Now when did Joe Namath show up in panty hose?

American workers revolt at a GM plant, complaining not over money but over work conditions. They have to punch out 101.6 Chevy Vegas every hour.

Have you ever driven a Vega? Riding a Sportster was a better option, especially since the '72 model year benefited from a displacement increase to 61 cubic inches while the wildly unsuccessful boat-tail rear end on the FX was sunk from sight, much to the happiness of all. AMF looked for ways to beef up their marketing position. One strategy was to get dealers to clean up their act, spiff up their showrooms to AMF standards, and upgrade their sales tactics. Those who rankled at the suggestions lost their franchises when renewals came up. Often veteran H-D dealers were summarily deleted from the rosters, as were small-town shops. AMF/H-D did not make many friends as a result.

Meanwhile America's air passengers were getting peeved as well. At U.S. airports we begin inspection of passenger luggage, in response to a growing number of hijackings. They aren't looking at shoes, yet. For some reason, vodka starts outselling whiskey in the United States. Some say it means more Russian spies have infiltrated the country. The Nicest People make *Jonathan Livingston Seagull*, the book about a bird, the biggest selling book since *Gone With the Wind*. In Alabama, Governor George Wallace is shot and paralyzed by a twenty-year-old busboy . . . from Milwaukee.

FOR SOME REASON, VODKA STARTS OUTSELLING WHISKEY IN THE UNITED STATES. SOME SAY IT MEANS MORE RUSSIAN SPIES HAVE INFILTRATED THE COUNTRY.

1973: The Metrification of American Motorcycling

An average house in 1973 cost $28,900 while a collector paid $153,000 for Hitler's Mercedes. Bros can choose from bumper stickers that read: "Beautify America—Get a Haircut" and "Don't Laugh, You Don't Know If Your Daughter Is in the Back of This Van."

Unfortunately, at least for H-D, that van might also have been carrying home a new Honda or Yamaha; sales figures were leaning largely to the Japanese side of the motorcycle pendulum swing. Not only were sales increasing but so were dealerships. What once were mom-and-pop Harley shops were becoming Japanese bike emporiums. With the U.S. economy in great shape, Harley sales held, more than seventy thousand bikes rolling out of the AMF reconfigured manufacturing facilities. Still, the Japanese bikes were gaining ground, both in the FL territory and as the cop bike of choice. Why? They were of advanced designs, offered high performance, and required far less frequent overhauls. So who were these interlopers, these invaders from the Land of the Rising Sun, that were, in the eyes of many, using two-wheels instead of torpedo bombers to undermine the United States?

In a nutshell, the competition had determination, organization, modern assembly lines and methods, high standards, motivation, and intelligence. And they had a plan. A long-term plan that saw beyond the first-quarter sales figures. Some say the Japanese were just good at taking someone else's idea and making it better. Maybe that was true at first, but eventually they would carve their own motorcycle destiny.

It's known that at the beginning of the twentieth century the developing Japanese industrial complex imported a number of foreign-made automobiles to see how they ticked; from them they picked out the best features as a basis for their infant car industry. A similar method was employed by the Japanese bike builders. The first Japanese car appeared in 1911; two- and three-wheelers became popular in the 1920s. Into the '30s, motorcycles built in Japan were usually powered by copies of both British motors (JAP) and American Harleys and Indians. After the destruction of World War II, cheap transportation was needed. Bicycles equipped with small motors was one way to go. A similar evolution had preceded in the U.S. development of motorcycles.

The Motorcyclist's Motorcycle Artist: Eric Herrmann

Eric Herrmann is what you would call the motorcyclist's motorcycle artist; literally hundreds of his creations hang in galleries, private homes, and corporate offices in eighteen different countries. His fast-lane schedule keeps him on the road two hundred days out of the year, otherwise he's working out of his home studio in the foothills outside Prescott, Arizona.

Photo: Jim Gianatsis

Eric recalls, "Growing up in Chicago with three brothers, I was surrounded by motorcycles and Easyriders *magazines, it seemed. I attribute my path in art to Dave Mann and his illustrations that appeared for so many years in the bike mags. I had studied art in school and worked in the commercial art field but was able to work for myself from the get-go. I'm not stuck in one mode but can paint about anything I want—a portrait, a landscape—as long as there's a motorcycle in it."*

If you're at Sturgis, Daytona, Myrtle Beach, Arizona Bike Week, or any of the other hot bike events, you'll find Eric and his artwork on display. He paints big canvases, and big bikes. Eric Herrmann has always set his own pace, in painting, in riding, and in setting new milestones in motorcycle art. For more information about his work, you can reach his studio at 888-200-6554 or 602-482-1421; or log on to www.ericherrmannstudios.com.

Whereas Mitsubishi had been making Zero fighter planes, it now turned out motorcycles, one, called the Rocket Queen, was built in the early 1950s.

Another postwar recycler of Japanese army pumps and electric generators was the legendary Soichiro Honda, who founded the Honda Motor Company in 1948 with about three thousand dollars. It was the first Japanese company to build both engines and frames. His first big success was the 50-cc, two-stroke Cub, sold by the thousands on a monthly basis (a total of 15 million sold!). His clip-on engines and mopeds evolved to a 150-cc OHV bike called the Dream. And it was, relatively speaking. One that had come true for Honda and generally for the rider, too. By the early 1960s Honda was amassing huge racing successes as well, adding to its prestige. The 250-cc, twin-cylinder Dream would start the revolution in the U.S. and European marketplaces in the late 1950s. Just two bikes arrived in 1958, but that trickle would turn into a tsunami, much to the chagrin of Milwaukee. In 1962 Honda sold 65,000 bikes to its burgeoning American customer base. By 1968 they had sold 1 million bikes in the United States! Accessories like electric starters and quality, leakproof engines made them especially appealing. As did their cost. Especially the cost. It all quickly began to affect all other manufacturers, including the Brits and H-D.

THE 250-CC, TWIN-CYLINDER DREAM WOULD START THE REVOLUTION IN THE U.S. AND EUROPEAN MARKETPLACES IN THE LATE 1950S.

In 1969 the motorcycling world was rocked by the introduction of the CB750, the four-cylinder "superbike" featuring disc brakes, serious power, and its own charisma. In 1970 a 750-cc Honda ridden by Dick Mann won the Daytona 200. Honda was winning on the track and also in the showroom with motorcycle success stories such as the 1975 Honda GL GoldWing cruiser, which met the FL head on; it continues to this day. During the 1970s Hondas were being ridden, in a wide variety of sizes, by all kinds of the Nicest People. Old, young, male, female—Honda had made motorcycles

J. P. Poland/Dan Meyer: Two-Wheeled Carousel Customs

These two Orlando, Florida, artists first teamed up in 1993 to build a "Tiger" bike for J.P.'s young daughter, who was afraid of bikes but liked big cats. That first bike turned into a business called Dream-Themes and a wild menagerie of other animal bikes, including prehistoric and mythological creatures, like the Saber-Toothed Cat and Dragon bikes.

Each bike is a one-off, with J.P. coming up with the concept and then Dan, a world-renowned sculptor by day, fabricating the bike; their shop handles all the mold making, welding, sheet metal, and painting to boot.

Artist: J.P. Poland
Photo: Don Rogers

easily accessible to all. But Harley riders weren't part of the "all." There was still a difference and, as they say, vive la différence.

Nineteen seventy-three also saw another H-D milestone of sorts, as President William H. Davidson retired, more or less because he was tired of being little more than a figurehead under AMF rule and wanted to concentrate on his civic and outside business activities.

In any case, other top dogs, even the prez of the USA, were feeling the heat as well.

1974: Dumping and Pumping

Tricky Dick left office in 1974, which was not as puzzling as the 50 to 70 percent increase in income reported by major U.S. oil companies. While we wait in gas lines, they're laughing all the way to the bank. Of course there is an oil embargo to blame. Dr. Heimlich comes up with his maneuver so we can puke out stuff that's choking us, and none too soon. The new president, Gerald Ford ("I'm a Ford, not a Lincoln") pardons Nixon.

David Mann: *Easyriders'* Exclusive Biker Artist

To quote from the pages of the magazine that brought his talent to Bros around the world, David Mann's art captures a lifestyle based on freedom, honor, and brotherhood. If we have to explain, you wouldn't understand.

David created his first painting of the motorcycle culture in 1963. That painting, Hollywood Run, *and his customized 1948 Panhead, accompanied him to the Kansas City Custom Car Show. There he met Tiny, an outlaw motorcycle club member, and a friendship that has now continued for over thirty-five years was spawned. Tiny sent a photograph of the painting to Ed "Big Daddy" Roth, a car customizer and publisher of* Chopper *magazine. Ed bought the painting (for eighty-five dollars) and a career was born. David went on to do ten more posters for Roth.*

In 1965 David went to work for Sheffer Studios in Kansas City, where he met Dave Poole, an architectural renderer who taught him how to use an airbrush and render drawings. David later studied at the Kansas City Art Institute, further refining his craft.

In 1971 he saw his first issue of Easyriders *magazine, and an ad for artists, cartoonists, and illustrators caught his eye. The publishers liked his work, and he was hired. His center-spread artwork has illuminated the pages of* Easyriders *since issue 3. David Mann's art is loved because of his uncanny knack for finding the essence of the lifestyle he portrays. His paintings derive from personal experience, and this honesty shows in his art. Imagination and wit, coupled with attention to detail, are hallmarks of his style, one that is wholly his own.*

A lot of styles in motorcycle customizing have taken off from paintings David created. He'd exaggerate a rake, or the length of a front end, and someone would build a bike to match that look. David says that his outlook on life is one of having fun, enjoying life and freedom, and don't let the bastards get you down.

David Mann's art appears in Easyriders *magazines as well as our other publications and will continue to as long as we have anything to say about it. David Mann forever!*

More bad news for H-D came in the form of a blunder in the courtroom. Believing the Japanese were dumping bikes on the U.S. market in an effort to sink H-D, AMF management decided to go after the Federal Trade Commission to help redress this wrong. Basically they wanted the government to order the Japanese bike makers to mark up their price tags or pay more duties on machines imported to the United States. The blunder occurred when the commission asked H-D for testimony from their dealers. Big mistake. The dealers were already pissed about dealing with quality problems, swallowing the warranty costs, and being made to buy H-D products they didn't want (like the Italian-made lightweight Aermacchi motorcycles).

The bottom line was the commission did not find in favor for H-D. They said, Yeah, the Japanese might have some dumped some bikes on the market, but nothing that really hurt the Motor Co., which actually hurt itself by not keeping up with the times and building more modern machines. Boy, did that sting, especially when you add in the lawyers' fees—the incredibly complex wrangling filled four volumes of testimony. The only good aspect, at least for the dealers, was the end of Harley's importation of Aermacchis. Also, there was a bit of a push to design and build something better. But it would not be until the '79 model year that something came of it, with a larger capacity engine and initial R & D for an updated 80-inch motor.

About the only good news coming out of '74 was the introduction of the thong string bikini. Yes, there is hope for America. A bumper sticker proclaims, "I'm Not a Dirty Old Man, I'm a Sexy Senior Citizen."

Back in the showrooms, it was not only the Hondas that were hurting Harley sales . . . and image. Another big hitter was the Kawasaki group, founded in 1949. Their first machine was a 123-cc, 8-hp two-stroke built in 1961. Two-stroke designs continued in various displacements, but there was a quantum leap in 1969 with the appearance of the fearsomely fast 60-hp, 497-cc, three-cylinder models. Even more scary was the 1971 746-cc triple. Riding one of the 125-mph beasts was not for the meek because of the mindblowing acceleration and less than stable handling. The legendary KZ series of formidable four-stroke, four-cylinder machines began with the 900 Z1, appearing in 1972, followed by the 1015-cc Z1000 in 1977.

ABOUT THE ONLY GOOD NEWS COMING OUT OF '74 WAS THE INTRODUCTION OF THE THONG STRING BIKINI.

1975: Detroit Bites the Bullet

In 1975 car sales, one of the barometers of America's economic health, were down, the excuse the auto industry used to can about 275,000 workers. Bumpers sprout "Eat Beans—America Needs Gas" and "If Everything Is Coming Your Way, You're in the Wrong Lane."

Harley's other Japanese competitor, Suzuki, was kicking up a storm on the international racing circuits at this time, eventually gaining the 1976 World Championship in the 500-cc Class. Suzukis were also doing it in the dirt, and doing it well. Their motocross racers brought home three world championships during the year. Suzuki, founded in 1936, has produced a variety of interesting machines, some would say weird, for example, the Wankel rotary-engined RX5 of 1975, with its Buck Rogers instrument pod, and the three-cylinder, two-stroke, 738-cc GT750, the venerable Water Buffalo cruiser, so named for its large radiator.

1976: Funny, I Don't Feel Two Hundred

We have a really big party in the spirit of '76. Not the seventy-third anniversary of H-D but America's Bicentennial Birthday Bash. Everybody's got a "handle," and we're all chattering away on our new CB's, grandfathers of the cell phone. *The Gong Show* is a hit, which says something about something, and the first drive-in-window funeral home opens in Louisiana. Nope, they still haven't found Jimmy Hoffa.

The major milestone for '76? It's gotta be Apple unveiling its first personal computer. Can you remember when people didn't use 'em? At least we're driving big, bad cars; 70 percent of all U.S. cars are powered by the good ol', ass-kicking Detroit V-8. And on the big screen we hear Stallone's Rocky Balboa utter the most famous of Americanisms: "Yo!" Bumper stickers meanwhile proclaim "Unemployment Isn't Working" and "Happy Birthday, America" in the same breath.

AMF was still calling all the shots, even to the point of pressuring H-D to pull an ad it ran in a 1976 issue of *Easyriders* magazine, the premier pro-Harley mag of all, but one that apparently offended AMF corporate suits. Another loss was the passing on December 17 of John E. Harley, son of Founder William S. Harley.

Mark Patrick: Road Warrior of Biker Art

When we interviewed Mark Patrick at his Colorado Springs, Colorado, studio he was working on a new addition to his extensive gallery of unique biker art. Mark laughed, a huge, hearty, good-natured laugh, and said, "I'm also working on another piece today called Daytona Daredevil. *It's a guy surfing his bike, you know standing up in the saddle as he's blitzing along, and his body is giving him the thumbs-up. Everything I sculpt, I've done. I've surfed my bike. You get it up to 70, and you stand up. And it's stupidity, but what a rush, man."*

In addition to his line of sculptures, which are limited to five hundred, Mark has created an ultralimited line of bronzes. Willie G. ended up with one of Mark's sculptures, a bronze of the Drifter, *the piece that originally brought attention to Mark's talents and put him on the map, so to speak. You can find Mark's sculptures literally all over the world, including Russia, Australia, and Japan; there's even one at a major distributor-dealership located in Opfikon-Glattbrugg, Switzerland, called Biker Art Europe. Mark says, "I'm supposed to be doing a life-sized bronze sculpture of Willie G. standing beside his favorite Knucklehead for the outside of the Harley headquarters on Main Street in Sturgis. I also did a custom piece for the Motor Company's CEO, Jeff Bleustein. I flew out to Florida and sculpted his whole family, all on their Harley dressers."*

Mark's also got a whole new series dedicated to vets. "I did a flathead bike piece for World War II vets," he says, "but I've been focusing on Vietnam, pieces that don't have bikes. I did the Leap of Faith *piece with a helicopter after talking to a friend who flew one in Nam. It really was a leap of faith. Without the vets we wouldn't be here enjoying the lives we have."*

The average price is about $200 to $300 apiece. One of his bronzes, like Wrong Turn, *will run about $4,400. And if you're into life-size animals—elk, bear, whatever—that jumps to about $75K. You can probably see Mark and his work up close if you make it to Sturgis, Bike Week, or Biketoberfest, or you can all him direct at 800-633-0670. To see more of his sculptured works, log on to either of his two websites: www.bikerarthd.com or www.bikerartonline.com.*

Rare Jewels: Don Nowell's Handheld Motorcycles

Think of them as Fabergé eggs in the collection of a Russian czar, priceless bejeweled creations, but now add wheels. The description aptly fits what surely is the ultimate motorcycle "model," although that term hardly applies to the mind-bending creations of Don Nowell, master craftsman in miniatures. These quarter-scale, museum-quality motorcycles take a degree of dedication long since placed on the endangered species list. Don, with years of experience restoring Pebble Beach–winning classic cars as well as racing dragsters at the other end of the spectrum, brings a passion verging on, well, lunacy, to his art. Even he admits it: "It takes some kind of weirdo to go to these extremes." It also takes weirdos to make the world a more interesting place. But we are talking extremes. Let's just talk nuts and bolts . . . like the 152 itsy, bitsy, tiny bolts Don hand-makes for each bike.

Building the frames was at least as difficult as, if not more difficult than making a full-size one. After a painstaking R & D period, Don bent the raw tubing, fabricated fixtures to hold the frame, then milled and mitered all the joints. Try welding with

1977: The Factory and Dealers Feud

Lucky numbered 1977 wasn't. Elvis is gone at only forty-two, and VW discontinues the Beetle. Detroit pulls a couple real stinkers, one being the "downsizing" of cars to meet the import threat, the other, GM's unleashing of the first diesel-powered American cars, supposedly to benefit from cheaper fuel costs. Bumper stickers have the last say, as in "May the Floss Be with You" and "Honk If You Love Cheeses."

Milwaukee was waging a market war on at least three fronts. The third in the trio of Harley competitors from Japan would be Yamaha. Back in 1954, and the newest of the Big Three, the parent company was already one of the largest manufacturers in the world, known for everything from world-class motorcycles to world-class pianos. Two-stroke Yamaha factory racers brought back boatloads of racing trophies, dominating the Nationals all through the '70s, and their famous line of TZ race bikes, sold to privateers, were the bikes of choice for years.

a magnifying glass. And then there was the engine. Don made the prototype components from 6061 aluminum billet, utilizing his well-equipped shop's milling machine and lathe. He then linked up with a foundry that was able to take the molds off the prototype engine, cylinders, transmission, and carburetor. There's front and rear working suspension, and Don cast molds for the headlight and taillight lenses. Colors, you want colors? The hand-rubbed paint schemes include pearl tones in candy orange, blue, red, and black, while the stunning Knuckle chopper comes in lemon yellow and fire engine red scallops.

Photo courtesy of Don Nowell

Don Nowell Design motorcycles are for a very special clientele; for example, the new Harley museum ordered one. For more information, contact Don Nowell Design in Granada Hills, California, at 818-363-8564; www.donnowelldesign.com and www.motorcyclefineart.com

Their street bikes are also known for muscle, and in 1977 the introduction of the four-cylinder, 998-cc XS1000 caused a sensation.

The formation of yet another organization had some long-lasting effects on H-D. In 1977 a Harley enthusiast, Carl T. Wicks, of Long Beach, California, sought to bring together all Harley owners, from dresser riders to bikers. The Harley-Davidson Owners Association as conceived would improve communications between riders and the Motor Co. and, it was hoped, resolve some of the now serious mechanical problems inherent in the bikes rolling out of Milwaukee. Wicks asked for support from H-D corporate but eventually ran afoul of their official policies when he began publishing articles on how to fix some of the glaring mistakes popping up and out of their bikes. One could say there was somewhat of a chasm growing between Harley enthusiasts and dealers and the Motor Co., a span that even Evel Knievel could not bridge.

1978: I Love the Smell of Catalytic Converters in the Morning

In 1978, besides some really bad cars, we got to see John Belushi in a toga in *National Lampoon's Animal House*, and disco music was in, thanks to the previous year's *Saturday Night Fever*. A bumper sticker says, "Live Dangerously: Take a Deep Breath." President Carter is coughing up a storm of environmental measures, resulting in changes in the automobile industry, which is ordered to address the toxic exhaust emissions polluting America. Motorcycles feel the crunch, too, performance being sacrificed in the name of healthier breathing.

1979: A Growing State of Crisis

There was a great moment, or two, in 1979, but we forgot what they were. The Iranian hostage nightmare, destined to last a year and indirectly cause Carter not to be elected president again, begins. A bumper sticker rubs it in: "Jimmy Who?"

AMF was thinking of moving away from the leisure products about this time, probably a smart move considering that, by the end of 1979, OPEC had upped the ante on global energy consumption, raising the cost of crude oil. However, the Japanese bike builders continued high production, offering a huge array of bikes to the public. Even in the face of the shift in world economic outlook, the Japanese did not blink. The aftermarket suppliers catering to Harley riders were having their parts made in Japan or Taiwan, further undercutting Factory product lines. Harley was offering 74- and 80-cubic-inch bikes, Police models, and the Fat Bob FX with a 5-gallon tank. In an effort to pump up brand loyalty, H-D staged a number of promotional events, many of which featured sledgehammer bashing of Japanese bikes. The dealers must have thought about doing some of their own bashing since the new bikes they were getting needed overhauls after only 5,000 miles because of defective components. Something really had to be done, or it was going to be all over. It came just in time in the form of the 1980 model FLT, a much needed improvement over the aging FLH. But we're still in the '70s, so make note and read on.

During this decade of AMF and the Japanese onslaught, it was war, and one of attrition. But for motorcycling in general this was a time of

Capturing the Image: Biker Artists

There are bike museums and art museums, and sometimes the two blend together as in the Guggenheim Museum's special exhibition, Art of the Motorcycle. While we can ride to some, others require a virtual trip on the Internet. Sometimes the artist works in metal, sometimes wood, sometimes a pallet of pigments, by traditional brush or high-tech airbrush. The tools may differ, but the end product speaks to the same issue, an effort to capture the magic of motorcycling.

Untold thousands, no doubt millions of photographs have been snapped of stock, dresser, chopper, custom, and racing Harley-Davidsons over the past hundred years, but as rolling works of art these bikes have inspired both amateur and professional artists to interpret what they themselves experience as machine fuses with art. While there are many talented artists out there in Bro-land using all kinds of media to express their motorcycle visions, some stand out from the crowd, and here's a look at some of their work, work that adds to the mystique and appeal of what we consider art on wheels.

healthy growth, with sales rapidly expanding and more people out two-wheeling. The Japanese expanded from lightweight bikes into the cruiser class, knocking on, then knocking down, the door on a market Milwaukee considered its own. Harley fought back with factory customs, although many said the design changes were superficial, the long-in-the-tooth V-twin Milwaukee mill a vibrating, gearbox-clunking anachronism. From the outside, it seemed H-D was locked in a mind-set of survival paranoia as it went after people using the logo or anything close to it.

By the mid-1970s, although sales of motorcycles had reached a million units during the peak years (70,000 Harleys for 1975, falling to 61,000 in 1976), AMF was losing interest in the H-D acquisition, one of many, all of which were responsible to shareholders. One sour point for AMF was the H-D workforce strike in '74, resulting in a three-month loss of bike production. Add in the realization that Harleys could not be mass-produced economically plus the belief that the Japanese had been allowed to dump their excess production in the United States at rock-bottom prices, and the picture looked bleak from a bean counter's perspective.

Now You Wear Von Dutch!

Bros wear clothes, too, well, not all the time, but generally. In any case, we like clothing coming in an enormous variety these days. Hell, even people who shake in their designer boots when they see a biker like the look. And since Von Dutch was such an important figure in custom everything, someone figured we'd like to wear duds inspired by his designs . . . or at least his signature, which was art in its own write or right—you spell it. Hook up with Von Dutch Originals in L.A. at 323-655-2222 or web it at www.vondutch.com.

The hard facts were that, with a market share of 5 to 6 percent, their product was outdated, its production limited, its consumer base split between the dressers and the cultists, and the Japanese pushing way ahead of the game. In other words, AMF wanted out. They began looking for buyers, even contacting John Deere, but no bites.

During the same period, the Japanese literally invaded U.S. territory, setting up their own facilities in this country. Honda bought property in Marysville, Ohio, where it began building cars and bikes. Meanwhile Yamaha was rolling its KZ machine from its plant in Lincoln, Nebraska. It was at this location that the Kawi police specials were produced, soon supplanting Harley cop bikes across the country, going for the throat of one of Milwaukee's most American monopolies. It was, as always, a matter of money or greed or whatever label you want to put on it. It was more important to save American dollars by buying foreign police bikes than to support an American icon. Of course, quality and dependability may have been factors, too. Around this time a new Harley cost about as much as a heavy-duty Dodge, another popular police vehicle. To make matters worse, the Italian bike builder Moto Guzzi was selling some of its 850-cc police specials to U.S. law enforcement. The company was in a state of crisis on all levels.

Against the background of corporate conflicts, the trend moved away from cutting up old bikes to customizing stock bikes with aftermarket parts, as more products became available. While Harleys were the principal recipients of the custom trends, both British and Japanese bikes were often treated to the personal touch, too.

As the 1970s ended, Hollywood would see its own dream fulfilled, fiction would turn into fact, and one of its own would become president of the United States of America. And Ronnie would take action, taking on the "Evil Empire" of the USSR and the faltering economy and still having time to give some much needed support to the longest-lasting American motorcycle company, in many ways a microcosm of the country itself. The AMF era was drawing to a close, and a whole chapter was about to be written in the Book of Motorcycle Destiny.

Leather List

You can look for leather in all the right places by referring to the following:

Custom Chrome. Check out their catalog of jackets or log on to their website www.customchrome.com.

Easyriders. Yes, they've got a bunch.
Phone: 818-889-8740.

Harley-Davidson Motorclothes.
Go to any Harley dealership.

InterSport Fashion West (makes many jackets, including jackets for Harley-Davidson). Phone: 800-495-5042.

Dave Hansen, Langlitz Leathers, 2443 Southeast Division St., Portland, Oregon 97202. Phone: 503-230-0959.

Route 66 Highway Leathers. Phone: 708-827-3300.

Schott Brothers. Another pioneer in biker gear.
Phone: 908-442-2486.

Vanguard Leathers. Phone: 516-420-1010.

Vent-Tech Leathers. Phone: 818-240-0226.

Freedom of Choice: "Helmet Laws Suck"

The issue of to wear or not to wear helmets is a hot and heavy one, with strong opinions on both sides. Here's one analysis of the facts.

American Bikers Aiming Toward Education (ABATE) is a nationwide organization of helmet-hating Harley riders. Mensa is an international organization of geniuses and near geniuses. Its members must score in the top 2 percent of the population on an intelligence test. The Gator Alley chapter of ABATE challenged its neighbors in the Southwest Florida chapter of Mensa to a whiz-kid test of knowledge. No bikes, no chains, no colors. Just tough questions, such as "What was established by the Lateran Treaty of 1929?" The showdown took place in Bonita Springs, Florida. It was a seesaw battle, but in the end the bikers won. To be truthful, Mensa played without the services of its president, Jeff Avery. Still, the ABATE team played without Avery also. He disqualified himself, being president of both clubs.

After their loss, the Mensans sat down with their opponents and listened to arguments for the bikers' favorite cause: the repeal of motorcycle helmet laws for bikers over the age of twenty-one. Several Mensans, even some who were not bikers, swayed by the logical arguments, joined ABATE. We cite the Mensa-ABATE showdown to demonstrate that not all anti-helmet-law activists are intellectually challenged, which is the prevailing media consensus. The TV reporter interviews a helmet-law advocate, a scientist (smart) in a white coat pointing to a hard, spiffy helmet. Then she interviews a drunken, tattooed biker (dumb) who screams, "Helmet laws suck!" as he falls off his barstool.

It seems intuitive that wearing something hard on your head would help you survive a motorcycle accident. Many state legislatures agree. As of this writing, twenty-four states and the District of Columbia have laws mandating helmet use by adult motorcyclists. The laws appear to work. A study by the Centers for Disease Control (CDC) indicates, quite conclusively, that motorcycle deaths per 1 million residents are lower in states with helmet laws.

That sounds good, but we could make the same argument for surfing helmets. Let's say Kansas, Nebraska, and Wyoming pass laws requiring helmet use by surfers. California does not. The CDC does a study, finding that states with surfer-helmet laws have fewer surfing deaths per 1 million residents than California does. This would be a ridiculous argument. People don't surf in Kansas and, if they did, surfing would be relatively safe, helmet or no helmet, there being no ocean. Similarly, you find fewer bikers in helmet-law states. For many bikers, motorcycling with a helmet is like surfing without an ocean.

Compare Florida, a helmet state, with Iowa, a no-helmet state. Florida has a beautiful, year-round riding season. Iowa has a long, brutal winter. Yet Iowa has more than

three times the number of registered motorcycles per hundred population as Florida. In California, a former biker paradise, registrations dropped by 22 percent (138,000 fewer bikes) in the first four years after the legislature passed a helmet law. Overall, states with no helmet laws had 2.6 motorcycle registrations per 100 population compared with 1.3 in helmet-law states. In other words, nonhelmet states have twice as many bikers.

Let's go back to those CDC statistics that show helmets prevent deaths. If we use the same statistics but count fatality rates per 10,000 registered motorcycles rather than per all residents, we find that helmet-law states actually suffered a higher average fatality rate (3.38 deaths per 10,000) than nonhelmet-law states (3.05 deaths). This is not sufficient evidence to prove that not wearing a helmet is safer, but it demonstrates that helmet laws do not reduce deaths.

Another way to measure the difference is to look at deaths per 100 accidents. Not even helmet advocates suggest that helmets will reduce the number of motorcycle accidents. The purpose of a helmet is to help the rider survive an accident. The numbers indicate otherwise. During the seven-year period from 1987 through 1993, states with no helmet laws or partial helmet laws (for riders under twenty-one) suffered fewer deaths (2.89) per 100 accidents than states with full helmet laws (2.93 deaths).

How can this be true? Is it possible that helmets don't work? Go to a motorcycle shop and examine a Department of Transportation–approved helmet. Look deep into its comforting plush lining and hidden amidst the soft fuzz you'll find a warning label: "Some reasonably foreseeable impacts may exceed this helmet's capability to protect against severe injury or death."

What is a "reasonably foreseeable" impact? Any impact around 14 miles per hour or greater. Motorcycle helmets are tested by being dropped on an anvil from a height of 6 feet, the equivalent of a 14.4-mph impact. If you ride at speeds less than 14 mph and are involved only in accidents involving stationary objects, you're golden. A typical motorcycle accident, however, would be a biker traveling at, say, 30 mph, and being struck by a car making a left turn at, maybe, 15 mph. That's an effective cumulative impact of 45 mph. Assume the biker is helmet-clad, and that he is struck directly on the head. The helmet reduces the blow to an impact of 30.6 mph. Still enough to kill him.

The collisions that helmets cushion effectively—say, 7-mph motorcycles with 7-mph cars—are not only rare but eminently avoidable. Another reason helmets don't work: an object breaks at its weakest point. Jonathan Goldstein, a professor of economics at Bowdoin College, in Brunswick, Maine, wondered how this could be. If fatal head traumas were decreasing, then some other kind of fatal injury must be rising to make up the difference. Applying his expertise in econometrics to those aforementioned CDC statistics, Goldstein discovered what was happening.

In helmet-law states, there exists a reciprocal relationship between death caused by head trauma and death caused by neck injury. That is, a 4-pound helmet might save the head, but the force is then transferred to the neck. Goldstein found that helmets begin to increase one's chances of a fatal neck injury at speeds exceeding 13 mph, about the same impact at which helmets can no longer soak up kinetic energy. For this reason, Dr. Charles Campbell, a Chicago heart surgeon who performs more than three hundred operations per year and rides his dark violet, chopped Harley softail to work at Michael Reese Hospital, refuses to wear a helmet. "Your head may be saved," says Dr. Campbell, "but your neck will be broken."

John G. U. Adams, of University College, London, cites another reason not to wear a helmet. In a study he found that helmet wearing can lead to excessive risk taking because of the unrealistic invulnerability that a motorcyclist feels when he dons a helmet. False confidence and cheap horsepower are a lethal combination. I called a local (Massachusetts) Suzuki dealer, said I was a first-time buyer, and told him I had only five to six thousand dollars to spend. The dealer recommended a GSXR 1100. He said, of course, that I must wear a helmet, especially with a bike like that. A GSXR 1100 is guaranteed to hit 160 mph.

Imagine: a novice on a 160-mph bike wearing a plastic hat that will reduce any impact by 14 mph. It's like having sex with King Kong but bringing a condom for safety's sake.

Why the enthusiasm for helmets? Mike Osborne, chairman of the political action committee of California ABATE, says insurance companies are big supporters of helmet laws, citing the "public burden" argument. That is, reckless bikers sans helmets are raising everyone's car insurance rates by running headlong into plate-glass windows and the like, sustaining expensive head injuries.

Actually, it's true that bikers indirectly jack up the rates of car drivers, but not for the reason you might think. Car drivers plow over bikers at an alarming rate. According to the Second International Congress on Automobile Safety, the car driver is at fault in more than 70 percent of all car-motorcycle collisions. A typical accident occurs when a motorist illegally makes a left turn into the path of an oncoming motorcycle, turning the biker into an unwilling hood ornament. In such cases, juries tend to award substantial damages to the injured bikers. Car insurance premiums go up.

Osborne sees a hidden agenda. "They [the insurance companies] want to get us off the road." Fewer bikes mean fewer claims against car drivers. Helmet laws do accomplish that goal, as evidenced by falling motorcycle registrations in helmet-law states. It is interesting to note that carriers of motorcycle insurance do not complain about their clients. Motorcycle liability insurance remains cheap. Osborne pays only $125 per year for property damage and personal injury liability because motorcycles cause little damage to others.

Keith Ball was one of the pioneers of ABATE, its first manager in 1971 and later its national director. What annoys him most is the anecdotal approach taken by journalists who have a penchant for reporting whenever the victim of a fatal motorcycle accident was not wearing a helmet, but when have you seen a news item that mentions that a dead biker was wearing a helmet? Which is not to say that Ball opposes helmets. He thinks anyone who rides in a car should wear one. After all, he points out, head injuries make up only 20 percent of serious injuries to motorcyclists, but they account for 90 percent of all car injuries. If Ball's idea catches hold, one day you might see angry men stepping out of Volvos with odd T-shirts beneath their tweed jackets. The T-shirts will read: "Helmet Laws Suck."

Photo: Big George Stine

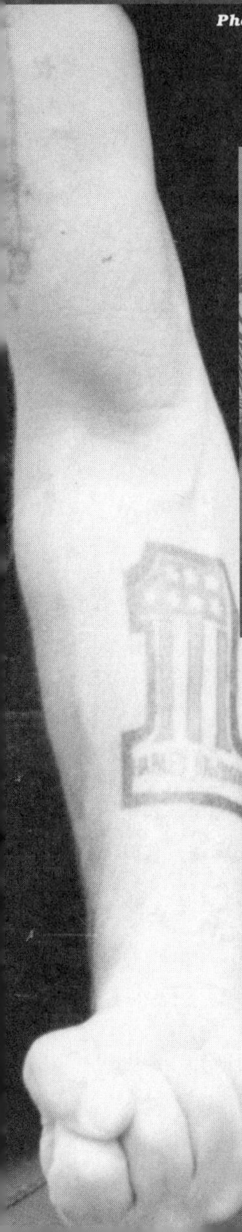

Skin Art: The Indelible Impression

Photo: Woody

Tattooing, an art form going back thousands of years, has always been a part of the Bro's world, way before it became chic and trendy. This is a subject worthy of numerous volumes itself; suffice to say that there's a lot of body art carrying dramatic imagery intrinsic to motorcycling. Many of the meister ink slingers and collectors have appeared in the pages of Paisano's Tattoo *magazines, edited by Frenchie Nielsen, and they sometimes crop up in* Easyriders *and its sister publications as well. A whole bunch of the photos are the work of ace photographer Billy Tinney, who has been documenting the world of wearable art for more than three decades.*

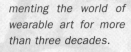

Photo: Jack Hughes

7

THE 1980s

HARLEY-DAVIDSON RECLAIMED

As Oscar Wilde said, "Nothing succeeds like excess," and we Americans take that as gospel; we made the 1980s excessively excessive. The decade of the '80s started out with the government coughing up $1,500,000,000—as in one and a half *billion* dollars!—to bail out Chrysler. The auto industry still loses $3 billion for the year—to imported cars. Built for the most part where? Funny, the government couldn't find more than a few bucks to help education or work up alternate fuels so we wouldn't still be kissing OPEC butts. But we could get some butt-ugly, gas-guzzling cars. The year 1980 kept our sights firmly fixed on such miracles of modern invention as the board game Dungeons & Dragons—what, you're still playing it? News turns 24/7 with the advent of CNN, and half of us are wondering who shot J.R. while the other half couldn't give J.S. The world is made a more organized place when Post-its appear on the market. Sexual harassment of women is made illegal in the workplace, but apparently everywhere else it's still open season. We crack up two helicopters and kill a bunch of good soldiers in an Iran hostage rescue attempt that gets FUBAR.

Crossword puzzles for the year feature *gridlock,* referring to traffic, ABSCAM, referring to politicians taking bribes, and *free basing.* The last thanks to the comedian Richard Pryor igniting himself while cooking up some cocaine. And in November, Ronald "20 Mule Team Borax" Reagan is elected the fortieth U.S. president and becomes the Great Communicator.

Against this background of turmoil, the world still rolled on, and, in showrooms across the country, Bros were giving the nod to the new FLT, brought out in the spring of 1980. The FLH replacement had some major improvements, including a new frame design that lightened handling, and the engine no longer transmitted as much fatigue (human and metal) causing vibration, thanks to being mounted so that it flexed longitudinally. Even the floorboards got the flexy, antivibe treatment. The icing on the cake came with the new five-speed transmission, which in top gear brought you loping along at 60 mph with the tach resting comfortably at 2900 rpm, which meant both your engine's longevity and your riding stamina were extended.

Harley Airplanes?

So if H-D wasn't selling golf carts anymore, what were they doing to make a few extra bucks? In the early '80s the company earned $39 million building shell casings for the U.S. Navy. There was talk of a contract to make small jet engines for drone targets, and apparently H-D got into the computer business by fabricating cable systems. Diversification, diversification, diversification. Wasn't that the plan back in 1965, when H-D started selling stock? But now it works.

A major upgrade was H-D's debut of the belt-driven FX models, with belts rolling both primary and secondary drives. The Gates Rubber Co. developed them for Milwaukee, and they were designed to last longer than any chain. While they also ran more quietly, the main idea was to reduce vibration. The idea wasn't new; several aftermarket sources had offered them previously. Called the Sturgis model, the belt-driven bike received favorable reviews for its improved comfort. And who was credited with coming up with the change? None other than Erik Buell, who was working in H-D's Engineering Department and would soon be one of the few men in history to have a motorcycle bearing his name.

The Japanese were already targeting the custom cruiser market when, in 1980, Yamaha brought out the first of their chopperish copycat V-twin Viragos, which H-D saw as a direct threat.

Even with the improvements manifested by the FX, AMF was freaking over the increased costs of production, a price tag that put Harleys on the heavy end of the competition stick, and a pitifully small profit margin. They wanted out big time. But the word was out—H-D had apparently put profits ahead of any kind of progress for decades, and no one wanted to take over a company that needed more than a makeover, call it a bull-dozing.

ERIK BUELL ... WOULD SOON BE ONE OF THE FEW MEN IN HISTORY TO HAVE A MOTORCYCLE BEARING HIS NAME.

At the end of their throttle cable, AMF talked with H-D top management, including Vaughn Beals, to see if they could put together a takeover of the company, in effect putting Harley-Davidson back into the exclusive hands of Harley-Davidson. That became official with documents prepared in February 1981.

1981: At Long Last H-D Comes Home Again

The year 1981 carries the onus of being the year AIDS was first diagnosed. Now about 50,000,000 people have the disease in Africa alone. Harrison Ford takes a break from space to play in the first Indiana Jones flick, and whip sales go up. Frantic and frenetic bursts of short-term-memory-friendly audiovisual stimulation occur with the debut of MTV.

Harley historians pinpoint June 1, 1981, as a day of rejoicing, for it was upon this spring day that Harley-Davidson became Harley-Davidson once again, its ties with AMF severed after eleven and a half years, much to the relief of all involved. The "buyback" was proclaimed all across the land, i.e., to the dealer network, that H-D was back in "family" hands. Each of the thirteen new group members (including Vaughn Beals, Jeffrey Bleustein, and Willie G. Davidson) paid from his own pocket, ranging from $75,000 to 150,000 each, and it appears that AMF wanted $80 million for their H-D holdings, a fourfold increase over the purchase price. Vaughn Beals as board chairman was chosen to father the company toward its new destiny. Among the new owners

Button Quotes and Bumper Stickers from the 1980s

Beam Me Up, Scotty—There's No Intelligent Life Here

Real Americans Buy American Cars

Bikers Do It in the Dirt

Gun Control Is Being Able to Hit Your Target

God Bless America—And Please Hurry

My Take Home Pay Won't Take Me Home

Don't Hit Me, My Lawyer's in Jail

If You Don't Like the Way I Drive, Stay Off the Sidewalk

When Times Get Tough, the Tough Go Shopping

You're Right—I Do Own the Whole Damn Road

You've Obviously Mistaken Me for Somebody That Cares

My Wife Ran Off with the Pickup Truck and I Miss It

My Other Car Is Up My Nose

My Lawyer Can Beat Up Your Lawyer

Die, Yuppie Scum

Girls Just Want to Have Funds

So Many Pedestrians, So Little Time

was Willie G. Davidson, backed by his father, William H. Davidson, who, according to Jean Davidson, "never gave up the dream that Harley-Davidson could be something grand. In his heart, he believed that Harley-Davidson could be what the founding Davidson brothers and their friend William S. Harley started and lived by so many years ago."

An ad campaign trumpeted the new company philosophy: "Motorcycles by the people, for the people." The company also pointed to a program aimed at creating more up-to-date products and improving dealer relations. The Motor Co. production facilities were rearranged into H-D Milwaukee, H-D York, and H-D International, in Connecticut, to handle exports.

Vaughn Beals had taken on what could easily be called a Herculean task: restoring Harley-Davidson to its rightful place in the American motorcycle industry. Many thought he'd never make it.

1982: Don't Falk with Me

We learned an interesting bit of geographical trivia in 1982 as Britain and Argentina did battle over the Falkland Islands in a scenario that about everybody agreed was really falked up. The biggest armed heist in history takes place in New York, the thieves bagging $9,800,000 as the Me Generation starts clicking into gear.

Apparently H-D got into the Me-thing, too, or at least the Us-thing, when they went full bore in legal actions against about three thousand unfranchised bike shops across the country that were using H-D logos and trademarks and not paying for them. This made some more enemies for H-D corporate, but it was a matter of fiscal survival. The country was reeling from the effects of the OPEC cartel's increased oil charges and high inflation. Also, when Reagan took office, he'd initiated the largest tax hike in history, only it was called Social Security. It hit the Bro market pretty hard.

The Japanese were affected, too, but instead of laying off workers or lowering wages, they accepted lower profits. This policy resulted in an overproduction of bikes, 80,000 bikes sold on the U.S. market at low prices in 1981 alone. By 1982 estimates pointed to as many as

The CIA and Harley-Davidson

Maybe you saw him at Sturgis in 1992. It would turn out to be Larry Freedman's last rally. He would have been another big guy with a beard going white riding a blackberry-colored FXRT Harley dresser. He probably wouldn't have told you he was an Army master sergeant and had earned his paratrooper wings and Green Beret as well as membership in the elite Delta Force. He for sure wouldn't have told you he was a CIA operative with numerous black ops under his trigger finger. Larry Freedman's covert life was often upstaged by his overt, pedal-to-the-metal approach to life.

An expert with all manner of weapons, from bow and arrow to sniper's rifle, Freedman was a skilled gymnast and inclined to Tarzan-like stunts that earned him the nickname Superjew, which he relished. While chasing girls and avoiding classes in college, he got into motorcycles with a passion. First it was a Norton, on which he often blazed his way from Kansas to Philly just to get a milk shake. After flunking out of college, he enlisted in '65 and volunteered for the Special Forces at age twenty-four. He had found his place in life, that of a warrior, honing his skills in parachuting, martial arts, intelligence, and weapons, becoming an ace sniper. Two Bronze Stars, a Purple Heart, numerous Good Conduct medals, the Humanitarian Service Medal, the Defense Meritorious Service medal, and a bunch more told the story.

After Nam, he joined the new Detachment-D, known today as Delta Force, where he trained in overseas hostage rescue and extraction. Already a trained medic, he worked both ends of the violence spectrum, healing and harming as needed with equal skill. Meanwhile, his wild sense of humor often got him in trouble with the brass.

Missions to Africa, the Mideast, and the Far East kept his talents well used in the field, and later as an instructor. Then, after twenty-five years in the military, he retired, soon joining the CIA. At age forty-nine, and still aching for action, he was considered one of the CIA's top operatives. In 1992 he arrived in Somalia with a sniper's rifle and a tan Harley-Davidson hat. He was wearing it on December 23 outside the city of Badera when the vehicle he was in hit a land mine.

Larry Freedman's name is inscribed in the CIA Book of Honor in the lobby of its Washington, D.C., headquarters. There's also a bridge named after him in Buundo, Ethiopia, which was built by U.S. troops and carried food to the starving inhabitants. And in Keystone, South Dakota, there's a small plaque just below Mount Rushmore with the words "In Memory of Larry Freedman." You'll find it at a picnic shelter where he used to take a rest stop on his way to the Sturgis Rally.

1,400,000 such bikes from the various Japanese manufacturers stuffed into huge warehouses around the country. The frenzy to sell them slashed prices as much as a third by Honda, even more by Kawasaki and Yamaha, and people were scarfing those bikes up by the bushel. Other bike builders, like BMW and Ducati, felt the squeeze as well.

Another factor hurting Harley sales was the incredible interest rates of the time, as much as 22 percent. Seven out of ten potential buyers were turned away as a result of these killer rates. In response, H-D brought out the new, relatively low-buck XLX-61 Sportster at $3,995 in '82, but with Japanese bikes of 750-cc going for half that, sales were less than stimulating. In fact, H-D had to shut down one plant in the early part of the year, and dealers were selling their bikes at dealer cost just to unload the crowded showroom floors. Vaughan Beals made a dramatic public announcement. Harley was facing bankruptcy. The auto industry was in the same fix, and all fingers pointed at cheaper imports. Both American management and American labor were united on one issue: put an import quota into effect and bring some relief.

HARLEY WAS FACING BANKRUPTCY. THE AUTO INDUSTRY WAS IN THE SAME FIX, AND ALL FINGERS POINTED AT CHEAPER IMPORTS.

Beals implemented various efforts to save the company, including a freeze on management salaries, layoffs (including John Harley, Jr.), and suspended production schedules until leftover stock was eliminated. He also instituted a very important new quality-control program to deal with the massive amounts of defective product, incorporating the famous MAD policy, materials on demand method of production and assembly. Meanwhile, the professional engineering staff was increased while the golf cart and industrial vehicle lines were sold off in order to concentrate on motorcycles.

Magazine articles began telling H-D's side of the import story, and backing for the company's point of view increased. The president and Congress were basically on the side of H-D and the rest of American business but were nervous about imposing trade restrictions, because history had shown they caused more problems than they helped. And it wasn't lost on the observant that, during the past ten years or so, the Motor Co. had been plugging in a lot of Japanese components, including Keihin carburetors and Showa suspension parts. And Italy was lacing up Harley wheels. The logic was that no American companies were making the products. In any case, H-D prepared to do battle again, as it had in 1951 and 1978, when it sought federal intervention to throttle back importation. A petition was prepared for presentation to the U.S. International Trade Commission for relief from "unfair foreign competition," which meant mostly Japanese products but others as well, except for Brit bikes, which by 1982 were virtually nonexistent. Triumph, BSA, and Norton were all "radically dormant" at this point.

1983: Japan Busted, Harley Wins . . . Kinda

Meanwhile, the Brits got to try out their expensive new war toys in the Falklands, so in 1983 you couldn't blame the United States for sending in troops to the island of Grenada. In all 8,612 medals are awarded, which is about 1,612 more than the number of troops that took part in the fray. Back in Milwaukee a group of young computer geeks hack into a bunch of high-security organizations, including the Los Alamos National Laboratory. They certainly give notice that security needs some beefing up. No word on whether they ride Harleys.

But the scene was set for a showdown between Harley and the Japanese importers. H-D, under Section 201 of the Tariff Code, was scheduled to take part in a hearing on January 15, 1983. In the formal proceedings, they focused on bikes over 700-cc displacement and promoted a sliding scale of import taxes over five years, the time they figured it would take to get the new and improved Motor Co. better prepared to meet the Big Four from Japan.

The facts presented by the more effective H-D legal counsel won the day. After three weeks of very costly deliberation, Japan was found guilty of dumping a glut of motorcycles on the American market. The penalty? Initially a tariff of 45 percent was added to the current 4.5 percent for bikes over 700 cc for all of the Big Four, the additional amount reduced incrementally during the following production years.

The Brits and Europeans were not subject to these increases. However, Hondas and Kawasakis built in the United States were exempted. But it was enough; Reaganomics saved the day for Harley and probably the future as well. The president signed the order, and it went into effect on April 15, 1983. An interesting side note was the Japanese consortium offering in March of a $200,000,000 loan and "technical advice." We don't think so, said H-D.

During 1983 the Motor Co. also continued their "seek and desist," or should we say search and destroy, campaign against the unlicensed use of H-D logos and names. They also told Carl Wicks, the founder and president of the Harley-Davidson Owners Association, that H-D was taking over his organization and replacing it with their own Harley Owners Group (HOG). Carl was understandably not pleased. But H-D was focused on their new lean, clean, mean motorcycling manufacturing agenda. And it was working.

Also during this year the rumors began spreading about some altogether new engine, a water-cooled one at that, code-named the Nova, that was being designed in cahoots with the Audi-Porsche people in Germany. Almost twenty years later that new engine would appear in the V-Rod. Meanwhile, H-D came out with the XR-1000 "superbike," a radically modified Sportster with special cylinder heads by the master turner Jerry Branch that helped push the beast to 120 mph. About 4,000, priced around $7,000 were built during '83–'84, most of them to sit in dealer showrooms gathering dust. Now, of course, they're hot-ticket collectibles.

On a much more successful note, rumors in 1983 of the new Evolution motor proved true. The new-generation Harley 80-cubic-inch power plant featured alloy cylinders with iron liners, flat-top pistons for a smaller, more efficient combustion chamber, plus improved valve gearing and lubrication. It still had the classic V-twin look but with modern microprocessor controls. H-D reported it had 15 percent more horsepower than its Shovelhead predecessor. It ran cooler, and looked cool all the while, although it still vibrated. After $15 million in R & D and a reported half million miles of testing, the new Evo motor was released in the all-new, custom-cruiser-inspired FXRS Sport Glide with Elastomer flexible motor mounts. The new engine also became standard in the FLHT and FLT models. The response to the new bikes with their Evo motors was exceptional. Vaughn Beals rightly received praise from all corners for the incredible turnaround his leadership had accomplished in such short order.

Back in the world of violence, a few seconds after stepping out of an airplane in the Philippines, the political opposition leader Benigno Aquino is shot dead. Poland's pro-Solidarity leader Lech Walesa is given the Nobel Peace prize. *Mouse* comes into the vernacular as a word referring to our little computer friend. By the end of '83 the U.S. economic picture was looking healthier, and while H-D posted losses in '82 and '83, 1984 was projected to look better. The proverbial light was growing brighter at the end of the Evo tunnel, though somewhat eclipsed by the feds' move to mandate gasoline vapor canisters. The costs hit H-D dealers already suffering from high interest rates and soft sales. Meanwhile, California enacts the strictest regulations, and "49 state legal" becomes a well-known phrase, meaning if you lived in California you couldn't own it.

1984: Harley Shapes Up with the Softail

We were given the immortal words "Where's the beef?" in 1984, and you could also say the answer came with Harley's softail model, another major step in the right direction. Bros are starting to find more money left over from their paychecks as the economy posts its best results since 1951, and we be feeling good. Big news from the Supreme Court: We can now legally videotape television shows for our own use. We are afflicted with a new life form: the Yuppie, or young urban professional, another term for trendy spender. And, yes, Bros are seeing a lot of Yuppies buying Harleys with just a pass of their credit cards. Lee Iacocca makes more auto history by bringing out Chrysler's minivan, sparking a whole new revolution in irritating vehicles. Speaking of irritating, the United States now has 490,000 lawyers, while there are about 685,000 people in the slammer. And our taxes are at work as the Air Force pays seven thousand dollars apiece for three coffeemakers. Well, it is before Starbucks.

Speaking of a pick-me-up, the new H-D softail was making friends fast. Based around the FX model, it sported a new kind of rear suspension system (invented by William Gray) in which the suspension springs are hidden under the engine, giving the bike the appearance of a '50s

The author test-rides a protype Super-Vee from Nostalgia Cycle
Photo: Steve Iorio

THE NEW EVOLUTION ENGINE, A.K.A. EVO, WAS NOW POWERING THE FULL HARLEY LINEUP, INCLUDING THE SOFTAIL CUSTOM, WITH AN MSRP OF $9,499.

hardtail chopper but with the comforts of full suspension—in effect, the best of both Harley worlds, past and present. With its nostalgic good looks, it quickly became the company's best seller, outdoing sales of the FL to the dresser crowd, a lot of whom were buying Honda GoldWings.

In order to keep above water, a number of the six-hundred-odd Harley dealers at the time also were selling one or more Japanese brands as well as ATVs, snowmobiles, Jet Skis, generators, et cetera. Entrepreneurs were going in an entirely different direction . . . like building their own V-twin engines to replace H-D motors or for use in creating scratch-built custom machines. This author rode one of the later evolutions of the Nostalgia Cycle 93-cubic-inch heavyweight cruisers, its innovative engine based on the tried and true Chevy 350 V-8 design and components. With remarkable diligence its creator, Steve Iorio, invested considerable talent, effort, and dollars into developing the rugged, dependable, easy-to-maintain, and cost-effective new power plant, despite taking considerable heat and gaining little support from the rest of the motorcycle industry or press. A number of people in the United States and overseas purchased the engine, and a controversial love-hate atmosphere developed relative to its assembly, but, bottom line, the owners loved the engine once wrenched to its potential.

By 1984 Factory bikes had reached new levels of quality and reliability, and announcements resumed again about German collaboration on a radical new high-tech engine design, but that program languished for several years, before it was resurrected into the remarkable new V-Rod.

But in 1984 Bros were able ride their new factory Softail Evos over to L.A., the stage for the Olympics, where all went smoothly, even with 5.5 million spectators minus the Soviets, who snub the event. *Ghostbusters* busts the movie charts and smokebusters celebrate the Great American Smokeout, 5 million using the excuse to quit smoking. Another form of toxic fumes kills thousands and blinds more in India as an American-owned Union Carbide plant spews out methyl isocyanate. Many of those 490,000 lawyers swarm over to Bhopal looking for clients. India asks for $3 billion in compensation, settles for $470 million.

1985: The Gipper Part Deux

Reagan got a second turn in the Oval Room in '85 and left flowers at a grave full of SS troops in Germany. *Nicht sehr gut*, Ronnie. But he does get $3 million for his biography before a word is penned.

1986: But Does She Have Dorothy's?

The year started off with 127 million faces glued to the tube watching Super Bowl XX, a record. A health report says moderate exercise can "significantly diminish the risk of death from all causes." That "all causes" seems too all-inclusive. Bullets, for one. We're told that the Philippines' Imelda Marcos has 3,000 pairs of shoes, but the fact is she has only 1,060 pairs. We thought inquiring minds should know.

1987: Vive la Evolution

The new Evolution engine, a.k.a. Evo, was now powering the full Harley lineup, including the Softail Custom, with an MSRP of $9,499. What was originally planned as an interim engine before the all-new, water-cooled Nova motor took center stage for the next fifteen years and was not replaced until the next generation of Milwaukee marvels, the Twin Cam, in 1998.

Bill Gelbke: America's Strangest Biker

You can thank Buzz Walneck, motorcyclist, collector, historian, swap meet promoter, and past publisher of Walneck's Classic Cycle Trader *for bringing to full light the truly fascinating story of "Wild Bill" Gelbke (1935–1978), who has to be America's Most American biker. And in so doing, resurrecting undoubtedly the strangest motorcycle ever built, and ridden regularly, in this country, and probably anywhere else for that matter. Maybe you've seen a photo of the bike. You couldn't miss it. Called* Roadog, *it was a monster of a machine, literally the world's largest motorcycle, measuring 17 feet in length and weighing 3280 pounds. Powered by a four-cylinder Chevy engine mated to an automatic transmission, it cruised all day at 90 mph. Four hydraulic jacks helped it stay upright when standing still, which it wasn't very often because Wild Bill was always blasting back and forth across the country from his home in Chicago—he'd been spotted from New Hampshire to California, logging over 20,000 miles on his creation.*

Bill Gelbke, with degrees in electrical and mechanical engineering, eventually worked for McDonnell Douglas and Hughes Aircraft. He had a brilliant but highly individualistic mind and was known for his stand-up character and fierce loyalty to his friends; he often came to their aid at his own peril. He also took no guff from anyone. Wild Bill built several other interesting bikes, but none quite so incredible as Roadog. *As Buzz writes in his book on* Roadog *and its owner, "He wanted something that would run forever and last a lifetime—this bike was built to do just that!"*

Unfortunately, the bike lasted longer than Wild Bill himself. Apparently there was a situation involving a girl and an old boyfriend who happened to be a cop. A bullet in his backyard ended Wild Bill's wild life. However, Buzz Walneck found the bike and put it back on the road, recovering a true piece of Americana and dramatic testimony to the fortitude and personal vision of one man, a true Bro.

You can get a copy of Buzz's book with lots of great photos and the complete story of Wild Bill Gelbke by calling Walneck's in Woodbridge, Illinois, at 630-985-4995. Roadog *has been passed on to Buzz's friend Larry Tarantolo of Iron Horse Clothing, who will soon be featuring it on display in a new store dedicated to Route 66 memorabilia and leather goods in the Chicago area. For more information log on to www.ironhorseclothing.com.*

1988: Harleys in Heaven?

So what were we talking about in 1988? Was it the new Buick Regatta two-door "sports car" with the TV-screen computer with forty-two readouts, or was it Ollie North's part in Iran-Contra? Maybe it was the buzz about the CIA's friend-turned-enemy Manuel Noriega down in Panama. Or Dustin Hoffman's performance in *Rain Man*. Or was the hot topic the newly detected greenhouse effect? *Good Housekeeping* magazine reports that 84 percent of all Americans believe in heaven, probably the same amount that believe in dusting the drapes every week.

1989: A New Kind of Flower Power

The IRS admits it loses about 2 million tax returns a year. Apparently not mine; how about you? Meanwhile the government allocates $7.8 billion to their antidrug campaign. Think a minute, guys. You could buy all the poppy fields in the world for that much money and still have enough to buy every U.S. citizen a new Harley. The end of 1989 thunks to a close.

Harry V. Sucher in *Harley-Davidson: Milwaukee Marvel*

When writing about the end of the 1980s and the AMF–H-D relationship, Harry V. Sucher in *Harley-Davidson: The Milwaukee Marvel* says that Harley-Davidson as a make had "joined the McCormack reaper, the Singer sewing machine, the Springfield rifle, the Concord stagecoach, the Model T Ford, the Curtis Jenny, the magnificent motor cars of August and Frederick Dusenberg, and the Stearman biplane, as an enduring example of Americana." *Enduring* is the operative word.

And as another decade slides under the continental shelf of dusty memories, almost taking the Motor Company's "unique antique" with it, Harley-Davidson's chrome begins to shine again under the new-old management . . . motoring into a brighter future, once again outdistancing the slings and arrows of outrageous misfortune.

8

Colorado Senator Ben Nighthorse Campbell

THE 1990s

HARLEY RULES (AND THE RULER AIN'T METRIC)

The 1990s saw a new Golden Age, make that Chromium Age, flowering for Harley-Davidson motorcycles in particular and the Brotherhood in general as literally millions of new riders joined up. By the end of the decade there were something like 30 million motorcyclists in the United States alone, not counting Harley colonies growing in billet abundance from Moscow to Melbourne to Montevideo and all points in between. To use one of those bean-counter terms, the demographics took on a whole new look. Whereas once Harleys were the manifest destiny of blue-collar working-class people, now it seemed every doctor, lawyer, accountant, and movie star, male and female, was hopping on the Harley bandwagon (and several falling off). The Harley-Davidson would become a badge of honor, a membership card, a trendy must-have, a good investment, and an American focal point all in one.

While the United States' national symbol is the eagle, it's more than coincidence that the primary image for Harley-Davidson is the eagle as well. In fact, take a stroll on a German strasse or an Italian piazza or a Spanish plaza and ask the natives for their opinion of what American means, and you'll no doubt hear Harley-Davidson included. It, like the dollar, has become the great common denominator, a bridge joining all kinds of political and ethnic differences. Just like Sara Lee, nobody doesn't like a Harley. Especially a customized Harley.

And with success comes the flattery of imitation; wanna-be Harleys sprouted up all over the place, not just the cruisers from Japan, the so-called metric cruisers, but also a slew of limited production motorcycles, appearing in numbers ranging from a few handfuls annually to several thousand units. Several of these V-twin-powered machines, variously referred to as customs, un-Harleys, and Harley clones have come and gone, caught up in the feeding frenzy of bike building spurred by the phenomenal success of Harley-Davidson. In addition, several have made names for themselves as quality motorcycles, themselves gaining loyal followings. The same spark that brought the H-D Founders to their little ten-by-fifteen-foot wooden shed burns bright in many others, and they had their go at realizing their own personal visions of the V-twin dream machine.

In the past customizing your Harley, (from just adding decals to making your own frame) was a given, but now those who'd rather have an instant custom can choose from a healthy list of premixed custom bikes from a number of sources. And for those wanting a bike built to their specifications or bearing the name of a famous custom bike designer, those options are limited only by imagination and pocketbook. Custom bikes now come in a wide range of "custom," from mild to wild, from refined to radical, from economical to grab your ankles and kiss your wallet good-bye.

And sometime in February 2002, while surfing the tube, we spotted a Harley as the main image in a Hallmark greeting card ad. Switching stations, we saw, on the Travel Channel, a sidecar Harley tour of the capital city of Tasmania. And what is the ride of choice for the Terminator? "I'll be back . . . on my Harley." What does Jay Leno auction off on national television . . . a Harley with the signatures of numerous celebrities. What does Colorado Senator Ben Nighthorse Campbell

JUST LIKE SARA LEE, NOBODY DOESN'T LIKE A HARLEY.

(Republican) ride to the Senate? Yeah, a Harley. What bike does the supermodel Lauren Hutton crash on? Yeah, a Harley. And so does Arnold while filming another movie. And who could forget Gary Busey's head crash, then born-again wear-a-helmet conversion . . . on a Harley. Harleys are literally everywhere. There's the story of the Russian bike club that had some thirty-five members and only one bike to share among them . . . a Harley, of course.

It's no wonder that Harley dealerships during the '90s were conducting lotteries to see which lucky customers could have their names put on six-month waiting lists to buy a Harley. Supply and demand was never more fully demonstrated than when Harley took off during this decade, creating a bubble that keeps on expanding like the universe. For years the naysayers have been standing around with their pin, predicting that bubble would be bursting. But with the hundredth anniversary coming up in 2003, that's one century down and another one just getting in gear.

The '90s, the era of Generation X (whose name had something do with the unknown commodity the generation represented), hit us with some hard facts of life: oat bran doesn't reduce cholesterol and Perrier is not naturally carbonated. It's not the first or last time we've been lied to (yeah, Milli Vanilli can't sing). In L.A. an amateur video of Rodney King being beaten results in riots when a not-guilty verdict is returned. Obviously, we all can't just get along. Unless we're on Harleys, where rubbies, yippees, yuppies, Rolex riders, vintage riders, even metric riders, now begin to share the road.

As *Easyriders* Editor Dave Nichols says, when writing about what he calls the dawn of the new Golden Age of Motorcycling:

In 1990 motorcycling lost one of its greatest ambassadors. Billionaire publisher and avid rider Malcolm Forbes traveled the world aboard Harley-Davidsons, presenting a very American image of independence, freedom, and goodwill. Harley offered up a tribute with the biggest motorcycle parade in history at that year's Daytona Bike Week, where H-D took the wraps off a new model in 1990 known as the Fat Boy. This stripped FL-style softail is still one of the factory's most popular models. Special for 1991 was a bike that harkened back to the Shovelhead Sturgis edition. The FXDB Dyna Glide Sturgis was a blacked-out factory custom featuring a totally new frame and rubber-mounted motor.

1990 was a banner year for Easyriders. With two hundred issues under our belts and having brought you the best of the biker world for twenty years, we were ready to do something big, something unprecedented. On July 14, with the sponsorship of American bikers everywhere, Easyriders went to the Salt Flats of Bonneville with our twin Harley Shovelhead-powered Streamliner and took the absolute Land Speed Record away from Kawasaki. The 322.150 mile per hour time is still the world record on two wheels.

In August of that year Sturgis, South Dakota, held its fiftieth Annual Rally and Races. Over 300,000 bikers rode in from all points on the globe to be a part of the event that the late J. C. "Pappy" Hoel and the Jackpine Gypsies started in 1936. Naturally. Hot on the heels of this scorchin' hoop-de-doo, Daytona had its fiftieth anniversary of Bike Week, and Laconia had its seventieth birthday.

By the end of 1991 Harley-Davidson had earned a whopping 62.3 percent of the market share in the 850-cc and larger motorcycle category and had the imported bike companies on the run. Just as with the Sturgis fiftieth, Harley came out with a limited-edition 1992 Daytona Dyna Glide with special paint and graphics to commemorate fifty years of the ultimate run to the sun. The Motor Company celebrated its ninetieth birthday in 1993 with specially trimmed models and began offering fuel injection on certain models. In 1995 annual production had reached 100,000 units, and dealers still couldn't meet public demand. With so many riders plunkin' cash down for American-made motorcycles, the climate was ripe for bike-buildin' entrepreneurs to step in and make a buck.

THE 322.150 MILE PER HOUR TIME IS STILL THE WORLD RECORD ON TWO WHEELS.

The Rebirth of the Golden Age of Motorcycling?

The midway mark of the '90s acted as the starting flag for a number of new motorcycle companies. The Indian motorcycle was trying to make a return, as was Excelsior Henderson. There was talk of a new Vincent, and Triumph *was* making a surprising resurgence. At the same time, several smaller companies—such as Titan, California Motorcycle Company, Big Dog, and Ultra—were rattling their bike-building sabers, using S & S motors and transmissions along with the best products from American aftermarket companies to produce complete custom motorcycles.

An Interview with the Chief: An *Easyriders* 2001 Interview with Indian Motorcycle's Rey Sotelo

At age twelve, Rey Sotelo remembers seeing the movie previews for Easy Rider *and, like every other red-blooded American kid that had a passion for motorcycles, he just had to see it, eventually dragging his father along to see the classic biker film that would leave an indelible impression. "After that I was hooked," says Rey. From living at the time in San Jose, he recalls a couple of the neighbors, who just happened to be members of the Hells Angels, riding Harleys. "We all grew up together in a tight little community back in the late 1960s. Because of this exposure, as soon as I was sixteen, I went out and bought a '53 Panhead. I was going into my senior year, so I rode it to high school, which really thrilled the teachers and the counselors.*

After working my way through school getting my business degree, I spent a couple years at Intel, at that time a new company, but figured out working in an office environment was not really something I wanted to do. I moved to a tiny little community outside San Jose called Morgan Hill, and the next thing you know I'm working on motorcycles for people in my garage. Three years later I rented a little shop in Gilroy, and I've been here ever since. We're going on twenty-four years being in the motorcycle business, counting fifteen or so years of retail business, which led into mass-producing bikes after starting up the California Motorcycle Co. And then Indian, which was being resurrected, found me, commissioning me to build the prototype Indian. Next thing I know Indian made me an offer I couldn't refuse, and here we are today, three years down the road and building Indians."

Now with some grasp of the man behind the rebirth of the classic Indian marque, Easyriders *came up with what we hoped were pertinent questions, and Rey, founder and chief of Indian Motorcycles, responded to them in his usual up-front and highly focused fashion.*

ER: Currently Indians are powered by S & S engines, but what's the status on your own proprietary engine, an Indian engine?

Rey: It's a pretty well-known fact that Indian is aggressively working on that power plant. Originally I was working on the project with CMC, and we just didn't have the money to fund a million-dollar investment. I think that was one of the reasons that attracted Indian to buy my company, seeing that we had a lot of things started but were just undercapitalized. Now that funding is available, and we're able to move forward. We've got running prototypes of the new engines and are in the process of conducting validation testing. If all goes well, we may have something to show the public by the end of this year. But we're definitely not going to make any mistakes by releasing this thing prematurely.

ER: Along with work on the new engine, what's happening with the new frame to go with it?

Rey: We have three chassis designs under development, with two prototypes completed and their validation testing finishing up as we speak. We've also petitioned for a patent for the rear linkage suspension, and have also designed a completely new proprietary front suspension. All of our business plans call for a 2002 release of those new designs.

ER: What have been, and have you reached, your production goals?

Rey: The first year we went pretty aggressively. We finished 1,100 of the Chief model in 1999. In 2000 we finished 5,200 units, then for the next three to four years we cut it back to about a 20 percent growth rate. We'll do approximately 5,500 this year, and about 8,800 next year, then 10,000 bikes the following year.

ER: How many models do you see in your lineup?

Rey: Right now we've got both the Chief and the Scout in production and available. We're also in the process of releasing the new Spirit model, which is a model that lies in between the Chief and Scout. In the next three years we plan to have two segmented platforms, one targeted for what you might call the more vertically challenged riders based on a smaller platform motorcycle. We also project various models based on the larger Chief platform, probably seeing six to eight different models in the Indian lineup.

ER: As far as retail outlets offering Indian motorcycles, how's the dealer network shaping up?

Rey: We have 225 dealers as of today. We're making a lot of headway and signing up a lot of top-notch players. We had our best month ever last January, which was saying a lot since it was the middle of off-season. We actually turned a profit that month, so that was great and the investors were happy. Right now everything is sold domestically, but we're trying to go international by the end of 2002. We're working on developing an EC (European Common Market) compliant motorcycle with their regulations and thereby enter the German market and let it filter down from there. It's definitely a challenge because of the various rules and regulations in the international arena, and what we don't want to do is build two different motorcycles, rather one that's EC compliant and can be distributed worldwide.

ER: What's your take on the so-called motorcycle bubble bursting?

Rey: I've been hearing that ever since I've been in the motorcycle business. I went through the recessions of the late '70s and mid-'80s and through the Harley transitions and it almost going out of business. Everybody kept saying the same thing. This thing's going to end, this thing's going to end. I see it as a transition of population. After experiencing the '50s, '60s, '70s, the era when I lived, an avid rider and enthralled with all the lifestyle, I can see how that's evolved, changed. I think middle America has taken over because they saw that it was always something they always wanted, and now I'm seeing a lot of middle-aged guys buying bikes for the very first time and loving it, wishing they'd done it thirty years ago. I don't think the bubble's going to burst. I think it's going to continue to grow. Hey, twenty years ago if they saw a Wall Streeter or doctor or executive riding a Harley, people were amazed, shocked; today that's commonplace. Now those guys want a piece of that freedom machine, and Indian has provided a real suitable alternative for that concept.

If you want more details about the Chiefs and Scouts (and the Spirit) you can reach the Indian Motorcycle Co. at 800-445-1759 or check their website at www.indianmotorcycle.com. You'll also find Indians on display at Bike Week, Laughlin, Myrtle Beach, Laconia, Sturgis, Biketoberfest, and the Love Ride.

Since this interview was done, Rey Sotelo has departed the company, and Indian has introduced their all-new Powerplus 100 V-Twin engine.

Of these new companies, Excelsior-Henderson and Polaris, with its Victory motorcycle, seemed to be the most promising and well funded. As the Excelsior-Henderson ad banners said in 1998 at Sturgis, "This ain't a one-horse town anymore." Seemingly overnight, more and more S & S–powered custom bikes started popping up The courts took the Indian name away from Eller Industries and awarded it to Indian/CMC. Suddenly it looked as if the Big Three would rise from the ashes like some motorized phoenix to create a second Golden Era of Motorcycling. (Sadly, Excelsior-Henderson would fall by the wayside in the late 1990s.)

Not that Harley was daunted by these upstart start-ups. The Motor Co. held the party to end all parties in Milwaukee in May 1998, celebrating ninety-five years of motorized excellence. The ninety-fifth anniversary models featured special paint and trim, and the Road King was the most popular bike in America. For 1999 Harley slapped the aftermarket with its completely new Twin Cam 38 motor, and a slack-jawed world could only look on in awe. This revolutionary 1450-cc powerhouse would rocket Harley into the new millennium in style.

The Sportster as a Musical Instrument

One day in 1989, Bill Davidson and his family were attending the Harley rally at Australia's Surfer's Paradise. Naturally there were a bunch of musical groups. One musician, an Aussie aborigine, was onstage playing the traditional didgeridoo. To add a bass line, he had stuck a microphone into the tailpipe of a Sportster. Now that's music to your ears, eh what?

The Custom Bike A-List

In order to get a handle on the custom scene, it's best to look at the work of the custom builders themselves, so we'll offer up brief bios of several of the leading talents and examples of their work. What do they have in common? V-twin engines. Everything else is up for grabs. Price tags for these dream machines start around $15,000 and have exceeded $125,000.

We'd like to quote the Ten Rules of Customizing, gleaned from the master builder Cyril Huze. This list seems to sum it up all nicely. Merci beaucoup, Cyril.

10. A good designer is not the one who takes you from "what you have" to "what you want" but the one who takes you from "what you want" to "what you didn't even know you wanted."

9. When you customize, don't follow the crowd. Just follow your dreams. A custom shop should be a dream factory.

8. Great mechanical skills can take a motorcycle only so far. Passion is the engine of creativity.

7. Designing and building a motorcycle is like composing and orchestrating a song. Everybody can use the same notes. But who is going to make a hit?

6. A good bike appeals to your reason. A great bike appeals to your emotions. There are so many emotions you can assemble on a motorcycle.

5. Just because an accessory fits doesn't mean it looks right.

4. Good ideas result from uninhibited experimentation.

3. Simplicity is the ultimate sophistication.

2. Good design is guts, brains, and soul.

1. Customizing. There are no rules!

It Takes Two to Tango

The other side of the equation is, Who buys these bikes? People who don't want their bikes lost in a sea of look-alike two-wheelers. People who want people to turn their heads when they roll by. People who want to attract the opposite sex (call it metallic sexual display: instead of bright feathers, rely on extrabright chrome). People who want to make a unique statement about themselves. People who want to cleave the wind and find a new path through life. People who feel claustrophobic in cars, a.k.a. cages. People who have to have the latest toy. People who view motorcycles as a legitimate art form. People who want to go really fast. People who want to annoy the establishment. People who like to stay in their garages and create, especially during winter. People who like to walk the fine line between danger and disaster. People who want to be someone other than who they were pre-Harley. People who saw *The Wild One* or *Easy Rider* and were indelibly imprinted. People who want to fly but don't want to leave the ground. Strong people who find peace when riding. Weak people who find strength when riding. People who want to stand out on a planet of 6 billion people. When it all boils down, a custom bike is about identity itself, a primal force.

There are as many different reasons as there are people who ride Harleys or any of the custom variations. The Recognition Factor is probably shared by all, to one degree or another. Recognition is a relative thing. Some need an entire industry to applaud them, others need only the approving glance of one special person. Still others are satisfied just to see the smiles on the faces of their children in the chrome. Some get their recognition via the subtle and seamless flow of metal and paint, others through raw horsepower and sound waves capable of knocking down the walls of Jericho. Sometimes recognition is based on adrenaline levels, sometimes on a simple nod of appreciation.

The men and women behind the welding torch and paintbrush are three-dimensional artists; their creations, greater than the mere sum of their parts, take art itself and plant it firmly between our legs and magically under the control of our own hands. This is beauty that truly is in the eye of the beholder. And here are some of the major beholders. Your own eye will determine the beauty.

The Master Builders

Please don't write or call if we forgot to include your name, because we know there are a helluva lot more great builders out there. Maybe the next book, okay? We give contact information, but this a book and, over time, phone numbers and even shops can change or disappear altogether. We gave it our best shot. Do the same if you're looking for these Master Builders. In any case, some bike builders, call 'em Master Builders, have been elevated to Olympian heights, that pantheon of metal magicians including such diverse dervishes of design as these.

Arlen, as in Arlen Ness

The Master Master Builder is synonymous with the entire history of custom motorcycling. From his San Leandro, California, location, he builds the leading edge into every bike that rolls out of the facility. Books have been written about him and his art. Go buy them if you want to understand the true meaning of form and function. Go buy one of his bikes if you can. That bypass surgery can wait. Phone: 510-276-3395, or log on to www.arlenness.com

DEC CA
DLR 2A 1983

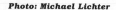

Photo: Michael Lichter

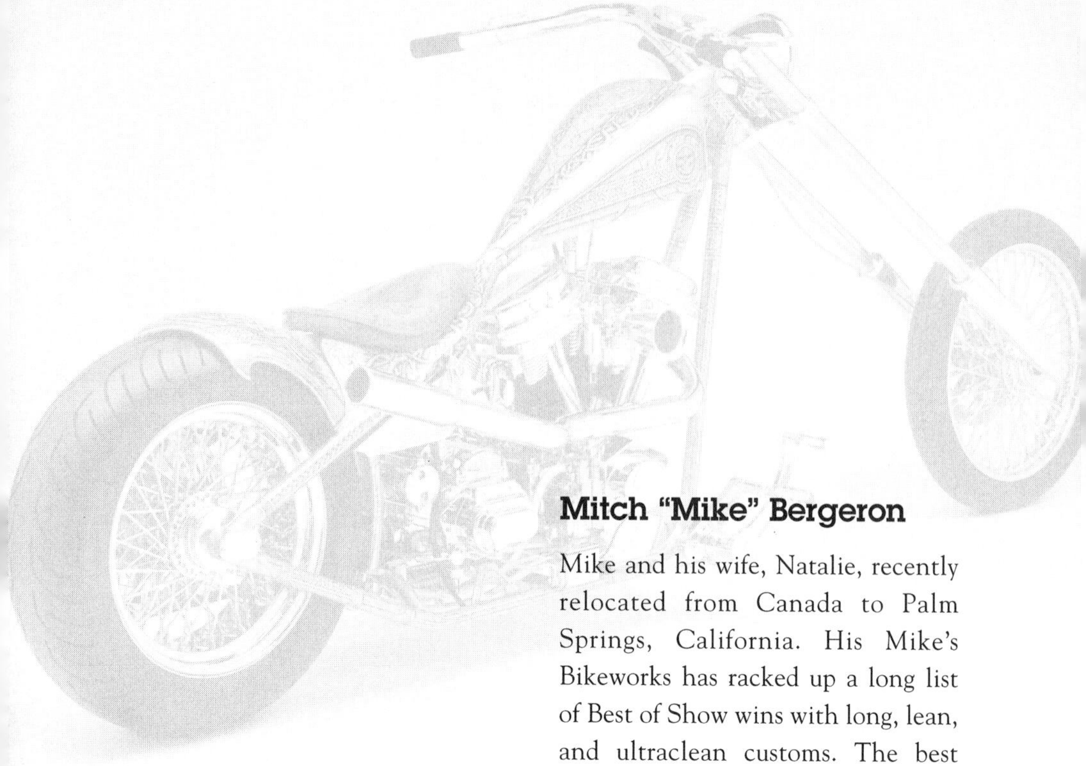

Mitch "Mike" Bergeron

Mike and his wife, Natalie, recently relocated from Canada to Palm Springs, California. His Mike's Bikeworks has racked up a long list of Best of Show wins with long, lean, and ultraclean customs. The best way to contact him is via his website, www.mitchbergeroncustoms.com

Roger Bourget

It's pronounced "Bour-jay." Bourget's Bike Works, headquartered in Phoenix, Arizona, has been known to roll out a hundred customs a year, ably assisted by Roger's wife, Brigitte. He's known for his radical low-slung frames and monstrously high-performance-oriented, fat-tired customs. Phone: 623-879-9642, or log on to www.bourgets.com.

Photo: Paul Martinez

Photo: Michael Lichter

Kenny Boyce

When you think custom frames, you think Kenny Boyce Pro Street Chassis Works of Rancho Cordova, California. One of the pioneers to use computers, Kenny creates megabyte customs as well as a custom parts line. Phone: 916-852-9116, or log on to www.Kennyboyce.com

Photo: Mike Chase

Carl Brouhard

Whether he's building bikes for the NBA or painting show-winning paint schemes for Arlen Ness, Carl's innovative and unique approach has added mystique to his Brouhard Designs shop, tucked away somewhere in the Sacramento, CA, area. Phone: 530-346-7582.

Li'l John Buttera

With a background in Indy cars, Li'l John is known for bikes that capture the essence of form, function, and flash and for their ultrasanitary "where are the lines and cables?" Phone: 714-220-6472.

With a radically different look, Chica imbues his bikes with both personality and serious attitude, a whip spin on the classic chopper unlike any other. Give Chica Custom a hoot at 714-842-9587, or check out their website at www.chicacustom.com.

Photo: Michael Lichter

Barry Cooney

Back in the '70s, Barry was the B.C. in B. C. Choppers, but now he hand-builds two bikes a year, one for himself and one for a friend. Buds with Arlen Ness, he designs radical shockers and high-visual rockers that are built to ride. Living near San Diego, he also still tears up the dragstrip for fun. Phone: 760-745-9442

Builders: Jerry and Kathleen Covington
Photo: Brad Haines

Jerry Covington

From his design shop in Woodward, Oklahoma, Jerry, "the man with the V-Twin eyes," focuses on big-inch, wide-tired, radical stand-out-in-crowd bikes and, as he says, "the crazier the better." With his wife, Kathleen, and a talented crew working on them, his bikes are consistent show winners. Phone: 580-256-2939, or log on to www.covington-cyclecity.com.

John Covington

The guiding force behind Surgical-Steeds customs, Master Builder John Covington carves his own vision into each of his often way unusual bikes, like the Stealth 2, Cobra, and Assassin bikes, plus his line of Steed-brand muscle bikes. More info at www.surgicalsteeds.com.

Photo: Paul Martinez

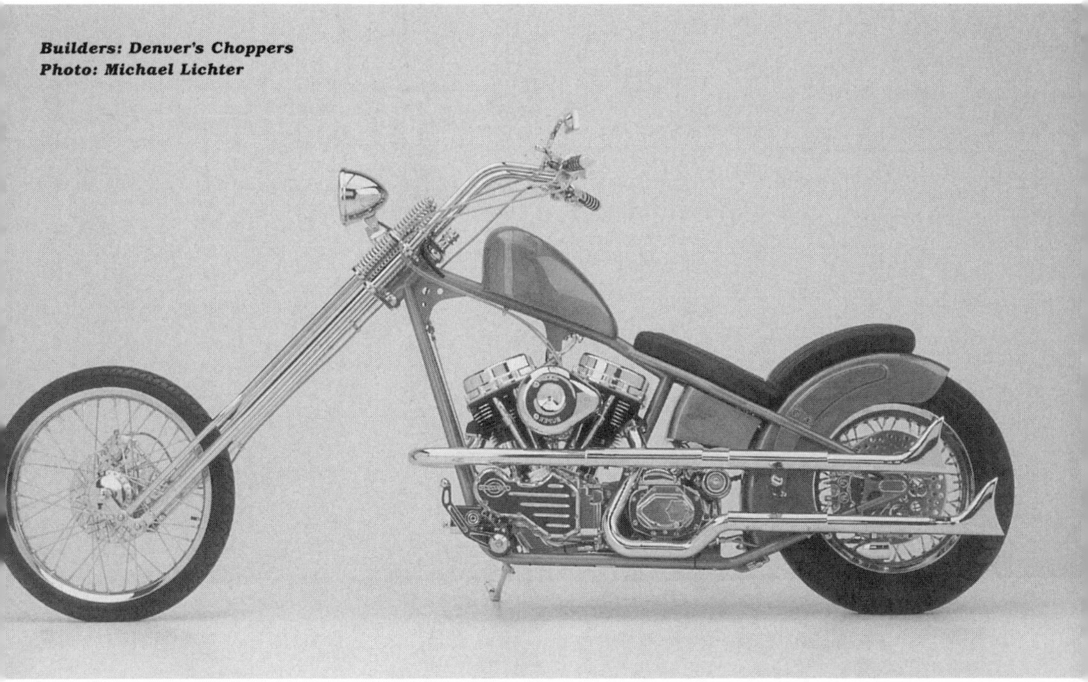

Builders: Denver's Choppers
Photo: Michael Lichter

Billie "The Kid" Craker

The Hogweiser custom show bike built by Billie Craker of Cycle Concepts for Julio Fernandez won Best Radical Custom award at the Easyriders Bike Show in Charlotte, North Carolina, and its painter, Sonny DePalma, took the ViQe Award for National Painter of the Year.

From his hideout in Miami, FL, Billie has unleashed such ultraradical customs as the famous Hogweiser, Terminator, and Porkunator show winners. When you call, say hello to Epstein and Hoodrat. Phone: 305-438-1511.

Damon's Motorcycle Creations

Tom Prewitt and Richard Perez build customs and create custom paint jobs from their location in Brea, California. Phone: 714-990-1166, or log on to www.damonsmc.com.

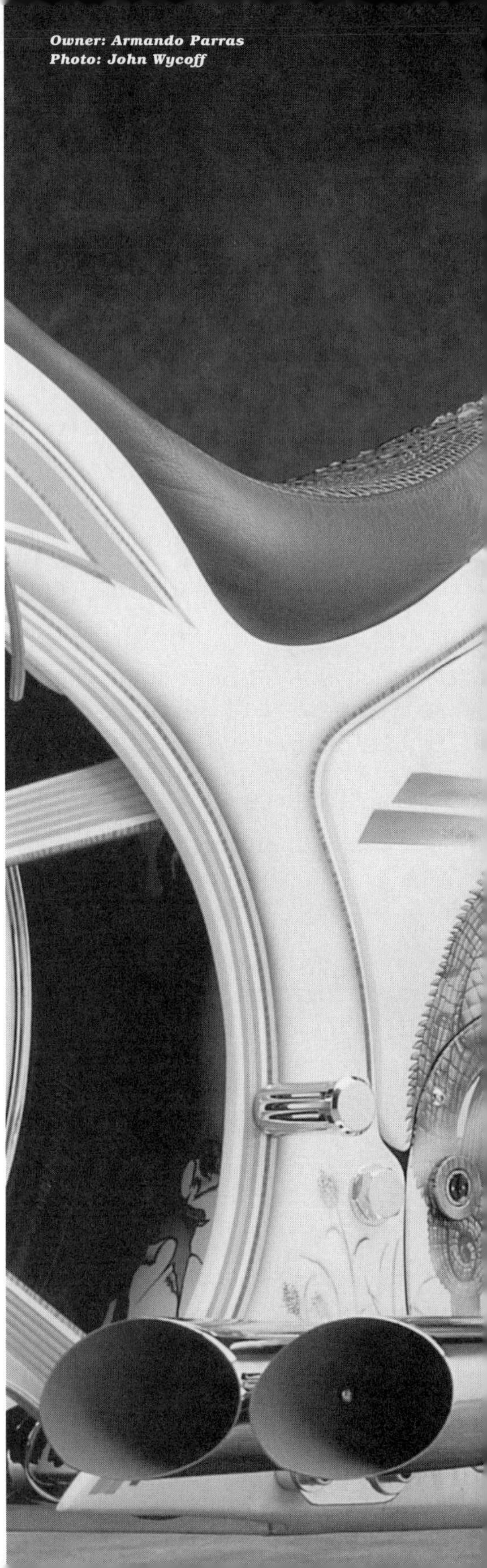

Owner: Armando Parras
Photo: John Wycoff

Denver's Choppers

A living legend in the industry, and now located in Henderson, Nevada, Denver's goes back three decades and counting. It's the home of classic choppers refined to the max. Call Mondo at 877-744-9412, or log on to www.denverschoppers.com

Photo: Bill Ellis

Rick Doss

"Really exciting stuff" was one way another master in the industry described Rick's work. And, "superclean and different than what other people were doing." There's also a comprehensive Rick Doss line of parts. Phone: 434-822-1790, or log on to www.rickdossinc.com.

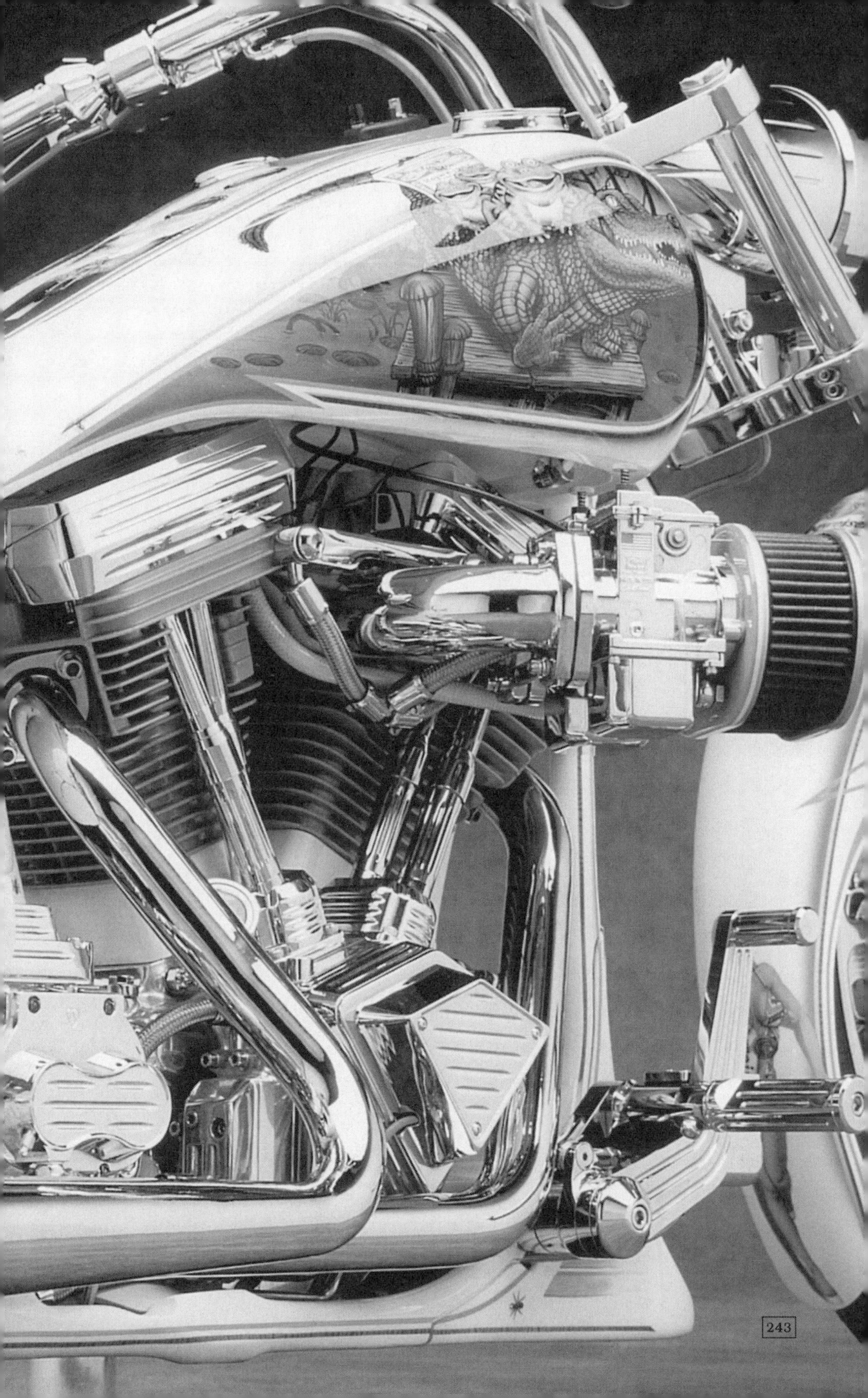

Bob Dron

The Bob Dron Design Center in Oakland, California, creates both traditional and prophetic customs. In 1997 a bike he built appeared in *VQ* magazine; it sure looks a lot like the V-Rod unveiled by the Motor Co. in late 2001. It was only one of many show stoppers. Phone: 510-635-0100, or log on to www.bobdron.com.

Tank Ewischer

From his ops at Tuff Cycle in Aurora, Ohio, Tank builds about a dozen bikes a year, including a Streamliner code-named Project Beer Can that measures 11.5 feet, every inch poetry in motion. And it's rigid, no less. Phone: 330-995-0775.

Louis Falcigno

Located on famous U.S. 1 in Fort Pierce, Florida, Louis started building choppers back in the mid-1970s. While the times changed, Louis's focus didn't. He stuck to his chopper guns . . . a classic who builds classics. Phone: 407-464-5623.

Photo: Don Rogers

Photo: Michael Lichter

Arlin Fatland

Creating his masterworks out of Denver, Colorado, since 1970, Arlin has been there, done that, from raw-boned choppers to high-tech Streamliner types. Yet all his bikes are stamped with his highly individualistic focus. Phone: 303-433-7025.

Ron Finch

Welding, painting, and serving venison chili to his customers, Ron of Finch's Custom Styled Cycles in Pontiac, Michigan, is an artist working in all kinds of materials, especially bikes that must produce a good "rap."

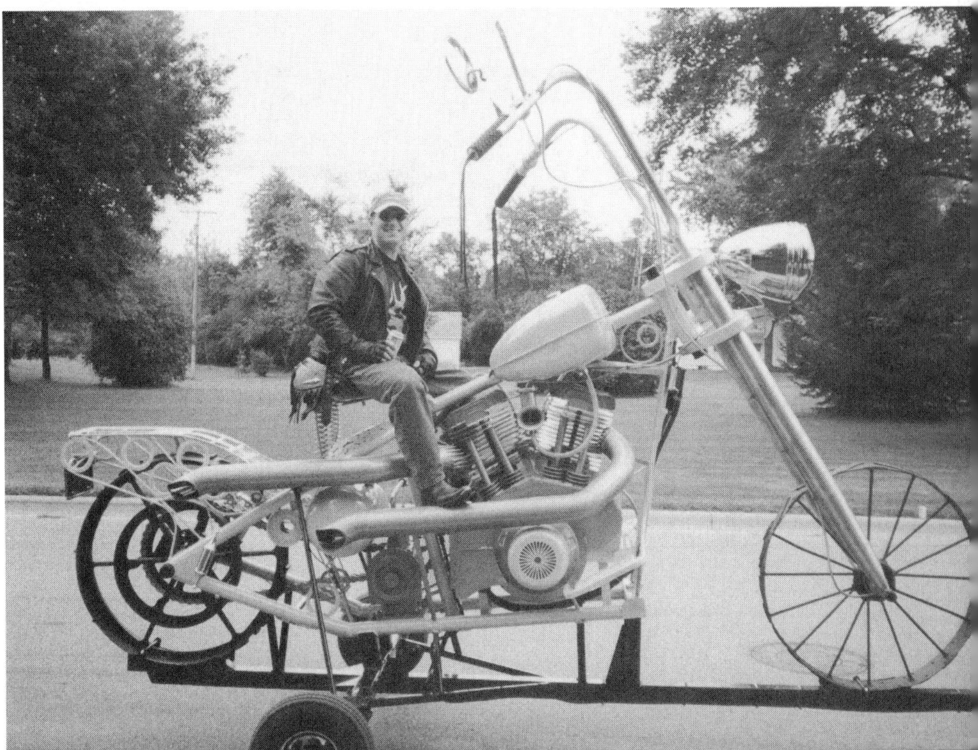

Photo: Rob Willard

Photo: Don Rogers

Matt Hotch

This Fullerton, California, custom builder is a master of invisibility, so clean is his concealment of lines and cables. Customers come in for a fitting, and even the handlebars are bent to their preferences, all dimensions matched to their body build and riding style. Call Matt and Hot Match at 714-680-4362, or log on to www.hotmatchcustomcycles.com.

Don Hotop

Another veteran builder from the mid-'70s, Don's known for his meticulous fabrication, ultrahigh standards, and corn-fed Iowa quality. His signature line of custom parts is also available through major distributors. Phone: 319-372-6216.

Photo: Michael Lichter

Cyril Huze

Living and working his wonders in Boca Raton, Florida, this French-born designer has a penchant for the elegance of art nouveau. His often thematically inspired customs feature many of his hand-fabricated components, now available through his signature line of specialty parts. Vive la diffèrence! Phone: 561-392-5557, or log on to www.cyrilhuze.com.

Photo: Michael Lichter

Jesse James

Jesse's the honcho at West Coast Choppers in Long Beach, California, home of some of the most outrageous and beautifully built bikes this side of the Pecos. He has become one of the Most Wanted builders, thanks to his creativity and the Discovery Channel. Phone: 562-983-6666, or log on to www.westcoastchoppers.com.

Pat Kennedy

This Tombstone, Arizona, bike builder builds long choppers in a direct tradition from the Old School, with an injection of modern super-sleekness that's distinctively Pat Kennedy. Keep it simple, righteous, and ridable. Phone: 520-432-1330, or log on to www.kennedychoppers.com.

Builder: Billy Lane
Photo: Michael Litcher

Billy Lane

The Choppers, Inc., philosophy: "Our interests lie in developing ways to chop stockers and build choppers faster, lighter, with more style, and with a show of class that the Factory should be embarrassed by. We will fearlessly take on any challenge." Phone: 321-757-7262.

Myron Larrabee

As a gym owner, Myron's heavy into weight lifting, but he's also dedicated to lightening up cruisers for the benefit of performance. Also the proprietor of Easyriders of Scottsdale, this Arizona Master Builder is adept at creating tastefully appointed muscle bikes. Phone: 480-970-0352 or log on to www.easyridersharleydavidson.com.

Bob McKay

Building rigid-frame, bar-hopper, hot-rod choppers, McKay's Cycle Creations in Shallow Lake, Ontario, has stayed true to that school for more than thirty years. In fact, Bob built the very first Twin Cam–powered rigid. Phone: 519-935-2241.

Photo: Paul Garson

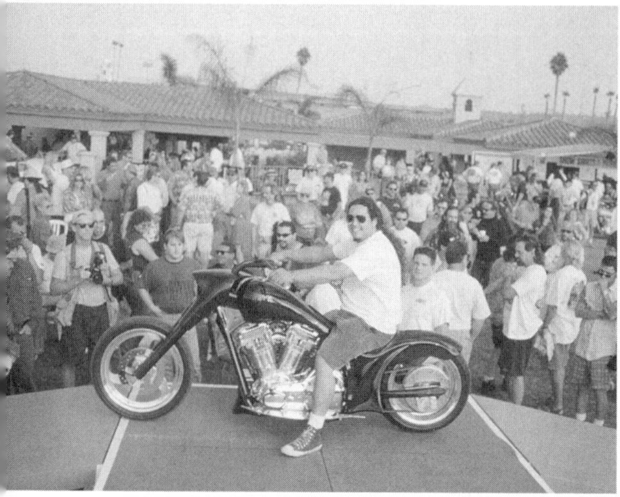

Mike Maldanado

Every time the SoCal master craftsman Mike Maldanado showed up at the Del Mar bike show, the paint barely dry on one of his supersvelt sleds, he took home the Best Concept award. He builds only a few, each a treasure of design and fabrication.

Eddie Meeks

Living and wrenching in Greensboro, North Carolina, Eddie, triply talented as designer, fabricator, and painter, has conjured up a new breed of radical customs with his partner, Simon Solomon, including such show winners as Hardly Civilized. Fax: 336-545-0412, or log on to www.hardlycivilized.com.

Photo: Bill Ellis

Photo: Markus Cuff

Russell Mitchell

From his Sun Valley, California, shop called Exile Cycles, Russell builds bare-to-the-bad-bone customs unlike any others. Low, lean, and mean, they don't even seem real at first glance. Not for the weakhearted. Phone: 818-702-7532, or log on to www.exilecycles.com.

Jim Nasi

From his skunk-works design headquarters in Scottsdale, Arizona, Jim is known for "clean cruisers that blend stylish sex appeal with rubber-burning grunt." He likes skulls in his paint jobs, too. Phone: 1-800-964-NASI.

Photo: Paul Martinez

Cory Ness

While both following and stepping out of his father Arlen's footsteps to do his own radical thing, Cory has designed his share of show stoppers, including bikes like *CurvaceousNess*, seen here. Wearing blue pearl paint by Jon Nelson and bodywork massaged by Bob Monroe, it has Nessian lines that are in a class all by themselves. Phone: 510-276-3395, or log on to www.arlenness.com.

Photo: Michael Lichter

Photo: Michael Lichter

Johnny Pag

Yes, they make custom bikes in Orange County, California, and Johnny's a past master at motorcycles that go as good as they show. Phone: 909-372-0676.

Ron Paugh

Ron Paugh's Paughco frames have literally framed the custom bike movement. He also makes some nice scooters himself. Phone: 1-800-423-2621, or log on www.paughco.com.

Dave Perewitz

Known for aeons for his fast and fabulous looking FXR "choppahs" as well as custom baggers, Dave's based in Brockton, Massachusetts, where his Cycle Fab facility offers a wide spectrum of custom parts. He's also known to move a mean paintbrush. Phone: 508-586-2511, or log on to www.perewitz.com.

Harold Pontarelli

From custom Corvettes to custom V-twins, Harold's ridable exotics are 98 percent hand-built by him alone at his H.D. Performance shop in Vacaville, California. Take for example this 113-inch-powered softail, stylized as a version of what a '54 Harley might have looked like. Phone: 707-453-1649, or log on to www.hd-performance.com.

Photo: Jan Haglund

Photo: Don Rogers

Royal Ryder

Randy Maneschalchi's exceptionally large and well-equipped manufacturing facility in Hudson, Florida, is known for chromoly frames that are 25 percent lighter and 33 percent stronger than steel tubing. Phone: 813-862-0444, or log on to www.royalryder.com.

Ron Simms

Ron's Bay Area Customs, a.k.a. Simms Custom Cycles, has sent seismic waves rolling through the custom bike world since 1977. BACC bikes are known for a combination of rugged, beefy functionality and attention to details, also a description of Ron himself. Phone: 510-537-3338, or log on to www.ronsimms.com.

Photo: Nick Cedar photography

Randy Simpson

Randy's Milwaukee Iron builds about twenty customs a years, including some totally cool retro-vintage customs. He's also heavy into sheet metal production, offering a wide assortment of cool components and rolling chassis kits. Phone: 434-845-7688, or log on to www.milwaukeeiron.com.

Donnie Smith

From his Minnesota shop, Donnie builds killer kustoms, high-tech, high-design bikes that favor big-inch TP motors, girder front ends, and his superclean signature frame. Phone: 763-786-6002.

Photo: Michael Lichter

Russ Tom

With two locations in Seattle, Russ and Brian Mitchell's Downtown Harley-Davidson have created daring new designs that are sizzlin' standouts, even in the rarefied world of the Master Builders. Phone: 800-474-HOGS, or log on to www.downtownharley.com.

Eddie Trotta

The Fort Lauderdale hotbed for pavement pounders par excellence, Eddie's Thunder Cycle Designs has garnered a wall full of Best of Show trophies and a long list of way satisfied customers. Phone: 954-763-2100, or log on to www.thundercycle.com.

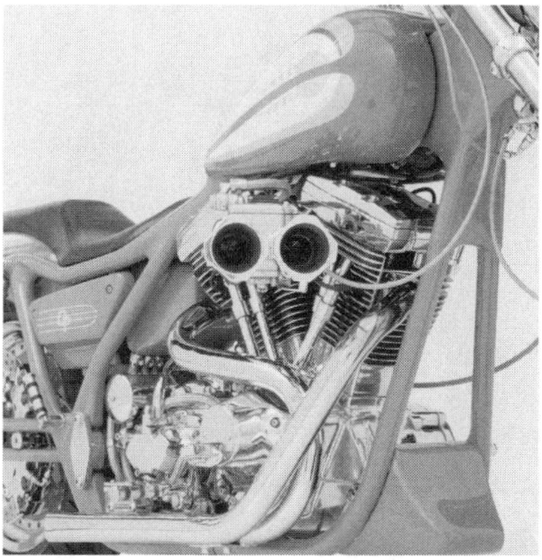

Billy Westbrook

This L.A.-based Master Builder is known for high-concept, hand-finished customs that will handle the real world in stride. A Westbrook bike is a work of both seamless design and simmering performance. Phone: 818-997-6040.

Paul Yaffe

The High End of high-end custom builders, Paul's won about every bike show, including the Oakland Roadster, and garnered *Easyriders'* Best Bike of the Year Award and Master Builder. He is an original, as is his selection of custom parts. Phone: 602-840-4205, or log on to www.pauleyaffeoriginals.com.

Owner: John Angel
Photo: Butch Lassiter

Mac Turnipseed

Since the early ’90s, this Tacoma, Washington, resident has been bolting on parts . . . his parts. Inspired by the Master Builders Ness, Simms, and Tom, Mac went on to create his own unique visions.

Photo: Michael Lichter

Meanwhile from the Factory, 1990–1999

New in the '90 model year lineup was the FLST Fat Boy, based on the Heritage Softail. The softails had been the hottest sellers since the late '80s, and in 1991 over 26,000 were built. New in '91 was the FXDB Dyna Glide Sturgis. For '92 there was also the new FXDB Dyna Glide Daytona, a limited edition model, as well as the new FXDC Dyna Glide Custom. For '93, H-D added the FXDWG Dyna Wide Glide, FXDL Dyna Low Rider, and limited edition FLSTN Heritage Softail Nostalgia. The year '94 saw the new FLHR Electra Glide Road King, while for '95 Bros got the new FXD Dyna Glide and black springer-forked FDXSTSB as well as the new base model FLHT Electra Glide Standard. There were new Sporties in '96 with the arrival of the XL1200S and XL1200c Sportster Custom. For '97 there was optional fuel injection on the Electra Glide plus the new FXSTB Night Train in an all-black treatment, and the new FLHCRI Road King Classic, complete with leather saddlebags, not to forget the new FLTRI Road Glide, which replaced the Tour Glide. Nineteen ninety-nine brought the hot new Twin Cam Evo engine to the streets and placed in all the tourers. There was also the cool new FXDXS, with its XR750 bars, Twin Cam, and all-black format. Taking a close look at the custom bike scene, H-D began, in 1999, producing its own line of custom bikes, with price tags hovering around $25,000.

TAKING A CLOSE LOOK AT THE CUSTOM BIKE SCENE, H-D BEGAN, IN 1999, PRODUCING ITS OWN LINE OF CUSTOM BIKES, WITH PRICE TAGS HOVERING AROUND $25,000.

By the 2000 model lineup, all softails were powered by the Twin Cam motor. For 2001 there was the new FXDXT T-Sport, using the Twin Cam B engine with balance shaft, and more fuel injection options on other models.

And here are the numbers that speak to the incredible success story out of Milwaukee production—1990: 59,207 bikes. Sales in 2001: 243,000. And more to come.

Master Painters

All that glitters is not chrome, especially in the custom bike world. A paint job can make or break a bike, and there are as many views on what constitutes custom paint as there are individual tastes. While some believe biker black is the only color, others reinvent the spectrum and go where no purveyor of pigment has gone before. Motorcycle paint offers perhaps the greatest latitude for creation, since there are no bounds. Today we have chameleon paints that change color in response to the sun, even stealth paint that allegedly confounds radar and, as for graphics or artwork, the scope defies cataloging.

From the minimalist approach as seen on Harley's V-Rod to the retinal-popping megamurals that would leave Michelangelo, Picasso, and Dalí gasping, today's painters create masterpieces destined not to hang on museum walls (well, no doubt some will) but to be traveling, kinetic art displays that bring art to the audience, often with the fanfare of trumpeting pipes.

Some, but certainly not all, of the world's Master Bike Painters have appeared in the pages of Paisano publications. Here are a few of them. Now phone numbers, like girlfriends and wives, tend to change over time, so if these don't work, there's always Information.

Andy Anderson

Nashville's Andy Anderson's been carving new milestones from the early days of custom painting and building, and still he brings a fresh and creative approach to his projects, making his own kind of multicolored music in a city famous for producing chart-topping hits. Phone: 615-255-4807.

Horst Baumberger

When Horst hits on something, everybody wants it. He works out of Albany, California, and has been called one of the most imaginative and creative motorcycle painters on the planet. Ask Ron Simms.

Photo: Bob Ellis

Cosmic Custom Airbrush

Honolulu's Dennis Mathewson and his team add color to over five thousand bike parts a year, not including five hundred complete custom bikes. Dennis counts thirty years of airbrushing experience and takes paint projects from 'round the world. Phone: 808-521-8833.

Teresa Crane

One of Rick Doss's and Randy Simpson's first choice in painters, Teresa has helped bring home numerous show trophies.

Photo: Don Rogers

CrazyHorse Painting

That's what JoAnn Bortles calls her Waxhaw, South Carolina, house of color. With paint jobs that have garnered numerous bike show awards, JoAnn is kept busy but finds time to ride her own bike to events, big and small, around the country. Phone: 704-843-3780.

Chris Cruz

Out of De Land, Florida, this world-renowned airbrush artist has been beautifying cars, trucks, planes, boats, motorcycles and walls since the late 1970s. His specialty is photo-realism. As one client commented, "The eyes of the things he paints look through to your soul." Phone: 386-734-3000.

Damon's

Who paints most of Jesse James bikes? It be Damon's. Phone: 714-990-1166.

Dennis Dardenelli

From his Campbell, California, paint shop, Dennis has done up several Arlen Ness project bikes, in addition to a wild assortment of show winners. A stand-up guy, he's known for his conscientious and timely approach to painting. Phone: 408-374-1213.

Sonny De Palma

Located in West Palm Beach, Florida, Sonny "the Doc" is a long-standing icon in the custom paint world, often called upon by Master Builders for his incredible graphics. He's also really into Rat Fink stuff. Phone: 561-615-0226.

Fitto

From Canada, Fitto is a national treasure, his work gracing innumerable show winners, including the bikes of Master Builder Mitch "Mike" Bergeron. You can hook up with him via Mike at www.mitchbergeroncustoms.com.

Dawn Holmes

A master or should we say mistress, Dawn's known for super tight airbrush work. Her talent is often employed by Master Builder Paul Yaffe.

Jon Kosmoski

Most people associate Jon with the famous House of Kolors, purveyors of all pigments possible, but he's still waving the magic paint brush when not penning How-to books through Wolfgang Publications on methods of custompainting for those who want to try it themselves.

Jeff McCann

Super meticulous in his execution (and a true master of the pin stripe), Jeff paints for the leading builders, including Arlen Ness, Battistini overseas, and Bob Dron. Setting many precedents, one if not the first to take the scroll and gilding designs from vintage carriages and applying them to custom bikes. Stockton, CA phone: 209-951-4715.

Al Martinez

The family owned business carries a 50-year rep in the custom paint world adding their magic touch to everything from radical Harleys to 18-wheeler trucks. Located in Orange, CA, the 10,000 sq. ft. facility is a scene of legendary show-and-go winning paintwork. Phone: 714-288-6700.

Kenny Morris

Located in Stanton, California, Kenny's Hot Rods-n-Hogs shop gets a lot of business from the famous H-D dealership Bartel's (Marina del Rey, California) and is known for precision color matching and artwork retouching skills. He builds bikes as well.

Mike Robins

Mike Robins, custom-painting motorcycles since the mid-'60s, has been there, done that . . . including bikes for Master Builder Don Hotop. Phone: 877-525-1888.

A Resurgence of All-American-Made Motorcycles—Other Than Harley-Davidson

At the beginnings of the twentieth century, there were three hundred or so American-made motorcycles. Ninety years later, there was one. That changed in the 1990s thanks in most part to the phenomenal resurgence of the fortunes of Harley-Davidson—i.e., public demand and enthusiasm. Numerous individuals and companies began producing their own visions of the Made in the USA motorcycle, based on the traditional V-twin engine configuration. Some fell by the wayside, others struggled along, a few prospered. Some of these bikes rolled out in droves, others trickled by the handful. Certainly the numbers did not threaten Milwaukee, but a new Golden Age

Arlen Ness Builds a Custom Victory

Says the maestro about his custom Victory bagger project built in 2000, "I guess you can say we're charting a new course here. I'll be doing design work on the 2003 model Victory, creating accessories for them, and acting in the capacity of spokesperson in addition to being an authorized dealer. It all generated out of some test rides I did through Victory. We began talking about me taking a Victory home and doing what I wanted to do with it. So they shipped me a bike, and we jumped on it to make the deadline for Sturgis.

"Sixty days later, we had finished the project. I rode it from Salt Lake City, and had planned to spend only one day on it. I didn't want to get it nicked up because it was to be displayed for promotions, so I had brought a second bike to ride. But the Victory rode so well, and I like riding it so much, that I ended up riding it the whole way out, including through rainstorms." So much for keeping it spic and span.

"The Victory ran 100 percent trouble free, was very stable, and the handling was such that I was very pleased all-round. It was especially comfortable for me because I had it stretched and lowered and set up the pedals and running boards to fit me, so it felt and rode hand-tailored."

Photo: Mike Chase

As for future predictions, Arlen says, "I see Victory evolving into a major motorcycle company. The first year they built 1,500, this past year 5,400, and for the new year they plan 15,000, then doubling production each year. I look at it this way. Many of my friends have more than one bike, some several; and now why not add a Victory? Don Hotop's built a smoking one, and Zipper's got one, too. All the right guys are getting involved, riding them, and hauling ass, so it builds from there. We and others will be making accessory components. That opens up the customizing horizons for Victory owners. In the performance department, it's even easy to see a blower on a Victory since it works so well with the overhead cam."

We thought we had a wild run in the twentieth century of motorcycling, but the twenty-first is already burning a new fast lane, and Arlen will, as usual, be leading the charge—his Victory assured.

Arlen now offers not only custom parts for Harleys but also for Victory, Yamaha, and Kawasaki motorcycles . . . yes, the metric cruisers.

of Motorcycling seemed to be dawning, and as result we were all enriched by the blood, sweat, and gears that went into these committed efforts.

First Off: The Buell

Yes, it is an "other than Harley-Davidson" and, yes, it gets star billing, although it's obviously a noncruiser and certainly not a "custom." It's been variously called a sport bike or a muscle bike, while the Firebolt model on introduction was dubbed a streetfighter by the company. Sticks and stones will hurt my leathers, but names will never . . . It just may be hard coming up with a pigeonhole name to describe a unique machine. Yes, I might as well say it right off. I am out and out bullish on Buells. Even before I rode one. And more so after the experience. Yes, they had teething problems. Yes, there were numerous recalls—paid for in full by the company warranty, by the way, without a whimper. But get over the niggling details and take in the big picture.

Erik Buell created a motorcycle that keeps on being created, which certainly makes sense in the face of rapid technological advancements and the thumps and bumps of real-world R & D-ing. I can hear the grumbling. Okay, so maybe it's a bike for people who like Triumphs, Nortons, and Ducatis (Erik did race a Yamaha TZ750 and a 900S Ducati). It brings a positive hell, yes, response from riders who enjoy nimble though rock-solid handling, and the feel of a torquey ruffian that slices through the air rather than pushes against it. It's obvious that Buells are bikes that are more like wild stallions than like Budweiser draft horses—not to disparage cruisers by any means, just different strokes for different folks. Or why not have the best of both worlds? Say, have a Road King in the garage alongside one of the new, as of this writing, ultracool XB9R Firebolt

Number 1 Product Introduction

Believe it or not, the most successful product introduction in history—not just the decade—is the Gillette Sensor razor, first seen in ads during Super Bowl 1990. By the end of that year, over 20 million were sold. But obviously not to us bikers, who like the face hair to do its own thing.

Buells. Like, why can't we just get along, cruisers and sport bikes?

Erik Buell first built race bikes, then went to the street in '87 with the XR1000-powered RR100 and later the Evo-powered versions. All shared their unique chassis design, including rubber-mounted engine and rear suspension mounted behind the motor for a shorter wheel base, trademarks that would continue on as the various Buell models progressed through the RR1200, RS1200, and then the S2 Thunderbolt, M2 Cyclone, X1, and Lightning, and the all-new Firebolt debuting in spring 2002.

The ABC's of Buell: lightweight, low-centered mass, simplicity, and the raw sensuality of power as close as your thought of it. Not one single doodad, either.

In 1998 Erik sold almost the whole shooting match to H-D, who had owned 49 percent since '93. In any case, the connection had always been there in a big way, i.e., the Buell's Sportster-based engine. The hookup with H-D did enable the production of Buells to jump from a few hundred annually to six thousand, effectively bringing the benefits, and some of the negative side effects, of transforming from a handmade to a mass-produced motorcycle. Many people like the S1 Lightning, a true all-muscle, no-frills bike looking like nothing else out there. Think of it as a sleek bulldog if that's possible. Then a lot of people like the Cyclone, because it carries the lowest price tag and is more of an all-around, for all the right reasons and seasons bike. And then enter the Firebolt that sent ... well, firebolts through the motorcycling world.

True, H-D assimilated Erik Buell's company into their corporate glom, but it still remains its own man or bike, distinctive if not quirky, a helluva lot of sheer fun to ride, and American-made as well.

And now back to our USA custom bike manufacturers:

"I Fell Off My Bike at 300 mph!"

As reported by Fastac Rinpoche in the pages of V-Twin *magazine, the first thing Dave Campos noticed was smoke in the cockpit. Then a violent shake. Soon the bike was on its side, and a pencil roll ensued. Campos remembers that just before the crash the air-speed indicator had hit 300 miles per hour. By the time the bike stopped rolling, his body was . . . well, actually, it was fine. Of course, it was no ordinary motorcycle. Campos was riding the* Easyriders Streamliner*, a fully enclosed (in an alloy skin) bike, 3 feet high and 28 feet long, owned and built by* Easyriders *magazine and its publisher, Joe Teresi. A year later Campos would ride the bike to a 322-mph world speed record. He also holds the unofficial record for falling off a bike.*

The spill came in October 1989 at the Bonneville Salt Flats. The smoke was the result of the front tire blowing out. The bike rolled maybe only four times, says Campos, because the skid controls dug into the salt. The following summer, Teresi replaced the conventional rubber tire with a rubberless aluminum wheel. It was a solution, but not a perfect one. The alloy wheel weighed 70 pounds, as opposed to the 13-pound rubber wheel. Between 280 and 290 mph, Campos felt a wobble, and again he went down, rolled right, and hit hard on the top of the Streamliner. Campos bruised the top of his head and got some salt from the flats into his eye.

Other than that, he was fine. After crashing at 300 mph, laying down your bike at 285 must seem tame. On the final run in that summer of '90, Campos broke the record. The front wheel wobbled again, but this time he pulled his elbows into his stomach to brace the handlebars and dampen the wobble enough to keep the bike upright.

What many bikers don't realize is that the two Harley engines in the nitromethane-burning Easyriders Streamliner *are Shovelheads, 90 inches apiece. Shovels take a lot of abuse and burn nitro well. The rider sits in a cockpit, his legs out in front of him, as in an easy chair, with the engines behind, wearing a three-layer fire suit.*

The Streamliner is "awkward at low speeds," says Campos, "not capable of being balanced." Driving a tow car, Teresi pulls the bike to about 100 mph, at which point Campos releases the tow rope, lets the clutch out slowly, and doesn't hit second gear until he reaches 200 mph (a long first gear!). He shifts into the third and final gear at around 280.

Campos, who lives in Albuquerque, is an inspector of transit coaches (buses), working as an independent contractor. Now fifty-eight years old, he has spent most of his life in New Mexico. He rode his first motorcycle, a Harley-Davidson 125, at thirteen, and ran his first race at sixteen. Campos became a fixture at drag racing tracks in Southern California during the 1960s and '70s. The Streamliner presented unique challenges. All motorcycles—and bicycles, too—are countersteered. That is, at riding speed, you steer the bike right by leaning right, but the handlebars must be subtly steered left to offset the lean. (Same deal vice versa, of course.) It's something the rider does without thinking. At very low speeds, however, a motorcycle or bicycle steers like a car. Steer right, go right. Steer left, go left. You notice this when you ride or walk your bike into the garage.

On conventional bikes, the transition from conventional steering to countersteering takes place at low speeds, and one doesn't notice it. But with the Streamliner, the transition kicks in somewhere around 60 mph, during the tow period, and if you're not prepared, disaster is imminent. Because it is so unwieldy, the Streamliner has skids, outriggers, that help balance the bike at lower speeds. With the skids down, it steers like a car. When the bike feels under control, Campos pulls the skids up, and—voilà!—countersteering rules.

The hardest part of riding the Streamliner? "You want to turn the throttle down," says Campos. No matter how experienced you are, nothing prepares you for a world record run, because no one has ever gone that fast before. Campos says his greatest challenge was to force himself to leave the throttle open because the speed takes you to unfamiliar territory. "Every time you get in the Streamliner," he says, "it might be your last time." Campos kept the throttle open. "If we didn't break the record, it wasn't going to be my fault."

American Eagle

This Hollister, California, company offers a top-drawer assortment of custom bikes in about any flavor. More info at www.americaneaglemotorcycle.com.

American IronHorse

This Fort Worth, Texas, company builds high-performance, customized bikes in the heavyweight, luxury cruiser class. More info at www.americanironhorse.com.

Big Bear Choppers

Kevin Alsop's $11,000 complete V-twin bike kit is hard to beat: an American Dream come true, an affordable chopper in every driveway. For more information, you can reach Kevin at 909-878-4340.

Photo: Jan Haglund

BigDog

Founded by Sheldon Coleman of Coleman sporting goods fame, this Wichita, Kansas, company produces over a thousand bikes a year. More info at www.bigdogmotorcycles.com.

The Boss Hoss

Not all American customs are powered by V-twin engines; a big case in point is the Boss Hoss, an American-made (Dyersburg, Tennessee) motorcycle powered by a small block Chevy 350 V-8 or 502 Big Block engine engineered into a 1100- to 1310-pound custom body. More info at www.bosshoss.net.

Photo: Michael Farrabaugh

Mind-Numbing Memorabilia

So you like to collect vintage biker stuff. Got a few rally pins and a can of Harley-Davidson beer, have you? Take a look at these two collections, one by the vintage bike restorer-historian M. F. Egan of Santa Paula, California, the other stockpiled by Norm Erlich of Seattle. Buttons, badges, books, tools, spark plugs, stickers, trading cards, watch fobs, postage stamps, ashtrays, trophies, oil cans, factory literature, shop signs, photos . . . you name it. So what are you waiting for? That next treasure is waiting for you at the next swap meet. Look out for the trophy Johnny tied to the front of his bike in The Wild One. *Or the football helmet Nicholson wore in* Easy Rider. *Hey, or a copy of this book.*

Photos: Markus Cuff

California Customs Cycles

With a total of seventeen different models as of this writing, this Mountain View, California, company dishes up both tasty chopper-style rigid and softail types, plus 240-tired bikes. More info at www.calcustom.com.

Confederate Hellcat

Confederate/CSA

This Louisiana company founded in 1991 builds a truly unique custom that's both dynamic looking and dynamite to ride. No cookie cutters here. More info at www.confederate.com.

Desperado Motorcycles

These customs from Woodlands, Texas, about three hundred handbuilt annually, include three rigid frame models and five cantilever dual hidden-shock rear-suspension (softail) models. More info at www.desperadomotorcycles.com.

Indian Motorcycles

This is the new, resurrected Indian. In the spring of 2002, Indian brought out new models, significantly, their all-new 100 Powerplus Indian engine, replacing the S & S power plant previously employed by their bikes. More info at 800-445-1759, or check their website at www.indianmotorcycle.com.

Photo: Teddi S.

Call it a contradiction in terms, this sleek and elegant Fatso Softail conjured up by Carl Brouhard of Brouhard Designs. Celebrating its tenth anniversary, the Auburn, California, custom shop is no stranger to show-winning customs, but even Carl was surprised when his latest work took home Best of Show from the Easyriders Sacramento Bike Show . . . and then scored with the NBA as well.

Of his goal for the bike's creation, Carl says, "I wanted to build something that looked like a big classic car that someone customized without going overboard on it. Just the right mix of chrome and simple paint with swoopy lines and body panels that accented it and gave it some flow. It was something a little different than what I'd built before, kind of the first big, 'bulky' bike that we turned out." Now Carl has painted a lot of full-bodied bikes for Arlen Ness and also some of Arlen's super swoopies, like the famous Smoothness *custom, but this was somewhere in between. "We got it finished up just before the Sacramento Easyriders Show. We took it there to show and to have a good time; not expecting to do as well as we did by winning the show. It was the Easyriders third show in Sacramento, and it was the second Best of Show we've taken there. And the year before my wife, Lynda, won the Sportster Class. [By the way, Lynda Brouhard did all the custom wiring on this bike, as she does on all the others that come out of Carl's shop.] So we were pretty excited about that. Then we showed the bike at the Sacramento Autorama, and it won the Outstanding Bike and Best Engineering award."*

Housed in the bike's Daytec frame is a Milwaukee Performance 100-inch motor with Evo Twin Cam heads, but it's the bodywork that seals the deal. "The most challenging part of the buildup," says Carl, "was getting all the lines to match up and flow toward where you couldn't tell where the tanks ended and the panels came in. The metal fabricator, Bob Munroe, is a master of creating that seamless look. If there's one thing I'd I really like to stress it's what a great craftsman he is and what a great guy he is as well. He takes my sketches, then turns them into reality. With these particular sketches, Bob worked up the body parts. I got it back at the shop and basically bolted all the body panels onto the frame and molded everything together in one complete piece. Then I split it all apart basically with a little coping saw where I had just a small gap between the panels, added all the other components, then sealed

Photo: Mike Chase

it back up together again. So I had several hours in that."

As for the bike's paint, Carl laughs again and says, "It's a color people either love or hate. I didn't want to use the traditional colors that everybody relies on. I also don't believe in ruining a bike with too much graphics. Since I do have a custom paint shop, people expect you to put fifty colors on every bike that comes out of your place. I don't do that. All the stuff we do is very clean, maybe some small graphics for accent if any at all. When I'm looking for a new look for a bike's paint, I go out and check out the car lots to see what's new and cooking. The color is a Lexus car color called Moss Green Metallic with pearl. I added some more gold pearl, a little silver, a little green, and kinda tweaked it around the way I wanted it. Basically when people walked into the shop and saw the painted frame, most of them said, 'Yow, it's the ugliest color I've ever seen in my life.' I just would say, 'Wait till it's all together.' I wanted something that was different, and if I took it to a show, no matter where they put me the color would stand out on its own, yet not be so bright and hideous that it took away anything from the motorcycle, but instead complemented it. And we got lucky. It worked at the shows."

Carl tells us the show winner is now in the hands of another winner, Lorenzen Wright, who was playing on the Atlanta Hawks. "He's already riding it back and forth to practice. The bike was actually built in partnership with Tom Gugliotta, who plays for the Phoenix Suns. This is the first custom project that Tom and I did together. He had bought a softail from me, and we'd become good friends, both having a love of bikes. It was a way for Tom to have more involvement, so we sit around and kick around ideas for bikes, and I go to work. Our plan is have as many of them out in the hands of NBA players as we can. Recently we've been talking to Shaquille O'Neal about doing a bike for him. We're currently working on another bike for a member of the Sacramento team.

"In addition to our NBA effort, we're busy building bunches of 250 bikes which are all the rage. And, like everybody else, we're waiting for parts." Carl laughs. "We're also getting more serious on a line of products that we're developing."

Panzer Motorcycle Works

The Canon City, Colorado, builders of the Neo-Pan, Panzer puts the past into the present. All its retro-customs are powered by its modern Neo-Pan 90-cubic-inch hand-assembled engines. More info at www.panhead.com.

Pro-One

These longtime makers of custom components got their federal license to build customs in 2002 and use their well-known products to build Show N' Go winners. More info at www.pro-one.com.

Pure Steel

The Phoenix-based Pure Steel hand-builds superstock custom motorcycles ranging from "extreme perfection" to "complete madness." More info at www.an-stuff.com/puresteel.

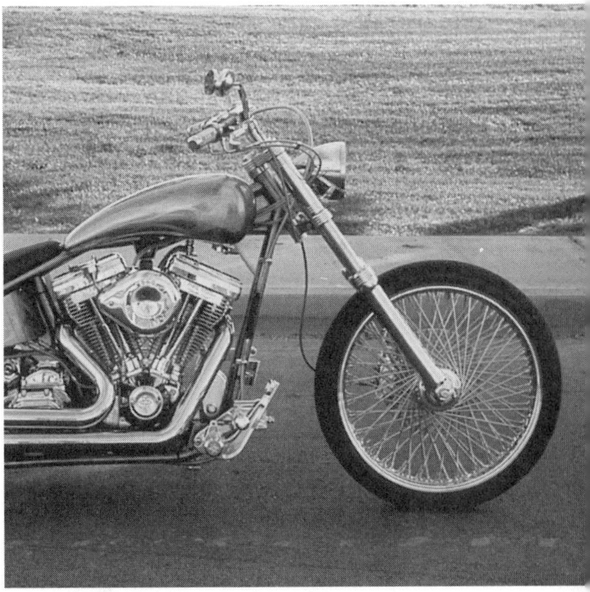

Photo: Paul Martinez

Surgical Steeds

Limited production bikes built in Scottsdale, Arizona, Surgical Steeds carry a reputation of quality and scalpel sharp performance. More info at www.surgicalsteeds.com.

Titan

With several models, both solid and rubber-mount designs, this Phoenix, Arizona, company has been a premier custom bike builder. Although they previously used S & S motors, in spring '02 Titan's all-new 1638-cc Big Twin made its debut. More info at www.titanmotorcycles.com.

Ultra Motorcycle Co.

This line of custom bikes out of Mira Loma, California, offers everything from bare bones to custom and sports cruisers. More info at www.ultracycles.com.

Last-Minute News Flash!

On February 21, 2001, it was announced that Fred Campagnuolo, an Ultra dealer in Florida, had bought up the assets and intellectual property of Ultra Motorcycle Co. from Finova Mezzanine Capital. Campagnuolo said it was going to streamline and upgrade the model lineup.

Victory

The Medina, Minnesota-based Polaris Industries, Inc., with fifty years in the business, is world famous for its snowmobiles. They also make ATV's and personal watercraft. In the early 1990s, with a sound infrastructure and dealer network behind them, their engineering staff set to work designing and fabricating an all-new American-made motorcycle powered by a fuel-injected, single overhead cam V-twin . . . and in 1997 the all-American Victory V92C cruiser was born. More info at www.victory-usa.com.

Metric Customs Arrive on the Scene

It's a fact of motorcycling life that the lines have blurred (and deliberately) between traditional Harley-Davidsons and the various Japanese cruisers, to the point where the novice motorcyclist, and sometimes even the veteran, might well mistake one for the other. Add the custom touch and the picture gets even blurrier or more interesting, depending on your point of view. The reality is that an increasing number of Japanese bikes are being customized, and the aftermarket industry, sensing a keen interest, has responded by producing an

Photo: Don Rogers

Shaq Attack Custom

Okay, so he's a celebrity athlete, but the bike deserves the spotlight on its own merits. The L.A. hoop star Shaquille O'Neal rides a long-legged bike built for him by Bruce Rossmeyer, owner of Harley-Davidson of Daytona Beach, with the substantial aid of Arlen Ness, who stretched the Road King frame and swing arm a whopping twelve inches to help accommodate Shaq's seven-foot-one, own 310-pound frame.

increasing amount of custom parts for these "metric customs." Yes, people are spending big bucks on their Yamahas, Kawasakis, Hondas, and Suzukis to add that personal touch previously reserved for Harleys. Major custom shops, dealers, and individual builders working out of home garages are creating a new direction in customs not originating in Milwaukee. Three representative examples follow, a customized Yamaha, Honda, and Kawasaki.

Scott Britt: The Master Builder Who Put the "Custom" in Metric Customs

Not only is Scott setting the trend in today's metric custom world but he is arguably the founding father of the whole movement, tracing his roots to the age of nine, wrenching at his father's Hodaka and Montessa bike shop in rural Tennessee.

In 1979 Yamaha started releasing cruisers, the 750 Special being first; at that time Scott, while working at his dad's dealership, began applying some custom paint jobs to the new model. He recounts, "In 1981 I met Mark Roberts and Gary Lane and both those guys are still with me today. I still do all the paint and molding, Mark does all the fabrication, and Gary does all the mechanicals on about every bike I've built. I couldn't do what I do without those two guys."

Scott came to the attention of Yamaha from the get-go. Even while in his early twenties, he was road racing on one of the only custom-painted racers at the time. "The quantum leap occurred when Yamaha introduced the milestone Royal Star model, but there were a lot of 1100 Specials and V-Maxes that took me up to that point."

When asked what was his favorite bike to customize, without hesitation Scott says, "The Yamaha Road Star. I love that motor. And I think the Road Star is the bike that helped close the gap where more people in general are accepting metric motorcycles than ever before.

Photo: Aaron Stevenson

"We're working toward giving people a place to start buying the more exotic parts, not just chrome pieces. We have kits where people can take their stock motorcycle into their garage and bolt on stretched gas tanks, custom rear fender kits, seat kits, and more. We also have a 230 rear-tire swing-arm for the Road Star. All these components are applicable to any Yamaha product, especially the Road Star, V-Star, and Royal Star models. I've got twenty-five years of history with Yamaha, and I'm just so familiar with their products that I know what works and what fits. Over the years, I have had a lot of support from Yamaha California and from their designer Jeff Pahlegyi. Yamaha probably recognizes that I'm doing more than any other dealer to promote this effort, and it works for both of us."

Scott has garnered his own share of awards and some unique recognition as the leader in his field of endeavor. One of his custom Royal Stars, called *Speed Star*, was the first metric bike ever to appear on the cover of an *Easyriders* magazine (V-Q, December 1999). He says, "We want to build new custom motorcycles, in various levels of customization, for people to buy right off our showroom floor, but moreover I want to build a custom showroom for metric motorcycles."

For more information, log on to www.brittmotorsports.com or call Scott's Wilmington, North Carolina, shop at 910-791-8321.

Yamaha's Concept Builder: Jeff Pahlegyi

It's pronounced "Pology," but there's no apology needed when you grasp the concepts behind this builder's custom Yamahas. It sounds like a dream job, and maybe it is, for Jeff makes his living building bikes for Yamaha as a regular day job. The talented designer also creates bolt-on components for his employers and still has time to wrench out a personal ride now and then, just for grins. He builds four or five cusoms for the Yamaha annually and has been at it for the past ten years or so, as of this writing. Lucky guy.

Homegrown Honda Custom

You don't have to have thousands of square feet and the latest in CAD-CAM CNC computers to wrench together a masterpiece custom. Just ask the Atlanta area resident Russ Austin. Russ's grandfather organized the first motorcycle police squad in Miami, Florida, and his father rides a custom Harley he had built for his own father, so motorcycles are part of the bloodline. Russ's whole family is involved in the floor-covering business and, in more ways than one, has covered all kinds of motorcycles. He says, "I've been tinkering on import bikes for about a few years now for family and customers. I've done an Intruder 1400, an Intruder 800, and am just starting a Marauder, and I have a Road Star lined up."

Photo: Mike Powell

The 1998 Honda 750 Ace seen here, dressed in elegant Chrysler Champagne pearl paint, has scored several trophies, including First Place in the Middle Weight Class and Third Overall at the annual Honda Hoot megarally. Attention to design and detail is readily

Bike Feature: Billy Lane's Swap Meet Show Winner

"Our interests lie in developing ways to chop stockers and build choppers faster, lighter, with more style, and with a show of class that the Factory should be embarrassed by," says Billy Lane of Choppers, Inc.

Milwaukee might be a bit red-faced after seeing Choppers, Inc., owner's red metallic rigid roller, the Motor Company's reflection thrown back by five grand worth of chrome. The embarrassment, more like envy, might have something to do with the very distinctive and very un-Milwaukee front end, in this case a springer transplanted from a 1940s Indian-Four. Billy says, "I'd seen a couple springer Indians and always thought it would be neat for a chopper. I found the front end at a swap meet down at Daytona Bike Week. It was all complete but bent really bad, so it took some rebuilding." Billy was into building hot rods before he got into bikes, transferring many of the skills he had developed from four to two wheels. He opened up Choppers, Inc., in 1993, eventually moving from the original Miami location to Melbourne, some miles up the Florida coast.

While he had the Indian girder in mind, the bike's overall design started with the back end. "I wanted to build the frame with no rear axle adjuster. I took a Paughco frame and cut it off from the seat post back, then redid the whole back to accommodate the front and rear belt drives. It was a lot of work. Lining up the chassis was very difficult. I had planned to set it up for a 240 Metzeler, but the release of the fat tire to the public was late, so I switched to a 200 Pirelli and ended up making the rearend somewhat narrower. The bike started out being built for a customer, but that deal fell through, and now I'm really glad it remained my bike."

The chopper was initially slated to be powered by a Knucklehead motor, but upon inspection Billy realized it required a complete rebuild, so he next opted to implant a Shovelhead. Then he saw that the look of the Shovel didn't match the look of the bike's design, so he traded it to a friend for a Panhead that fit the bike's personality. As far as the dramatic paint scheme, another five grand investment, Billy says, "I liked the vintage look of the pearlescent white and with the burgundy I wanted a deep, deep color to set off against the white." Wearing that pricey but eye-popping paint, the gas tank was a five-dollar can of rust, a Sportster peanut, which Billy found at another swap meet and which required a whole lot of massaging. The grill piece is another swap meet find, this time "treasure" from the Laughlin River Run. Says Billy, "It's from a 1941 Ford pickup. I like old cars and stuff, and thought it would look cool as part of a motorcycle gas tank, in this case the dash. Of course, it was a lot bigger, and I had to cut it down to fit. I used car parts for the headlight, a unit from a '59 El Camino, and mirrors from a Model A."

And, speaking of that 200 Pirelli, it's been boiled down to a slick thanks to Billy's 7000 miles of travels. "It rides really smooth because of the belt-belt setup. And the springer rides incredible. When I first saw it, I thought, Well it's going to look cool but ride like hell. The springer had three or four times the number of leaf springs that it has now; the bigger Indian-Four needed all those springs. I also had to mess around with the shoulder springs to adjust the dampening. I had it out in Sturgis and rode it through Spearfish Canyon, Needles Canyon, and out to Wyoming. It also sounds really cool with the 'flappers' on the pipes, because you can really hear the cams."

Speaking of those flappers, they direct the loud *sound from the pipes away from the rider's ears. Billy, who came up with the pipes, inspired by Funny Car designs, says, "People were freakin' out over the pipes at the Cincinnati Dealer Expo." While Choppers, Inc., offers a number of cool parts, Billy has plans to offer soon the pipes as well as the bike's trick forward controls to the public.*

Billy's Pan Chopper took Second Best of Show at the Charlotte Easyriders Show, then went on to the Columbus Easyriders final show of the season, where it took home a First Place in its class. You'll be seeing it in the photographer Michael Lichter's Journey Museum exhibit and, while he's had a lot of offers, Billy wants to hold on to this bike. Asked about the Indian front-end theme, he says, "Right now I'm doing a hubless wheel bike, a twin-carb Knuckle, and I actually bought a couple Indian springers at a swap this year and am thinking about maybe doing one up with a turbo Evo motor."

And, yes, they'll all be choppers. Hey, whadya gonna build when you got such a cool name as Choppers, Inc.?

apparent, plus it was no easy task finding custom parts for the Ace. Russ recalls, "I wanted a Kuryakyn Hypercharger, but they didn't make one for my bike. So I called up Mike Farley, who makes trick custom parts locally and told him, 'Hey, I need some help with this thing. I can't get anything to mount up.'" Mike conjured up the necessary pieces from raw billet while another local artisan, Ray Welsh, modified the rear fender and fabricated the special polished neck section. The bike's distinctive sound issues from a set of DG Hard Krome two-and-a-half-inch drag pipes. In addition to replumbing all the electronics and doing all the final assembly, Russ designed and prepped the seat based on the stock pan, then had Gary Long stitch on the leather. Further pieces were gleaned from Cobra, Pro-One, Jardine, Ness, Legends, White Brothers, and Headwinds. Russ and his wife, Jana, enjoy riding their custom Ace up through the green hills of northern Georgia.

Texas High Plains Drifter Kawasaki Custom

As manager of Grapevine Kawasaki in where else but Grapevine, Texas, Steve Crawford has seen a lot of stock metric bikes. As the designing hand behind Rolling Creations Custom Motorcycles, he's created his share of metric metamorphoses, taking the stock out of stockers. After researching the marketplace, he chose the Kawasaki Drifter, a retro homage to the classic full-fendered Indian motorcycle popular in the '40s, based on its engine, which he considered as "good as it gets." While well aware of the huge Harley custom market, he read the handwriting on the wall and saw a large movement toward customizing metric bikes.

Photo: Frank Merott

With few custom parts available and a bike that had a lot of black to begin with, Steve knew he was in for a challenging experience. Now you have to know what a stock Drifter looks like to really appreciate the "fine tuning" Steve accomplished with his smooth makeover. He massaged the gas tank by rolling the edges and french-flushing the filler neck. Other subtle but significant changes included the relocation of the ignition switch from its less than user-friendly stock position. He did find some Longshots pipes through Vance & Hines that seemed to be the look he wanted, but they were back-ordered for four months. To get the right seat look, he transformed an old Cobra custom seat intended for a Vulcan into a solo saddle with concho accents. Speaking of accents, you'll note the classic rear teardrop taillight with the blue dot center.

To add to the performance upgrades, Steve had a fuel injection intake prototype fabricated by CS Designs. He also put on a Kuryakyn Hypercharger to back up that trick intake.

But all eyes are on the supersleek red pearl paint with the ghost flames licking the length of this Texas High Plains Drifter, a retro metric custom cruiser that perhaps signals a whole new species. For more of the same, hook up with Steve at 817-481-2500.

Easyriders
JUN
Dell D.
Beau
Chopp
in Co
he
ing
r
World's
Ugliest Trike
Rock Stars and
their Choppers
Sissy Bar
sign Contest

Easyriders Magazine Celebrates Its Twenty-fifth Anniversary in 1996

Launched in June 1971, *Easyriders* magazine, in this writer's unbiased opinion, joined the ranks of other milestone publications like *Life*, *Playboy*, and *Screw*, magazines that somehow captured the uncapturable of America.

One man started it all, and kept it all going strong . . . the late Lou Kimzey. He had already created and published *Drag Racing*, *Drag Strip*, and *Big Bike* magazines. He was the leading force, with emphasis on force, behind what would become a publishing milestone. The "chopper pro" staff member way back then was Joe Teresi, a designer and builder of choppers and drag racer who was the owner and publisher of Paisano Publications. Another bike builder who formed that first nucleus at *Easyriders* was Mil Blair, whose talent with the camera helped put the publication on the map.

Easyriders is recognized worldwide (and no doubt beyond in Harley Heaven) as the ultimate Harley-Davidson lifestyle magazine. Always imitated, never duplicated as they say. Weathering its own cycle of ups and downs, *Easyriders* (a.k.a. Paisano Publications) has made it, along with the Motor Co., into the twenty-first century.

As *Easyriders'* current editor, Dave Nichols writes,

Just as Fonda and Hopper's film Easy Rider acted as a microcosm of the hippie and biker culture, so Easyriders focused on this wild lifestyle and defined it. The first issue didn't offer a biker chick on the cover, just a wild chop job. Soon, the boys realized that sex sells and made sure there was always a pretty girl seen with the motorcycle. Easyriders had a definite and tweaked point of view, from the wonky "Takin' It Easy" column of bizarre news stories and weird tidbits, to mind-bending art direction and quirky cartoons. They even invented oddball characters like Miraculous Mutha, who was the embodiment of the whore with a heart of gold. The first issue jumped off the shelves, and soon the magazine had a life of its own.

Early issues of Easyriders carried the tag line "For the Swinging Biker" (though this soon changed to "Entertainment for Adult Bikers") and conjured images of wild parties and fast rides on unimaginably customized machines. The magazine created an image of hard partyin' bikers, a life where beautiful women were plentiful and begging to go for a ride on a chopped Hog or between the sheets. The first issues were published bimonthly, with the very first David Mann centerspread appearing in issue three.

THE OUTLAW BIKER IMAGE, LIKE IT OR NOT, WAS GOING MAINSTREAM IN A BIG WAY.

Another artist to join the staff early on was Hal Robinson, whose leg-wettin' cartoons only served to further create the image of what Easyriders was all about. Very early on, Easyriders established ABATE, which at the time stood for A Brotherhood Against Totalitarian Enactments. Today, the organization's acronym stands for A Brotherhood Aimed Toward Education. The idea was to create a body that policed governmental policies regarding custom motorcycles and acted as a watchdog for new laws that restrict bikers' rights and freedom. At present, ABATE has chapters all over the country, with membership in the tens of thousands.

The magazine was, and is, a sounding board for readers who kept the lifestyle alive through Harley's lean AMF years. Easyriders readers have always been very vocal. There's never been any guesswork in finding out what they want, and so Easyriders' success has been the success of the American biker, independent, fiercely loyal, and proud.

Always wanting to give readers what they want, Easyriders magazine went monthly with the November 1976 issue. By now, the rag had gone from sixty-eight pages to ninety-four and would soon jump to over a hundred. Loyal readers had gotten into the act of preserving their biker lifestyle and were sending in artwork, photographs, poems, fiction, true road tales, jokes, and cartoons that exemplified the Easyriders way of life. In fact, by 1978 there was so much good scooter photography coming in that we gave birth to another magazine, In the Wind. Both publications continued to feature the coolest custom bikes and hottest Harley honeys on the planet.

Easyriders has always been about reflecting the motorcycling world, and as the custom bike scene changed and evolved, so did Easyriders. By 1980 the rag was already going through refinements, adding more tech tips and legislative news, offering more color photography, more big bike events, runs, and parties, more gorgeous gals and wilder art. Cool products produced by bikers for bikers began to appear, beginning with Easyriders T-shirts, belt buckles, boots, and more. This would soon mutate into an entire products division, including everything a biker needs, from leathers and riding gear to tools and bike lifts.

By the mid- to late 1980s, Easyriders continued to grow as well, adding Biker and Tattoo to our stable of magazines, and we were offering $100,000 sweepstakes to win new Harleys and Fly & Putt Trips to Europe. New riders on new Harleys couldn't help but notice our coverage of such traditional biker parties as the Sturgis Black Hills Classic, Daytona Bike Week, and the Laconia Rally and Races. These new riders joined the old-school bikers at rallies in droves, and the times, they were achanging. Easyriders continued to echo these changes, becoming the largest-selling motorcycle magazine on the newsstands while still offering its whacked-out point of view to scooter tramps worldwide. The outlaw biker image, like it or not, was going mainstream in a big way.

—*Dave Nichols Editor*, Easyriders

Cool Bikes Not Built by Famous People

This writer is known for his inclination toward the unique—others call it weird . . . so be it. But here are a few of the bikes that have grabbed his attention, designs that pushed an already well-pushed envelope, standout customs in an increasingly difficult-to-stand-out-in world.

Photo: Micahel Farrabaugh

The Millennium Cruiser

This totally time traveling bike is the creation of Brian Olson, Mike Kennison, and Bill Holler of Peru, Indiana, who drag-races cars and runs a paint and body shop in addition to Brian Olson Bikes, Inc. When first shown at the Indianapolis World of Wheels, it took top awards in Radical Class, Best Bike of the Show, Best Paint, and even Best Display. A one of a kind that certainly deserves its name.

Outadisworld Ottawa Radical

Sometimes a radical bike ups the ante on "radical," and such was the appear ance of the Canadian Mitch Roberts's ultimate creature feature. "I've hac a couple Harleys over the years," he says, "but I've never made anything radical. But then my buddy Scotty and I sat down one day and I said, 'You know, man, I want to build something that will blow people's minds away wher I go up the street.' 'I agree,' says Scotty.

"We handmade the frame from cold-rolled seamless steel and machinis tubing as well as the tank, fenders, oil tank, and seat. We hung the frame fron my garage ceiling on a nail and decided on the rake—something crazy like fifty eight degrees. And because we wanted the most radical thing on the street we made it only fourteen inches high at the seat. My knees are about twc inches above the seat when I ride."

As for the paint job, Mitch was referred to another guy who worked out of his garage, a Master Painter by the name of Fitto, who lived in Montreal. "I wanted a wild, biomechanical monster look, so you'll notice the stainless vertebra up the center and a rib cage attached to it."

The first rule when riding this thing, what with its 113-inch S & S and the blower, is to hold on tight. Mitch estimates 200 horsepower launching a bike weighing only 450 pounds. Funneled through a set of 2.25-inch shorty straight pipes and a lumpy cam, it sounds like a top fuel dragster. By the way, this is the first bike that Scotty's ever built. Nice first effort, eh? "Yep, we're just a couple of backyard guys from Canada," says Mitch.

Two-Wheeled Cadillac Eldorado

Spin of D & S Enterprises (Anaheim, California) designed this Eldorado Custom Conversion based on a stock Harley softail. D & S made the classic valenced fenders, mufflers, stainless mufflers, gas tank, pegs, seat, and grafted on a Wide Glide front end and 16-inch whitewall towers. Now you're stylin'.

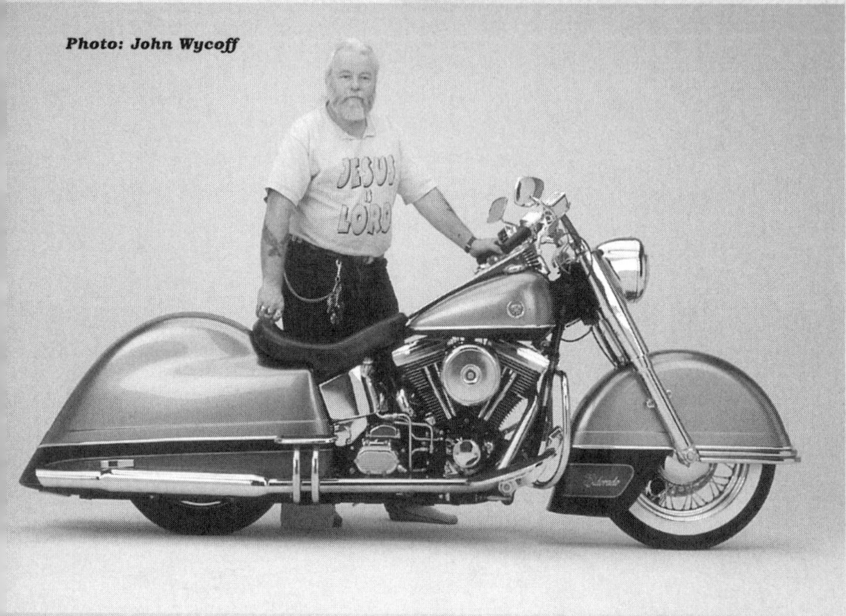

Photo: John Wycoff

Zyborg

Built and fabricated by its owner, Paul De Meester, and Fred and Ingrid Muehlenhort of Race Tec, Zyborg, *with its bizarre physiognomy, does have that* Alien *film look. The hand-hammed, black porcelain–coated aluminum body panels and sculpted lines are backed up by a supercharged 89-cubic-inch engine. How much to realize this futuristic flier? Try $125K.*

Photo: Paul Garson

The Bike the Borg Built

Well, it was actually the aircraft mechanic James Hines. Powered by a dual supercharged nitrous-oxide-injected Chevy V-8, this monster has won numerous awards and caused several neck injuries when people take a double look as it thunders by.

Farra's Flyer

Farra and Steve Cook and their sons, Steven and Taylor, live in the Atlanta, Georgia, area. Steve keeps busy running his own shop (Steve Cook Racing), where he wrenches on Winston Cup race cars. "When Farra decided she liked bikes," he recalls, "I said, 'Okay, I'll go get us a bike to ride on.' But I couldn't find anything that I liked because I'm a little radical, so I decided to just build my own. I had built the softail that I ride and, in my spare time, two or three bikes for other people. Then Farra said she wanted her own bike. She designed the bike, picked out all the pieces, and I did the special fabrication work."

Photo: Mike Langello

Says Farra, "People look at me and say, 'How in the world can someone so small (five-foot two) handle something so big?' I tell them, 'Once you get the hang of it, you know what you're doing.' I was kind of a tomboy, and always loved motorcycles. Growing up, I had a favorite uncle who had a Harley, and I've always wanted one myself. Knowing that this bike was what I had chosen, and that my husband had built it, and I had helped put it together gave me the greatest feeling." Among other awards, Farra's Flyer *won Best of Show People's Choice at the Atlanta Easyriders Show and a Second at the Charlotte Show.*

Photo: Paul Martinez

"Cashmere"

The Springfield, Missouri, custom car and bike enthusiast Bob Lowe has built only a few bikes, but each is a masterpiece, often with radical bodywork fabricated by Ron Englert of Reno Engineering. One such bike is his Cashmere*, a custom that perfectly mixes elegance with performance.*

Photo: Jan Haglund

Terry's Titanium Terror

Keith Terry of Terry Components (805-376-2700) in Newbury Park, California, went so far as to team up with tank builders in Russia to build this totally mind-blowing and beautiful titanium-enhanced V-twin engine, thus resolving the heat problems plaguing performance engine builders for aeons. The superhigh-tech engine revs from 1500 to 6000 rpm in under three seconds. Want one? Terry can make more.

Watch Out for Woodpeckers

The L.A. bike fan Barry Weiss likes the warm look of burled walnut, so he carved what has been dubbed the Harley-Davidson Corniche, *with simulated walnut veneers, the illusion created by the painter C. D. Hall on a set of fiber-glass repro Indian valenced fenders with Damon's custom painter adding the brass screws and gold pinstriping. A 1350-cc Big Twin motor pushes the wood down the road.*

Photo: Paul Garson

Gold Bullion: Rick Squadrito Rides a Fred Kodlin Custom

Voted Best Radical at Daytona Bike Week, this bike was created by the German Master Builder Fred Kodlin for the Colorado resident Rick Squadrito. Fred's design innovations include a twist-grip clutch integrated into the hand-built bars. As for the "invisible" rear brake, Fred designed and fabricated a jackshaft system to make it fade away from sight. And the carburetor's also outasight, hidden within the gas tank. Fred literally handmade everything except the Twin Cam motor. Asked what he didn't make on the bike, he laughs. "The tires." Oh, and he did take the taillight lens off an Opel car to create the bike's rear lighting. Fred is known as The Builder in Europe, a well-earned reputation for unique mindblowers and show stoppers. Oh, and when Fred focuses, he really focuses. This bike was built in six weeks flat.

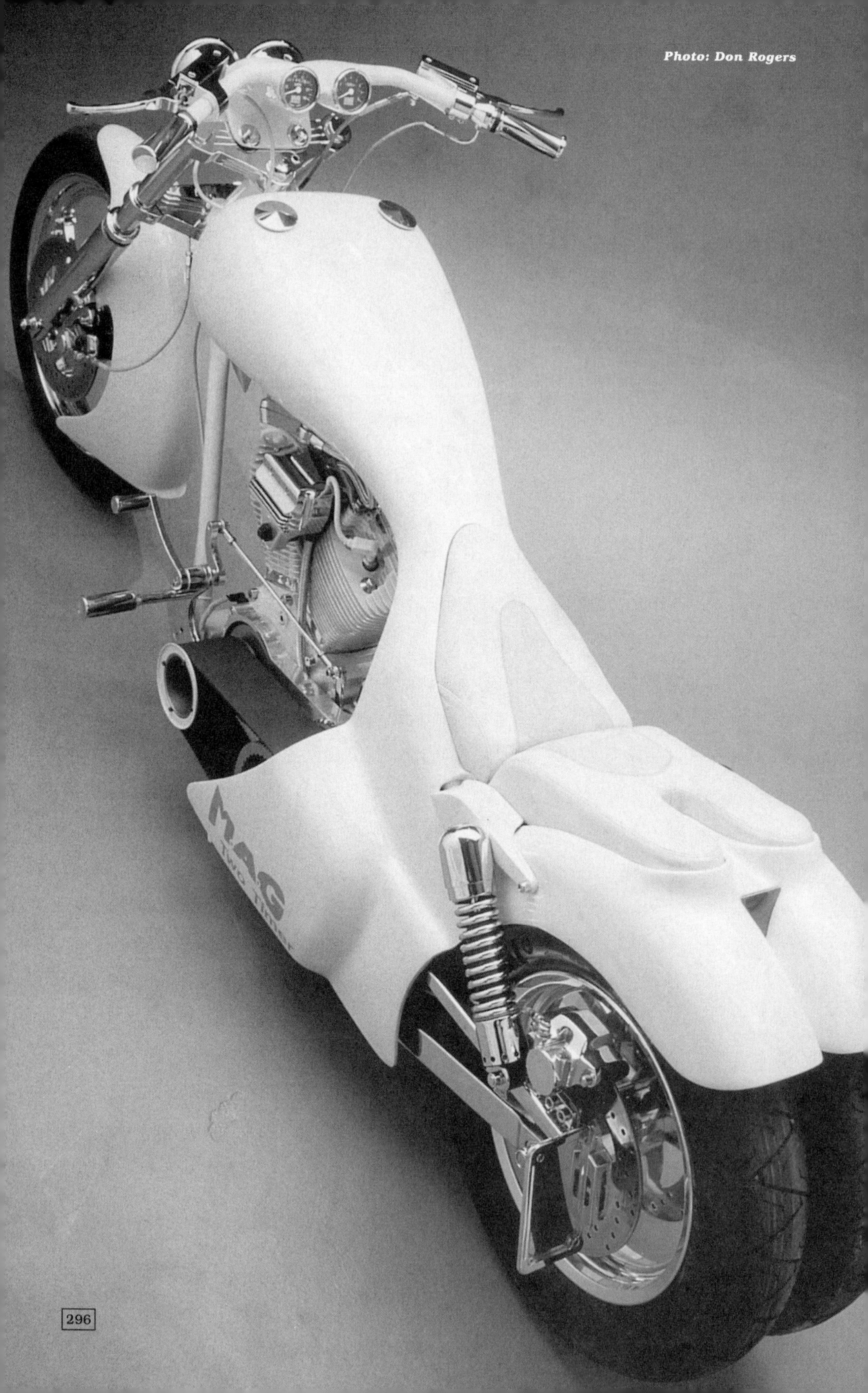

Photo: Don Rogers

Ultimate Radical Trike

Glenn Kottmann builds customs out of MAG Cycle in Pompano Beach, Florida. Look carefully. This bike has not two but three wheels, two squeezed together in the back. So impressed were they by its technical brilliance, the Germans paid for its flight to the famous Essen show so that Europeans could appreciate Glenn's work. Coincidentally, the master craftsman Kottmann had relatives in Deutschland, so that was wunderbar.

Olson Ford V-8 Custom

Some Bros not only march to a different drum but often focus on a different drum altogether. In the late 1970s Dale Olson started working in a motorcycle shop, then took a twenty-year break, restoring classic automobiles and building hot rods. "I wanted to restore motorcycles," he says, "but then I saw how high the prices were, even the basket cases, so I decided to build my own antique. I built the motorcycle the way I would like to see one, in a vintage style."

He wanted something with vintage character and appearance. "I chose the 1930s Ford V-8 '60' engine, and thought it would make a good power plant for a motorcycle because of its compact size, V-8 smoothness, and torque." The Ford Motor Co. manufactured these engines from 1937–1940. They powered full-size cars, the "60" referring to their rate horsepower. Most were scrapped during World War II. But they became popular for use in midget car racing, where the 60 hp combined with the small size and light weight made for great racing.

Photo: Dale Olson

In his Maple Hills, Illinois, shop Dale takes about a month to build each bike. He uses a 750 Honda as a donor bike, from which he harvests the neck, fork, and rear wheel, which helps make everything easy and legal at registration time. The exhaust system is handmade from stainless steel, and the sound is like that of a sprint car. Says Dale, "I have built one with a softail frame, and it rides like a Cadillac." The bikes hover around $20,000, no two exactly alike, and are built to the same standards Dale dedicates to his prize-winning hot rod and classic car restorations. For more information, call Olson Auto at 815-827-3110.

Photo: Michael Farrabaugh

Jaxports Streetster

This Lansing, Michigan, company builds these Harley-powered '32 Ford Highboy custom cars in three-quarter bantam-scale size. The 1200-pound two-seater can hit 90 mph and gets you 40 mpg cruising at 65. There's even a trunk. Contact Jaxports at 517-886-9301 or log on to www.jaxports.com.

Bertaut & Sons

From New Orleans, the Bertaut & Sons Eco-Matic 25 is a beautiful leap backwards, a single-cylinder, 341-cc, single-valve, 12-hp flathead, Made in the USA. Featuring a continuous variable transmission, it's totally automatic. Just twist and go. It can carry a 250-pounder all day at 60 mph and return 80 miles to the gallon, not to mention tons of fun. For more info, call 800-511-2524.

Photo: Bertaut

Photo: Michael Lichter

Harley Bumper Car

Forget your little electric commuter cars, here's the real deal, San Diego area resident Tom Wright's 1200-cc, Sportster-powered 1929 vintage bumper car. The original parts were rescued from a long extinct amusement park, then treated to a radical restoration. It can cruise at 50 down the freeway, anything faster . . . well, it is a bumper car.

Photo: Paul Garson

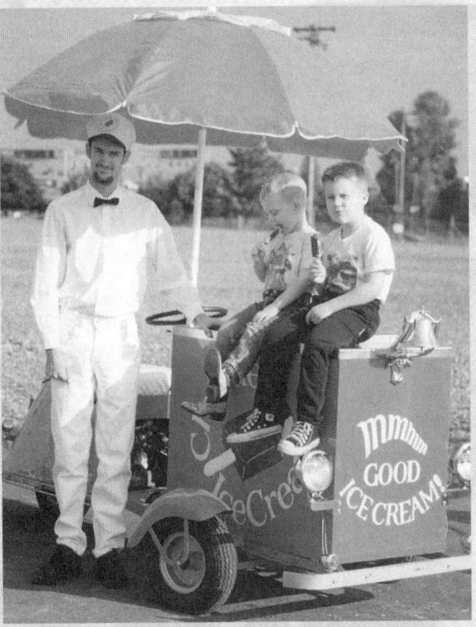

We All Scream for Ice Cream

At the ripe age of thirteen, Charley Smith completed this 1941 Cushman Ice Cream cart, his very first restoration. Originally used to haul artichokes, it was a rusted-out hulk when turned over to him by his father, the Oregon-based Master Restorer Mike Smith. Charley beat out all the metal parts, rebuilt the engine, and even applied the paint. His mom, Roseanne Smith, hand-painted the lettering.

Okay, So It's Bike Furniture

This 74-cubic-inch desk was made for Jims, a well-known maker of special tools and engine parts for Harleys. In this case the past Easyriders *editor K. Randall Ball sourced out the frame and springer front end from Ron Paugh (Paughco frames), engine parts from STD, pipes from Samson Exhaust Systems, fasteners from Gardner Westcott, and chrome goodies from Custom Chrome.*

Photo: Markus Cuff

9

Harley-Davidson V-Rod
Photo: Ken Ross

"WE SAW THE FUTURE, AND IT WAS OURS"

On January 1, 2000, the world celebrated the new millennium with parties all around the globe, but what the hey? Milwaukee was celebrating by way of its year 2000 models, including the completely new Twin Cam Softails with the Twin Cam B motor, guaranteed to be "smooth as glass on an emerald pond." The big news for the new millennium came in 2001, with the introduction of the radical, especially for H-D, V-Rod. The 110-hp, 140-mph silver sensation sent a tsunami-size ripple through not only the motorcycle industry but the Harley family as well. Bros were stunned. A radiator on a Harley? And where's the paint? It looks like a Ducati and a V-Max mixed up together? Others just nodded, commenting that the new bike from Milwaukee was a jewel, a true twenty-first-century Harley, and a high-tech masterpiece. In order to survive, all things evolve, and so it is with H-D as well. The bottom line was, all the dealers who got the first production of V-Rods had takers lined up even when they were slapping thousands of dollars on top of the MSRP of $17,000. Time will tell the effect of this major fork in the Harley road.

As CEO Jeff Bleustein said, "The V-Rod is a signal to the world that the hundredth anniversary for Harley-Davidson is not an end point, it's a milestone."

And, speaking of milestones, it should be noted that, while H-D will celebrate its one hundredth anniversary in 2003, the year also marks the tenth anniversary of its acquisition of Buell, the "other high-performance Harley," although the names are kept very separate but not necessarily equal. The big break for Buell could well be the Firebolt model introduced in 2001, a sport bike that immediately attracted attention not only by its aggressive and unique looks but also by its level of technical development and performance. And, with a $10K price tag, it seems a blast of a bargain. And, yes, in 2000 H-D did bring out their super-econo ($4,400) single-cylinder, entry-level, 492-cc Blast! aimed at new riders and women, who have no problem handling the lightweight, minimal maintenance machine. And, yes, we know a lot of ladies are easily handling Big Twins as well. By the way, the Blast! is a Buell product, technically speaking.

In fact, 45 percent of the people taking the factory riding course, the Rider's Edge program, offered at forty-two H-D dealers in twenty-three states ($225 for a twenty-five-hour class), were women. The course supplies each rider with a Blast! which makes sense.

We're not saying the Blast! is only for women riders. It also would seem to lend itself to some creative customizing, since thumpers have been around since the beginning of motorcycling and have many attributes. A retro-Blast! could be one way to go, like a Silent Gray Blast! or something along those lines.

From this point in time, the future looked bright indeed as the Motor Co. entered 2002. For one, they got a big nod from the establishment.

Investing in Metal: H-D Chosen as Forbes Company of the Year

IN FIFTEEN YEARS H-D STOCK VALUE ROSE BY 15,000 PERCENT! LIKE WE SAY, INVEST IN METAL, HARLEY METAL.

From newsstand shelves across the country, from Barnes & Noble to Borders to your favorite grocery store, Harley-Davidsons blast across the covers of all kinds of bike magazines, and now the prestigious *Forbes* publication. While the late Malcolm Forbes was a big fan of motorcycles, Harleys in particular, the fact that the new V-Rod and CEO Jeffrey Bleustein ("Father of the Evo motor") were filling the cover of the January 7, 2001, issue had more to do with big business. The Motor Co. had been voted the Forbes Company of the Year.

The article itself, "Love into Money" by Jonathon Fahey, ran five pages and carried images of the V-Rod and scenes from Harley history, which the article traced with a graph, of course. Got to have a graph. Especially when it points out that while the rest of the country's companies were hit hard by a recession, the 2001 stats reported a 15 percent sales increase for H-D, for a total of $3.3 billion, with earnings cranked up 26 percent to $435 million. If you owned shares in H-D you were beaming, as they were up 40 percent in 2001. Did your 401k include H-D stock? Don't think so.

If you had bought some of the first shares offered to the public in 1986, you would be sitting pretty, and probably on a new Harley, because you would have benefited from a 37 percent average annual earnings growth. In fifteen years H-D stock value rose by 15,000 percent! Like we say, invest in metal, Harley metal.

As we hammer out the last words of this book, the future offers . . . well, the future. With every passing day, new technology is developed that will shape the destiny of motorcycling. What's in store just over the horizon? Your guess is as good as ours. We do think that the two-wheeled, think-and-go Segway people mover with its "intuitive" computer-assisted controls could find its way into motorcycles. While bikes are already extensions of our bodies and spirits, future tech may take that relationship to a whole new level. Then again, forward thinkers such as Craig Vetter, a pioneer in motorcycle design, have got that contest going with a big cash prize for the first homegrown inventor to come up with a functional hovercraft-type motorcycle. And who didn't want one of those antigravity flying "speeder bikes" as seen in *Star Wars?*

Will we really take the wheels off motorcycles and take to the air? Hey, look at Jet Skis. We'd just be moving from one environment to another . . . land, sea, and air. If we can imagine it, we can eventually build it. And now the time lag is growing shorter between the thinking and the creating.

Can't you just see a Dave Mann illustration of a bunch of Bros blasting over—literally *over*—the countryside on their Harley Hoverbikes? We can. And look around at your kids or grandkids—which one of them will have his or her name inscribed in the history books as the first human to motorcycle on another planet?

Harley-Davidson and Bros and Bro'ettes around the planet have seen a century of motorcycling, and when the two hundredth anniversary rolls around, who knows what marvels will have

AND WHO DIDN'T WANT ONE OF THOSE ANTIGRAVITY FLYING "SPEEDER BIKES" AS SEEN IN *STAR WARS?*

rolled or flown out of Milwaukee. And yet the cement that holds it all together—the unique blending of man and machine called motorcycle—will still be the defining element.

Let's call the following our last comments, at least for this particular book, and as a good a way to end as any:

In the first three months of New York's Guggenheim Museum's display of motorcycles in their Art of the Motorcycle exhibition, over 300,000 visitors flocked to see the 101 bikes set in a dramatic panoramic setting in the structure designed by Frank Lloyd Wright. The visual feast included everything from an 1868 Michaux-Perreaux steam velocipede to a 1998 MV Agusta F4, as well as eleven Harleys, including a Captain America replica and an '89 Buell RS1200. The Chairman of the AMA, Carl Reynolds, summed it up, saying, "At last, the Guggenheim has demonstrated to the public what we motorcyclists have always known: Motorcycles are not just machines . . . they are works of art that have heart and soul."

During the past fifty years we've seen the evolution of the Bro from outlaw to pillar of the community. But whether you're a traditional biker with years of riding or a particle physicist who just bought his first hawg, when you throw your leg over the saddle, the same magic still happens. You become Johnny in the *The Wild One*.

Girl: What are you rebelling against, Johnny?

Johnny: Whataya got?

The author's son, Grant Garson, ponders the future-past of motorcycling while enjoying the radically realized vision of L.A. resident Barry Weiss's ultimate 1970s Triumph hotrod.
Photo: Paul Garson

Future Bikes

What is the shape of things to come? Here are just a few flights of fancy, a mere hint of what the future may hold.

Photo: Paul Martinez

Stealth Fighter on Wheels

From the mind and hand of Master Builder John Covington of Surgical Steeds, this F-117A–inspired Stealth Custom *actually foils radar . . . not that Bros would want to circumvent the speed laws, would we?*

Virtually Reality Custom

The Canadian computer and multimedia artist Barry Garnder, a Harley enthusiast, conjured up this radical and future-ridable concept bike. Now when is someone going to build those supercool bikes in the movie Tron?

Photo: Paul Garson

Corbin-cycles

The famous motorcycle saddle maker Mike Corbin, headquartered in none other than Hollister, California, designs and manufactures the Sparrow electric vehicle and the gasoline-powered Merlin, both classified as motorcycles. The three-wheeled, single-passenger machines offer economy, performance, and heaps of attention-getting charisma. The Merlin comes in coupe or radical roadster models powered by an 88-inch twin-cam H-D motor producing 75-bhp and four-speed manual transmission. Price tag is $23,900 at this writing. More info at www.corbin.com or call 800-538-7035.

**Future Shock—
The New Electric Bikes**

Electric Motorcycles

A company called Electric Motorbike Inc. (EMB) embarked on an interesting foray into electric-powered motorcycles in the mid-1990s, eventually producing the futuristic Lectra24, with a top speed of 41 to 50 mph, a range of 35 miles, and a recharge time of about four hours. Maintenance costs were low since it had no spark plugs, carburetor, oil filter, gas filter, air filter, exhaust pipe, or gas tank. A Lectra was a grand prize on the Wheel of Fortune *game show in 1999. EMB was bought by ZAP, who say they no longer offer e-mc's. But you can still get some info about them via Scott Cronk at scott@ebike.net.*

Photo: Paul Garson

Car-Bikes

A blend of automobile and motorcycle could be one wave of the future as evidenced by several creations, including Hogzoom, *the shark-finned Chevy V-twin-powered custom built in 1995 by Ultra Custom Cycles of Riverside, California. Inspired by the classic styling of the '57 Chevrolet, the bike is powered by an 80-inch S & S motor. Ultra Custom Cycles also created the Bat Bike suitable for Batman's cave garage.*

Egg-Bikes

Photo: Paul Garson

Fred Ferino believes the egg is nature's perfect design, so the Yugoslavian-born California resident set out to build several vehicles emulating that shape, including a Honda-powered Exert motorcycle, running on both gasoline and electric power and capable of 100 mph. His Carfly, another gas-electric hybrid, featuring a four-cylinder Ford power plant, appeared years ahead of other such experiments. Fred says, "To build the future, we need ideas. Young people should educate their minds but also cultivate their creative side. The world will always need inventors, in every field, and with every good invention, there is further opportunity." Fred is open for discussions at 619-295-6455.

Showdown with the Future

As a student at London's Royal College of Art, Cesar Muntada got an A+ for his master's degree project with a concept bike he called Showdown. He dispensed with forks and went with leading link suspension controlled by hydraulic steering. The wheels are also driven by hydraulic motors, and the bike's height and length are adjustable. Oddly enough, it has the same wheelbase and seat height as a Sportster. His inspiration? The "culture culture." Check out the saddle seat and other gunslinger cues.

Photo: Cesar Muntado

Photo: Paul Garson

Three Cylinders

Evolution is based on healthy mutations, accidents in the gene pool that create something different, something with a higher performance level. Such may well be the case with Feuling Advanced Engineering's new W3 radial triple engine. The Ventura, California, firm, headed up by Jim Feuling, created this exotic power plant, which can displace anywhere from 142 to 245 cubic inches. The 142-incher itself makes 150 mph. The engines are marketed with a frame and swing-arm package, all ready to build a way radical custom. More info at www.feuling.com.

Two Wheels Rather Than Four?

At the 1995 El Camino Motorcycle Show and Swap Meet (held annually in Torrance at El Camino College), the author tries out a pre-Segway homemade contraption. What the future holds is anyone's imagination.

Building Your Dream Bike

Piecing together your own custom bike takes research, dedication, patience, and money. While we can't list everything out there, here's a sampling of some of the bigger pieces. Consult your bike mags and distributors for the myriad components and services available, and then go at it.

Frames

The bones of your bike, on which you hang the rest of the parts, determine its personality. Frames come in near infinite variation when you factor in rake and stretch options on top of no-suspension, some suspension, lots of suspension designs. Cruiser, muscle bike, sport tourer, full radical, fat tire, café, pavement hugger, dragster, or a mixture of some or all—you've got quite a selection to choose from. Here are some of the people who are ready, willing, and able to frame your image of the ultimate custom bike. The big distributors also carry frames, while individual builders can carve you out a handmade custom as well.

Atlas Precision—760-242-9111

Kenny Boyce—916-852-9116

Chopper Guys—707-557-2400; www.chopperguys.com

Daytec Center—760-244-1591

Kosman Engineering—www.kosmanracing.net

Paughco—775-246-5738

Pro-One—www.pro-one.com

Pro-Street Frameworks—918-652-9606; www.pro-streetframeworks.com

Thunder Cycle Designs (Eddie Trotta)—954-763-2100

Custom Wheels

American designers and manufacturers have reinvented the wheel in an almost infinite variety, and as the, uh, pivotal parts of any motorcycle, wheels, be they spoked, solid, or custom cut, get a lot of attention. Here's a list of places that roll out some of the trickest variations on one of humankind's most important inventions.

American Made, Rancho Cucamonga, California (909-944-5837);

American Wire Wheel, Denton, Texas (940-898-1400);

Black Bike Heavy Equipment, Northridge, California (818-341-2550);

Carriage Works at www.carriageworksinc.com;

Eurocomponents at www.eurocomponentsusa.com,

Excel Chrome Aluminum Wheels, Oceanside, California (760-732-3161);

Hallcraft's, Gainesville, Texas (940-668-0771);

Harley-Davidson (800-443-2153);

Pat Kennedy, Tombstone, Arizona (520-432-1330);

Performance Machine, La Palma, California (714-523-3000);

Arlen Ness, San Leandro, California (510-276-3534);

Pro-One (800-884-4173);

Sturgis Wheel Co., Rapid City, South Dakota (605-394-9525);

RC Components, Bowling Green, Kentucky (270-842-6000);

and RevTech, Morgan Hill, California (408-778-0500).

Custom Doughnuts

Naturally you need tires to protect your expensive custom wheels, so here are a few. There are a lot of manufacturers who make all kinds of treadware, and the following focus on what the coolest custom cruisers are wearing. **Avon Tyres** (Brit spelling for tires) began making tires in 1885, pneumatics in '01, so they've got it down. Info at www.avontyres.com. **Bridgestone-Firestone:** World-class tire makers since 1931 and 1900 respectively, the former Japanese, the latter American, joined forces in 1988, so East does meet West, or two stones are better than one. Info at www.bridgestone-firestone.com. **Continental:** This German company founded in 1871 makes more than just tires, but they do make good ones for motorcycles, including Harleys and metric cruisers. Info (in English) at www.conti.de. **Dunlop Tires:** Selling the only tires made in the United States, Dunlop rolled out its first tire in 1888 thanks to the Scots veterinarian John Boyd Dunlop, who wanted better tires for his kid's bicycle. Dunlop is OEM for H-D and Buell and many others, including the new H-D logo tires. Info at www.dunloptire.com.

Maxxis Tires: This Georgia-based company, while relatively new (1967), is the world's largest manufacturer of bicycle and specialty tires, and they make some technologically very advanced motorcycle tires. Info www.maxxis.com. **Metzeler Tires:** Another German manufacturer, they go back to 1863. A part of Pirelli since 1986, they offer a selection of wide cruiser tires. Info at www.metzeler.com. **Michelin Tires:** Yep, the French folks with the famous chubby tire guy; they've been around since 1832. In 1903 they came out with their first motorcycle tire; the radial bike tire appeared in 1987. They'll be celebrating their hundredth along with H-D. Info at www.michelin.com. **Pirelli:** A world-famous name in tires, Pirelli was founded in Milan, Italy, circa 1872, and started on bike tires in 1974. Info at pirelli.com.

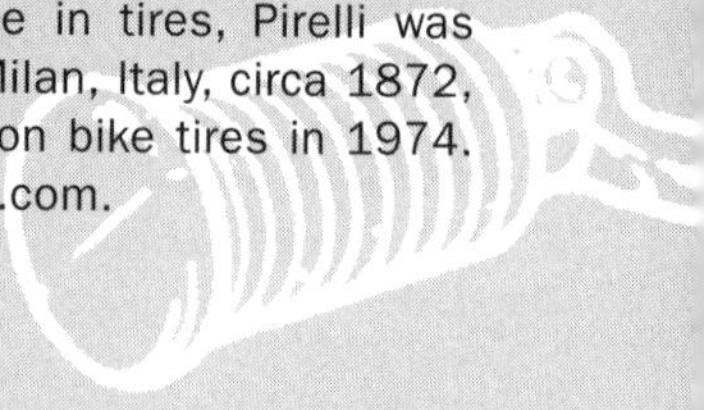

Custom Engines: The Heart of the Beast

In order to roll those custom wheels and tires, an infusion of power is needed. The following folks have harnessed up the horses in a number of high-performance packages. Since times and prices change, call for the latest price tags.

Delkron

Delkron Competition Eliminator Series billet engines bolt directly onto any Big Twin frame and come in two configurations: 100 cubic inches with a two-cam valve train or 131 cubic inches with a four-cam (Sportster style) valve train.

Competition Eliminator motors come assembled, using CNC-machined billet crankcases, specially tuned high-flow heads, and many other high-quality components, such as a flat-slide performance carb, specially ground cams, ultralight adjustable push rods, and viton O-ring seals. Combine all that with the rigidity of Delkron's 6061-T6 billet aluminum cases, billet covers, and billet camshaft support plate, and you get a Competition Eliminator.

The square 100-cubic-inch Competition Eliminator two-cam yields a remarkable 116 pounds of torque and 116 horsepower at the rear wheel. Delkron's also planning to release a more powerful square 120-cubic-inch version of the two-cam soon. With the 130-cubic-inch, four-camer in your bike, you could be boasting well over 150 horsepower at the rear wheel. Delkron, Sacramento, California. Phone: 916-921-9703; fax: 916-921-5209.

Harley-Davidson

Harley-Davidson's New Era Twin Cam 88 Engine Program offers new Twin Cam 88 and Twin Cam 88B engines, available through authorized H-D dealers. The Twin Cam 88's are available in the Dyna configuration in black and chrome or silver and polished. The Twin Cam 88B (counterbalanced) is available in the softail configuration in the same colors. Carb and manifold not included. Contact your Harley-Davidson dealer, or go to www.harley-davidson.com.

Merch Performance

The popular 120-cubic-inch Merch Performance's engine package features a 4.25-inch bore by 4.25-inch stroke for smooth, reliable service. All 120-cubic-inch engines feature MP crankcases, flywheels, heads, connecting rods, cylinders, rocker boxes, push rods, push rod tubes, and oil pumps. Additional features include forged pistons, O-ring base gasket stainless steel bullets (inserts in cases for increased stud strength), 9.81 compression ratio, 1.940-inch intake and 1.625-inch exhaust valves, compression release valves for easier starting, 110-horsepower, 125-foot-pound torque at the rear wheel, and a six-month, 16,000-mile limited warranty. This engine fits into all Evo and Twin Cam frames. Call 888-637-2448 USA or 877-637-2448 Canada, or log on to www.merch.performance.com.

Panzer

Panzer's 90-cubic-inch Neo-Pan motor was made specifically for Panzer by Accurite Engineering. It features an Andrews BH Grind bump stick, a tried and true S & S Super E carburetor, S & S cases, black-powder-coated 3.625-inch-bore cylinders with S & S pistons and rings, Mallory ignition, S & S flywheels, S & S 4.375-inch stroke, a 12-volt generator or alternator options, plus many more go-fast goodies. Panzer's Neo-Pan *is* much more than a trick-looking Panhead engine. Aside from its appearance, there's nothing vintage about the Neo-Pan; it's a totally new power plant that's capable of running wide open to Tuesday, just as you would expect from any modern motorcycle engine. Panzer manufactures EPA- and CARB-approved motorcycles, and uses their Neo-Pan motor on all their production bikes. Call 719-269-7267 or log on to www.panhead.com.

RevTech

Custom Chrome's RevTech engines use components that are made from all-new tooling in a state-of-the-art ISO 9000 manufacturing plant. Some features include increased cooling fin surface area and ultrahigh-temperature O-rings that are used in place of head and base gaskets. There's also a high-performance computerized ignition that controls and monitors break-in. RevTech engines are available (at this writing) in displacements of 82 and 100 inches, and in two finishes: black with chrome covers and natural with chrome covers. The engines are compatible with original equipment and custom frames that accept Evolution engines. Contact your Custom Chrome dealer for information.

S & S Cycle

S & S's Super Sidewinder motors with BFD (Big Fin Design) heads and cylinders increase cooling area. They have longer, 7.658-inch connecting rods and pressurized piston oilers for extended engine life, while a pressed-in 1.5-inch crankpin increases crankshaft rigidity and engine smoothness. All the new engines feature highlight fins on cylinders and heads. Displacements include 100, 107, and 115 inches. Inch for inch, power outputs are virtually identical to those of the early style engines. Most S & S Long Blocks are available complete, minus ignition, exhaust, and charging system. S & S Cycle, Viola, Wisconsin. Phone: 606-627-1497; www.sscycle.com.

Sputhe

Alan Sputhe and his team build conventional forty-five-degree Evo-style V-twin engines, in sizes up to 109 cubic inches, as well as Fat Head Evos up to 107 cubic inches. But a sixty-degree engine is their flagship. Their production 104-cubic-inch is equipped with dual 41.3 mm Keihin flat-slide carbs and is rated at 141 horsepower. It fits in a stock FXR, FLT, or Dyna frame, has stock-type motor mounts, and bolts to a stock Evo.

Sputhe built a sixty-degree, 120-cubic-inch injected-alcohol engine for the racer Danny Grotto in Australia, and he's been running the sucker full throttle for many years without a single failure. In other words, this handsome engine is tough as nails. Alan Sputhe mentions that his mean 60 is capable of running in the 10's in the quarter mile, has been clocked at 171 mph on the Bonneville Salt Flats, and is smooth enough so you can putt-putt to the corner store to pick up a slurpy and the latest issue of *Easyriders*. Sputhe Engineering, Grass Valley, California. Phone: 530-268-0887; fax: 530-268-3024.

STD

STD Development offers STD High-Performance Street and Strip Engines available in both 97-cubic-inch and Long Rod 100-cubic-inch configurations. Each engine is carefully machined and assembled to exacting tolerances by STD's staff of experienced builders. Engine assemblies come complete with full electrics; all oil system components, including steel braided lines; and a Mikuni HSR45 carburetor with an exclusive-design STD chrome filter assembly. S & S states that it is the strongest, most powerful and reliable turnkey Big Twin engine available to the public. STD Development, Chatsworth, California 91313. Phone: 818-998-8226; www.stddevelopment.com.

Terry Components

Terry Components builds the Boxer, a titanium-enhanced forged billet aluminum engine. Features include proprietary aluminum alloy forging that's heat-treated to a Brunell specification of 145! Hey, it's important metallurgically speaking. Terry Components' high-tech manufacturing process is applied to the rocker boxes, cylinder heads, tappet blocks, oil pump, cam cover, and engine cases. In addition, the cylinder heads, cylinder bases, and tappet blocks are O-ringed to ensure positive seal for no-leak operation. The Boxer engine runs 30 to 50 percent cooler than others in the marketplace. Terry Components, Newbury Park, California; Phone 805-376-2700 or www.terrycomponents.com.

TP Engineering

TP Engineering's A TP Pro-Series engines are built with TP-manufactured parts that when combined result in an aggressive power plant with a lot of attitude. Cases are formed from A356-T6 aluminum, featuring an integrally cast-in hub that ensures the steel hub that houses the crankshaft support bearings will not move. Extra material has also been added at strategic points in the crankcases. Oil is supplied to the power plant by a TP Pro-Series patent-pending billet oil pump, giving the crankshaft a constant flow of oil at any rpm. Anchoring the TP flywheels is TP Engineering's designed pinion shaft with a diameter of 1.625 inches, giving the engine more stability and less vibration. TP Engineering, Danbury, Connecticut. Phone: 203-744-4960.

Zipper's

Zipper's produces complete 107-inch Twin Cam engines that routinely achieve 120-plus foot-pounds of torque and horsepower with compatible exhaust systems. Dyno charts show a power curve that's immediately vertical and flat all the way to red line. Zipper's Twin Cam arrives with all-new aluminum 4.125-inch bore cylinders. Four-inch stroke with liners that are over 50 percent thicker than stock OEM castings provide the ultimate in cylinder stability. Zipper's CNC ported heads with oversize valves, Red Shift cams, and ignition system are included, along with forged pistons and top-quality chrome-moly push rods. A ThunderJet-equipped S & S G carb and a round-style air cleaner with Zipper's filter upgrade finishes off the look of a sleeper. Zipper's Performance, Elkridge, Maryland. Phone: 410-579-2828; www.zippersperformance.com.

Feeding Your Beast: Carburetors

These potent projections from the sides of your engine take on their own personality and are as much form as function when it comes to the elements of show and go. Here are some of the fuel feeders out there in custom bike land. Just hook up your throttle and cables, then twist away.

Atomized Fuel Technologies—CNC-machined carbs work as good as they look. Call the Apple Valley, California, company at 760-240-5903.

Carl's Speed Shop—After years in SoCal, Carl moved down to sunnier Daytona Beach, the center of East Coast bike action, but he still offers his hot-looking Typhoon carburetor and lots of other go-fast goodies. Check 'em out at www.carlspeedshop.com.

Edelbrock—A legendary performance name, this Torrance, California, company offers their famous Quik-Silver carbs and all the trimmings. More info at www.edelbrock.com.

Mikuni—An industry standard, this Northridge, California, company makes the very popular HSR43 and 45 smooth-bore carbs for H-D engines utilizing flat-slide technology. More info at www.mikuni.com.

Rivera Engineering—For decades this Whittier, California, carb mecca has offered the full spectrum of carb choices.

You name it, they got it, including their trick Ram-effect intake manifold. More info at www.riveraengineering.com.

Screamin' Eagle—These Harley-Davidson carbs come in CV, flat-side, and Holley Performance variations for all things H-D. More info at www.harley-davidson.com.

S & S—Arguably this Viola, Wisconsin, company manufactures the most famous V-twin carburetor of all. The S & S E and G models are available for almost all H-Ds, past and present. More info at www.sscycle.com.

Terry Components—These guys in Newbury Park, California, are the only manufacturer of Weber carb kits for Harleys thanks to their special intake manifold, including the wild dual Weber setup as well as chopper downdraft models. More info at www.terrycomponents.com.

Distributors: Parts Is Parts

Sure, you'll need a bunch more parts before your sled is scooting down the street, like brakes, handlebars, fenders, suspension, gas tanks, cables, instruments, exhaust systems, forward controls, seats . . . which we don't have room to showcase. That's what the bike mags are for. But for access to the ultimate in parts wish books, go to the major distributors, who carry about everything known to relate to motorcycles. In addition, many custom builders are now supplying their signature parts through distributors, but there are still plenty of individual shops cranking out their own one-off pieces. Check out the bike mags and the Internet for an almost infinite array of possibilities.

Chrome Specialties—
www.chromespecialties.com

Custom Chrome—
www.customchrome.com

Drag Specialities—608-758-1111 or www.dragspecialties.com

J & P Cycles—www.jpcycles.com or 319-462-4817

MID-USA—www.mid-usa.com

Books We Thumbed Through to Write This Book (Bibliography)

Bolfert, Thomas C. *The Big Book of Harley-Davidson*. Harley-Davidson, 1991.

Brown, Roland. *Classic Motorcycles*. Hermes House, 1996.

Clarke, Massimo. *100 Years of Motorcycles*. Portland House, 1986.

Clymer, Floyd. *A Treasury of Motorcycles of the World*. Bonanza Books, 1965.

Daniel, Clifton. *Chronicle of the Twentieth Century*. Chronicle Publications, 1987.

Davidson, Jean. *Growing Up Harley-Davidson*. Voyageur Press, 2001.

Dickson, Paul. *Timelines*. Addison Wesley Publishing, 1990.

Emde, Don. *The Daytona 200*. Motorcycle Heritage Press, 1991.

Engelbert, Phillis, and Diane L. Dupuis. *The Handy Space Answer Book*. Visible Ink Press, 1998.

Griffin, Al. *Motorcycles*. Henry Regnery, 1972

Gup, Ted. *Book of Honor*. Anchor Books, 2000.

Henshaw, Peter, and Ian Kerr. *The Encyclopedia of Harley-Davidson*. Chartwell Books, 2001.

Maltin, Leonard. *Leonard Maltin's 2000 Movie and Video Guide*. Signet Reference, 1999.

Mitchell, Doug, et al. *American Motorcycle Classics*. Publications International, 1994.

Rafferty, Tod. *The Complete Catalog of Harley-Davidson*. Lowe & B. Hould, 1997.

Rafferty, Tod. *The Illustrated Classic American Motorcycles*. Motorbooks International, 2001.

Stolley, Richard B., editor. *Life: Our Century in Pictures*. Little, Brown, 2000.

Sucher, Harry V. *Harley-Davidson*. Haynes Publications, 1985.

Sucher, Harry. *Inside American Motorcycling*. Inforsport Publications, 1995.

Tragatsch, Erwin, editor. *The Complete Illustrated Encyclopedia of the World's Motorcycles*. Holt, Rinehart and Winston, 1977.

Ward, Ian, editor. *The World of Motorcycles*. Orbis Publishing, 1979.

Williams, Mark. *Road Movies*. Proteus Books, 1982.

Wilson, Hugo. *The Ultimate Motorcycle Book*. Dorling Kindersley, 1993.

Wright, David K. *The Harley-Davidson Motor Company*. Motorbooks International, 1983

Wright, John W., editor. *The Universal Almanac 1993*. Andrews and McMeel, 1992.

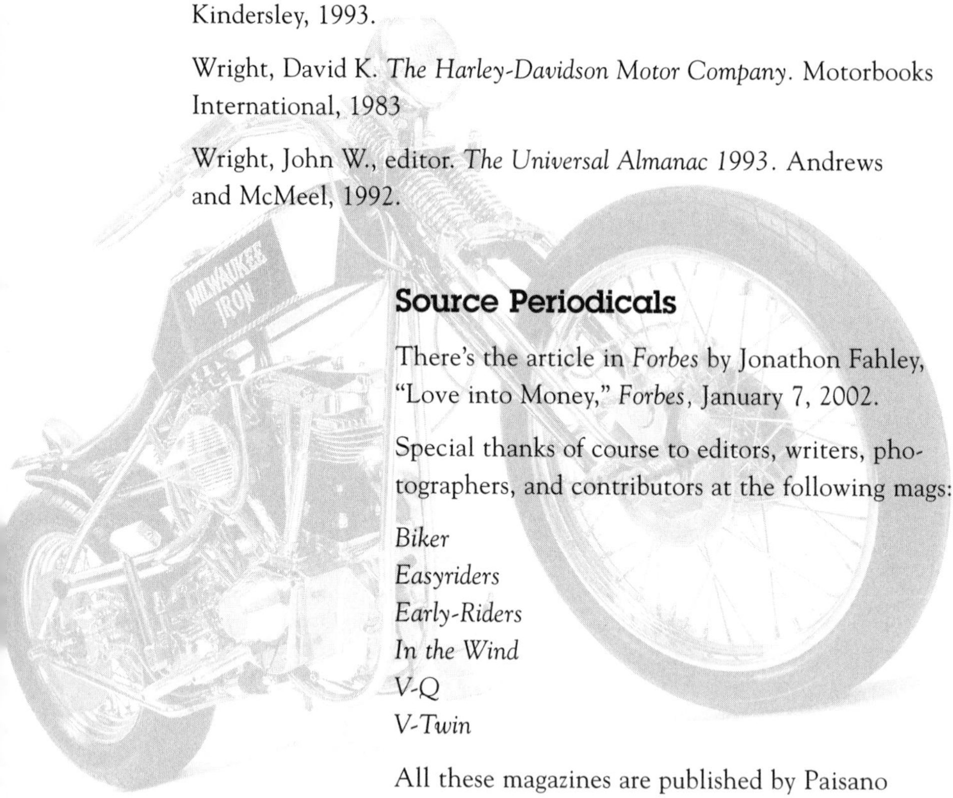

Source Periodicals

There's the article in *Forbes* by Jonathon Fahley, "Love into Money," *Forbes*, January 7, 2002.

Special thanks of course to editors, writers, photographers, and contributors at the following mags:

Biker
Easyriders
Early-Riders
In the Wind
V-Q
V-Twin

All these magazines are published by Paisano Publications, 20210 Dorothy Drive, Agoura Hills, CA 91301; 818-889-8740.